Originally from North Yorkshire, John Holroyd  and religious studies at King's College, Londo taught religious studies and philosophy in l schools and was Head of Religious Studies at S London for over twenty years. He currently lectures at the London School of Philosophy and teaches philosophy for the Workers' Educational Association. He has published articles with *Philosophy Now* magazine and *The Ethical Review*.

John Holroyd

JUDGING
RELIGION

A Dialogue for Our Time

SilverWood

Published in 2019 by SilverWood Books

SilverWood Books Ltd
14 Small Street, Bristol, BS1 1DE, United Kingdom
www.silverwoodbooks.co.uk

Copyright © John Holroyd 2019

The right of John Holroyd to be identified as the author of this work has been asserted in accordance with the Copyright, Designs and Patents Act 1988 Sections 77 and 78.

All rights reserved. No part of this publication may be reproduced, stored in a retrieval system, or transmitted in any form or by any means, electronic, mechanical, photocopying, recording or otherwise, without prior permission of the copyright holder.

ISBN 978-1-78132-863-7 (paperback)
ISBN 978-1-78132-864-4 (hardback)
ISBN 978-1-78132-865-1 (ebook)

British Library Cataloguing in Publication Data
A CIP catalogue record for this book is available from the British Library

Page design and typesetting by SilverWood Books
Printed on responsibly sourced paper

*For my wife Helen
and my good friend
John Moss Smith*

Contents

Acknowledgements		9
Preamble		13
1	Introduction: How Can We Judge Religion?	17
2	Through A Glass Darkly: Religion In The Media Spotlight	35
3	Religion Before The Ethics Tribunal: Four Contexts Of Religious Life And Practice	49
4	Religion Before The Ethics Tribunal: Four Elements Of Religious Life	86
5	Within The Faiths: The Upbringing And Schooling Of Children	115
6	Islam From The Foundations: Qur'an And Hadith	131
7	Islam Today: Attitudes Towards Women	163
8	Islam Today: The Making And Countering Of Militancy	189
9	Problems Of Evil And Suffering: From Theory To Practice	226
10	Beyond Conclusions	246
Endnotes		256
Bibliography		284
Index		296

Acknowledgements

I would like to thank many friends and colleagues for their help and support as I have put this book together. The process of copy-editing and proofreading has also been a collaborative one. In particular I would like to thank Shumaila Ahmed, James Blackstone, Stephen Bushell, Martin Muchall, David Solomon, Anja Steinbauer, Steven Turner, Michael Wagner, Nadine Wilstead, and my wife Helen Dyer for the very careful attention they have all given to reading and commenting on the manuscript.

Thanks are also due to Helen Hart and her publishing team at Silverwood Books. Any faults or errors that remain in the text are my responsibility alone.

'There may be few more urgent fields of study in the world today than the "science of the sacred".'
Scott Atran[1]

'We move forward faster and live better when we seek doubt.'
Fatema Mernissi[2]

Preamble

Making judgments about the truth or falsity of religion, about its ethical profile, about where and how it is cause and/or effect among global geopolitics, seems more than commonplace today, at least in the West. In this book I seek to examine some of the claims made against religion, and to look with an equally critical eye at defences of its role and significance in our time. My motivations for doing this have gathered pace over recent years, drawing upon a number of considerations:

Huge judgments and generalisations have been made about religion by people who have not spent their lives studying it, who are not religious scholars and who have not had an experience of being religious in anything but a nominal sense. I am thinking of the new atheists Richard Dawkins, Christopher Hitchens, Daniel Dennett and Sam Harris, to name but a few. Yet despite their lack of qualifications in these respects, their views have gained great publicity and had a considerable effect over the past decade or so.

Less-well publicised defenders of faith are in turn engaged in apologetics.

Some are, in an academic sense, extremely well-qualified to reach judgments about religion but, like their adversaries, they appear well 'dug in'. Both sides, akin to squabbling politicians at the despatch box, attack and defend thereby polarising debate and perception in the public arena, where they seek our support. What is needed in current discussion and reflection about religion is a more disinterested intent and a keener desire to understand rather than conclude on the part of all those so engaged.

Amid all this, the world is not becoming less religious. Even in parts of the world heavily dominated by a particular religion, contact with and awareness of other religions is growing, alongside the forces of globalisation and digital media. Religious multi-cultures on all scales, up to and including the global, are becoming the norm.

The Western media in its routine coverage often pours scorn upon religion, especially on Islam. News items about Islam for example select and highlight militancy and extremism, however unrepresentative this is of the religion as a whole. This often leads to division and mistrust within and between communities, thereby undermining some of the best community and educational work that has helped build creative and collaborative multi-cultures across the planet. This type of negative journalism does not need censoring, but rather vigorous, well-publicised critique and debate.

There clearly is cause for alarm, but also for analysis, as we consider how sources of militancy, terrorism, misogyny and oppression of the worst kinds are sometimes more and sometimes less reflective of religious faith. I am concerned that in our understanding of these things we get the right culprit(s) because if we don't, not only are we responsible for a gross injustice, but the real culprits will remain at large. Mistaken judgments about religion can do real harm. If, as Christopher Hitchens maintains, 'religion poisons everything', we need to know that. Equally, if it does not, with the potent forms of harm lying elsewhere - for example in extreme forms of nationalism - then we need to be alerted to that too. If we can be accurate about the dangers we can be best prepared for them.

Happily, religion has been and continues to be studied with academic rigour in many quarters[3], and such study can significantly eschew prejudice, but these points are insufficiently appreciated. There has never been a more important time to understand religion and to apply this understanding.

In the light of these remarks, my overall approach to understanding and evaluating religion will seek to bring together the various voices of believers, of the victims of religion and of academic experts of various kinds into a form of dialogue that is at once about interrogating both the evidence and the arguments, while also being open-minded to the variety of conclusions that after careful consideration remain available.

1

Introduction: How Can We Judge Religion?

Making judgments is part of the routine of life: whether we're thinking about what to buy at the supermarket or how to budget for the month, we can hardly escape making these sorts of judgment. On a wider scale, judgments frame our life. We make choices about a career, a partner, somewhere to live and work, yet despite the magnitude of these decisions, they are often accompanied by a sense that time is pressing. We don't quite manage to weigh up all the pros and cons, we make our decisions on the hoof. The philosopher Martin Heidegger described this life situation or condition as a 'living unto death'. We can't take in all the relevant information all the time and yet we had better get on with it, whatever it is, because both it and we will not wait forever. Yet 'getting it right', making the correct judgments, is all the more important exactly because life is not a dress rehearsal. Life is now and we don't get a second chance.[4]

Many feel so overwhelmed with all of this within their own lives that making judgments about politics or religion is more than their life is worth. Others regard religion as enough of an existential threat to press for its immediate public appraisal where, as far as they are concerned, it can be condemned for all to see and for all to benefit. If, as many of the new atheists believe, religion is a serious moral hazard, we had better sit up and take note. It might inform who we choose as a partner or friend, how we bring up our children and where we send them to school and the sort of schools we wish to see founded and closed. It will also affect how we view history and the sort of future we want for ourselves and the world.

This book will refer in a number of places to the views of some of the new atheists, since they offer so much by way of critique of religion. However, its focus is religion, not the new atheism which has been discussed at length elsewhere. I shall look most especially at an ethical appraisal of faiths, and while I mention a number of religions, my attention will be directed mainly towards the Abrahamic faiths of Judaism, Christianity and Islam as they are practised today. I shall identify some sample perspectives and issues that begin to indicate the scope of what is to be evaluated. An ethical appraisal of Islam will form a case study within our discussion, since it is at the heart of so much on-going dispute and debate. Islam is also important because, according to some estimates, such as the findings of the Pew Research Center, the Muslim population of Western Europe including the UK is projected to grow steadily within the coming decades.[5]

To achieve all this, three preliminary issues need to be addressed. First, what do we mean by religion? What is it we are making judgments about? Second, because this book focuses on ethical judgments of religion in particular, we need to ask what is an ethical judgment and how it differs from any other sort of judgment. I shall also consider what is the purpose of an ethical judgment. Third, what is the status of an ethical judgment? Is such a judgment valid for all times and places; or are ethical judgments merely applicable to the time and place, culture and religion from which they originate? Towards the end of the chapter I shall suggest further options as to how ethical evaluations of religion can best proceed, that see certain types of dialogue, what I shall call a 'way of dialogue', as being at the heart of the process.

Preliminaries

What is religion?

Judging religion in an ethical or any other sense cannot begin unless we have an understanding of what religion is. This first preliminary consideration, though, presents immediate difficulties. For example, in his book *The Myth of Religious Violence*, the theologian William Cavanaugh argues that we cannot define religion in a way that satisfactorily separates it from secular ideology and practice. On this basis he claims that we cannot therefore consistently distinguish between religious and secular violence. As such, judgments about religion can also at times be considered to be judgments about nationalisms and political ideologies such as Marxism. According to this reasoning, there are many circumstances in which we are unable to say that it is religion that is to be praised or blamed rather than some form of political ideology. To reach these conclusions, Cavanaugh contends that definitions of religion that are *substantive*, focusing on the *substance* of belief or practice, fail. For example, to define religion as, among other things, involving belief in God, excludes most of Buddhism, Taoism, Shinto and Confucianism, which don't generally share this belief. Yet these practices are usually referred to as religions. On the other hand, more inclusive definitions of religion that define it as involving a belief in the transcendent carry the opposite difficulty of including too much. For example, some ethnic nationalisms, with their beliefs in imagined communities; and forms of Marxism with beliefs about historical determinism and a future communist destiny, both hold onto a form of non-empirical truth about the way things are.

If, by contrast, religion is defined *functionally*, in terms of what it does, by reference that is to its role in the lives of people and communities, then its peculiarity in relation to other things begins to fade. For example, if religion is more about *how* people believe than *what* they believe, then it is hard to see why football doesn't count as a religion in some respects. As Bill Shankly, manager of Liverpool FC in the 1970s remarked, 'Some people believe football is a matter of life and death. I am very disappointed with that attitude. I can assure you it is much, much more important than that.' In a functionalist sense, football offers communities a sense of belonging, a kinship and an identity, all brought together through commitments that can reasonably be described as forms of devotion. Yet this doesn't seem right either; football is not generally viewed to be a religion.

The word 'religion' is problematic. Its meaning is an on-going subject of dispute among philosophers and sociologists of religion. For example, some scholars have written their beliefs into their definitions of religion. Nineteenth century philologist and orientalist Max Müller saw religion to be 'a disposition that enables men to apprehend the Infinite under different names and disguises'.[6] Both non-believers and less liberal forms of believer would reasonably object to Müller's definition as it violates their beliefs by assuming on the one hand the existence of 'the Infinite' and on the other that the Infinite can be variously apprehended. A further difficulty about defining religion is that what 'religion' refers to or denotes can also be a political issue, as when someone defending their faith protests that a terrorist attack was not carried out by members of their religion, 'they're not true believers if they do that, whatever they say'; or when the Chinese communist authorities refuse to accept Taoism or Confucianism as religions; or again as the Indian BJP government refuses to accept Hinduism as a religion, claiming that the concept is a colonial imposition.

Before we despair altogether, though, about being able to understand the word 'religion', it is also clear that people are not constantly at cross purposes in using the word for all that it remains contested, otherwise a meaningful conversation about religion could never take place. And yet, such conversations do take place, all the time.

With this thought in mind an alternative approach to understanding religion is to move away from seeking a precise definition of the term. The philosopher John Hick has offered what has become known as a family resemblances approach to understanding the word 'religion' .[7] The focus in this approach is on the use of the word 'religion', on what it refers to (its referent) rather than on its meaning or dictionary definition. Hick suggests that if we look at how people use the word 'religion' today, it is part of a dialogue of understanding. For example, religious and non-religious people might at times use the word differently, but usually not so differently that they fail to be able to hold a conversation on the subject. In this way the use of the word 'religion' can be said to follow an implied set of rules organised around a variety of characteristics that religions may be said to have or to lack, to a lesser or greater extent. Examples of such characteristics include: beliefs and myths about the origin and meaning of the cosmos and humanity, beliefs about destiny including life after death; a system of values and ethics; a set of ritual practices like prayer, meditation, rites of passage, festivals and pilgrimage; institutions and communities that regulate such practices and beliefs, and that refer to forms of authority such as founders, messengers, texts and very often a God, along with a theory and practice of liberation or ultimate salvation (known as a soteriology). Further characteristics include being engaged with ultimate concerns and commitments that trump all other considerations, a system of law and an expressive dimension in art, literature, music and architecture.

Two points should be made about this set of characteristics. They are descriptive, not evaluative. The more we write into the characteristics of religion ethical or cognitive evaluations of it - for example in the way that Müller in his definition implied that there is 'an Infinite' - the more people will be talking at cross-purposes about what they mean. For this reason, it is best to avoid evaluations of religion within definitions of it. Including evaluations in this way begs questions about the appraisal of religion that this book seeks to address. The other important point being made about the characteristics of religion offered is that not all religions will necessarily have any one attribute in common, although quite a lot of these features will be found in most religions. In this way, like a set of family resemblances, we come to use the word 'religion' in a way that is identifiable and accurate without being precisely definable. The list of characteristics includes many substantive features (such as a set of ritual practices) alongside functional ones (such as engagement with ultimate concerns).

This kind of approach to understanding words and phrases like 'religion' and 'political ideology' means that while they are not hermetically sealed in separate boxes, they are still distinguishable to a fair extent. Marxism for example - for all its this-worldly theory of liberation; its sense of destiny unfolding within the historical process; and its civic rituals paying due respect to some of its founders and leaders - still lacks a number of very widespread substantive characteristics of religion, including belief in an afterlife and belief in a God alongside notions of cosmic meaning and origin. It therefore doesn't qualify as a religion to anything like the same degree as, say, Islam, Christianity or even Buddhism. The same can be said of political ideologies such as nationalism, and even more so as regards supporting a football team, which can be said to lack most of the substantive characteristics of religion, short of a highly interpretative account of them.

Of course, there are blends of politics and religion, as we shall see for example in certain forms of Islamism, but the kind of characteristics that we have identified here will help us, even in such cases, to pick out when and where religious factors are broadly at work, and where other factors are more salient. The substantive features of religion are particularly helpful in distinguishing it from political ideology. In this way, problems of understanding what is being referred to by 'religion' as distinct from other things can be largely overcome.

So, the word 'religion' does have meaning, despite evading a precise definition that fits all instances of its use. We can meaningfully apply it to the phenomena we call Christianity, Judaism, Islam, Sikhism and Buddhism for example. Each of these faiths is characterised by the vast majority, if not all, of the features we listed above. I would agree with Cavanaugh that the word as it is often used today stems from the Reformation and the early modern period of the seventeenth and eighteenth centuries, when special focus on specific beliefs as distinct from others came to the fore in the Christian West. In this sense, 'religion' is broadly a modern category or lens through which Western scholars in particular have come to see the world. Nevertheless, it is not, for all of this, a fiction. That would raise too many questions about why the word 'religion' and its cognates have come to be used and continue to be used not just in the West but worldwide alongside very similar words in many other languages. 'Religion' is not a fiction in the minds of radical atheists, nor in the minds of believers from a wide variety of traditions, nor in the minds of the general public, nor in the minds of many Religious Studies scholars.[8] Good judgments, however, begin with specifics, and I have sought to be specific throughout the book by referring to particular religious practices, attitudes and contexts. We shall also see that lines of reasoning weaken the more they build up from specifics towards generalisations about whole religions and 'religion' as a whole.

What is an ethical judgment and what is its purpose?

A second preliminary issue is to do with the nature of judgments. Judgments can be about facts, for example the date of the battle of Hastings or Jesus's birth. By contrast, judgments can also be about values, including moral values, for example about whether cannibalism or assisted suicide can ever be right. Assessing these two types of judgment involves different procedures. Judgments about, say, historical facts can in principle be confirmed by historical investigation and evidence. Value judgments, including moral judgments, by contrast involve appraisals about 'the good life' or 'the good society' or some other measure for assessing how we know the good. Many critics of religion want to make both types of judgment about it; they want to critique its claims both about what is true and also what is good. We shall be focused on the second issue, but we shall occasionally touch on the first, because to be committed to the good would appear to imply, all other things being equal, being committed to the truth as well.

A further point about judgment is that it can have many purposes. I shall seek to be accurate and fair in my observations and in my selection of institutions, scholars and victims of religion as I discuss the evaluations being made. All the same, I shall want to draw particular attention at times to some of the moral failings of faiths, because religions in various ways and for a variety of reasons see themselves very often as key generators of morality, offering a vision of the good. In this sense I want to track down evidence while also engaging with questions about how religions can morally improve. There is tension between these two objectives within ethical judgment, that of being fair and that of seeking improvement. Still, I believe that for ethical reasons we can't really let go of either goal.

There will be those who ask 'who am I to ethically evaluate religion?' I don't regard myself as having a more privileged position than the reader in this regard. I believe we can all make our contributions and this leads on to the issue of the status or validity of ethical appraisals of faiths. In what respect can we know that we are right in our ethical judgments or what does 'being right' in our judgments mean?

What is the status of ethical judgments?

This then is our third preliminary consideration: the question of the status of ethical judgments about faith. This issue has often divided philosophers into two camps. When a religion or an aspect of religious practice is praised or blamed, some think that such judgments - when they use the correct logical procedures - are valid for all times and places. Philosophers who hold this view are ethical absolutists. Other philosophers take the opposite view and see ethical appraisals as only relating to the time and place in which they are made, and perhaps only to the specific cultures and religions from which they originate. According to such an ethical relativism, ethical judgments are not valid universally and do not apply beyond the limits of the time, place, culture and creed where they begin. We shall look first at this last view - that religions and cultures cannot judge each other, that, for example, a Western rationalist cannot judge the ethics of a religion or culture from a very different time or place.

Let us initially be clearer about the nature of ethical relativism. Ethical relativism is the claim that the only way the practices of a culture, tradition or religion can be judged is from within that domain. This is because from beyond any such culture, religion or tradition there can be little or no understanding of it and therefore no valid judgment made. Ethical relativism is often motivated by values of tolerance and has been found, ironically, in many different times and places, as this ancient Japanese sentiment makes clear, 'Nor let us be resentful when others differ from us. For all men have hearts, and each heart has its own leanings. Their right is our wrong, and our right is their wrong.'[9] Clearly, if this view were to prevail, it would undermine a great deal of judgment about religion that is being made, so let's examine cultural and ethical relativism a bit more closely.

Cultural relativism raises key questions about where cultural and religious boundaries lie. People have regional or tribal identities, usually supplemented by a nationality. Then of course there are ethnic and religious identities, as well as the important communal markers of language and dialect. All of these features are in constant change, and many concepts, ideologies and traditions bridge cultures and get exported and fused with others elsewhere. Now for cultural relativists, cultural boundaries cannot be identified or defined from beyond any culture, because for them such a point of view is inaccessible.

Yet neither can such boundaries between cultures be defined from within a culture because, as we have just seen, such boundaries exist on a spectrum of ever-changing borders that interact with each other. At best the boundaries are blurred. They are also in dispute.

Before all these questions can be answered, there lie some more basic ones, such as what is a *specific* culture or religion. Like the abstraction 'religion', such matters are understood, debated and mutually intelligible, as we saw earlier, not only within particular cultures, but across cultures - contrary to what cultural relativism would suppose.

Furthermore, in very practical, real-life situations, any significant amount of cultural relativism would mean that we would need to treat people from other cultures and religions as living in parallel, irrelevant universes. We might be curious about lifestyles but we would be right in thinking that generally speaking no one had anything to learn from other cultures. As regards ethics, this would mean that there were many truths and we simply found ourselves living within a particular set of them. Yet this is false. The issue might be whether someone is a freedom fighter or a terrorist; when, if ever, is abortion justified; or how far the UK government should spend money on aid to sub-Saharan Africa. The fact that such questions are hotly disputed both within and across cultures indicates that cross-cultural interaction is a mainstay of moral debate, not the limit of it. Different cultures, however they are defined, do reach understandings, whether it is the Good Friday Agreement in Northern Ireland, or agreements about land rights for the aboriginal peoples of Canada or Australia. Cultural and moral universes are integrated, not parallel.

Connected with this point is the issue of praise, blame and learning. Logically, praise and blame are two sides of the same coin. It makes no sense to be able to do the one without the other. The logic of cultural relativism is that we could do neither with regard to other cultures. Yet we and others not only praise and blame other cultures, we also learn from each other pragmatically – and morally – as well. It might be to do with education or policing, agriculture or literature, aesthetics or commerce: thoughtful cultures that can afford it go and find out about these things elsewhere precisely because it is widely appreciated that we can all learn from each other both about facts and values. If that is true, then any thorough-going cultural relativism is false.

There are also two connected philosophical arguments against cultural relativism.

First, the notion that each culture or religion is inaccessible to the outsider for any sort of judgment needs justification across the very cultural/religious barriers being asserted, otherwise it would convince nobody who needed convincing that such barriers were there. Yet if, as the relativist maintains, such barriers to understanding and judgment do exist, it would follow that they could not be crossed so as to communicate this fact.

Second, cultural and moral relativism also self-destructs because the claim that all cultural perspectives are true only within the limits of that culture is a claim that if relatively true can be ignored beyond cultural limits; or if universally true proves false the claim it seeks to assert, since then we would have found at least one, universal, non-culturally relative truth.

So, when it comes to being clear about the ethical status of our judgments about religion let's conclude that there are real problems with a full blown cultural and ethical relativism, and look instead at its opposite, moral absolutism.

Absolutism asserts the existence of a valid, true standpoint of judgment that is not relative to time or place. In its stronger form, it also asserts that people can find and use this true standard to gain knowledge. Many of us are absolutists in some respects but not in others. For example, many scientists and some philosophers of science would argue that when we measure the speed of sound or light we gain objective knowledge. Yet, when we begin to look at ethics or aesthetics this sort of absolutism is harder to find. For example, is there an absolutely best way to parent children irrespective of the culture around them? Can we be absolutist about a question like that? Surely questions such as 'what is appropriate dress?' defy absolutist judgment. Or do they? Many argue for example that the radical seclusion of women by the Taliban and ISIS violates their human rights: in this way, they are arguing that absolutist judgments *can* be made about a religion's practices.

One key argument in favour of absolutism has been well expressed by the political philosopher John Rawls in his *A Theory of Justice*. Rawls conducts a thought experiment that runs as follows. Let us imagine that we live at present in some sort of 'pre-world' or prequel to a world into which we are about to be born. In this pre-world – what he calls the original position – we have all of our faculties; we are able to reason perfectly well. The task we are all given is to agree with those others in the original position about the rules that will govern this forthcoming world. Crucially, however, we do not know who we will be there. We may or may not be able-bodied, We know nothing about what our natural capacities will be, our strength or intelligence. We know nothing either about what will be our conception of what is good and we are ignorant of our own psychology, for example we may or may not be a risk taker or an optimist. The circumstances of the society and our circumstances within it are also hidden from view in the original position. As such he calls the people behind this veil of ignorance a 'legislative council of equals' equalised by their ignorance of their place in this coming world. Rawls notes that self-interest cannot be separated from benevolence in the decisions made by the legislative council of equals because they don't know who they will be in this society. He concludes that the decisions made will be impartial and rational and therefore fair and just. The main barriers to a complete absolutism would be our mental faculties, but the implication is that if we could reason well enough, we would be able to gain a strong insight into rules for the best society that would be meta-cultural. Behind this veil of ignorance, we could, in principle, judge all ethics, all religions and all cultures.

The implication and hope within Rawls's thinking is that in practice, whatever the world that we are currently in, we can imagine ourselves behind this veil of ignorance, looking out at our universe and its possibilities. In that thought experiment, we could see past our own self-interest and that of others and so approach a more bird's-eye view or absolute perspective that is both rational and impartial and as such universally applicable. We would then have available to us a means of judging a culture or religion, without any kind of bias.

I want to argue that Rawls fails to offer us a viable route to anything like absolutism that can then be used to make valid ethical evaluations of religions. This kind of rational alchemy whereby we relieve ourselves of all but pure reason would be hard to check. How would we know when we had distilled our minds of all but this, and achieved an absolute, objective perspective?

The history of ethics in the West, at least since the Greeks, has been full of scholars seeking the best possible methods for deciding objectively and impartially what is right and what is wrong, and even those who largely agree that this can be done disagree about how to achieve this. Very broadly speaking, philosophers today – such as Rawls, or the famous Enlightenment philosopher Immanuel Kant – stand out as deontologists who think that reason will objectively and impartially tell us our duty and give us rules that should be kept. By contrast, ethicists such as Jeremy Bentham, John Stuart Mill and Richard Hare are utilitarians. They regard the consequences of actions and decisions as more important than the rules that actions and decisions follow. For Kant, for example, 'Do not murder' might well follow from his mother of all laws, called the categorical imperative, which states 'Act on that maxim whereby you can at the same time will that it should be a universal law.' So, for example, according to this principle, murdering Hitler would have been wrong because we could not morally will that there were a universal law according to which people could murder each other. By contrast for Bentham 'Do not murder' would very much depend on the consequences, because he would apply to it his principle of utility, which asks 'What would bring about the greatest amount of happiness for the greatest number of people?' In this case, murdering Hitler may well have been morally permissible if there had been good reason to judge that his murder would have resulted in greater happiness for more people than would have been the case otherwise.

My point is that if we imagine Kant, Rawls, Bentham and Mill among our legislative council of equals all using reason alone in order to reach an absolute objective view about how the world should be, they are not about to agree. They will be divided about whether principles or outcomes should take priority as an ethical guide. Their perspectives tell us that there are significantly divergent ways of applying reason to questions of ethics. What we have after hundreds, indeed thousands, of years ever since Plato, is a variety of judgments about what an absolute objective judgment would involve. And that is so after but the briefest possible glance at only the Western philosophical tradition, leaving aside the many perspectives other cultures have to offer.

There are additional problems about the attainability of objectivity and absolutism. The philosopher Paul Feyerabend, a fierce critic of concepts of objectivity, absolutism and pure reason writes that 'cultural variety cannot be tamed by a formal notion of objective truth because it contains a variety of such notions'.[10] This applies quite forcefully to John Rawls's thought experiment about his legislative council of equals in further ways than the one I have suggested about the deontologists and utilitarians. Let's imagine that behind the veil of ignorance our decision-makers are people from the rich variety of human cultures both past and present. These decision-makers would bring to the legislative council of equals their own languages, concepts and senses of belonging. They would very probably view the legislative council of equals differently. They would come to it with their own experience, both good and bad, of society and the individual. They could not come without these things otherwise they would have no concepts, language or experience with which to think about the legislation which it is their job to enact. These considerations indicate that the concept of the original position is itself deeply flawed. Further, what about simple preferences and tastes? Should we make decisions for a society without reference to these things? What about feelings and emotions? Should these also be banished? Someone who is a risk-taker compared with a more cautious individual is for example going to make different judgment calls. Rawls clearly thinks that none of these biases would feature in our deliberations in the original position. Yet how can he be so sure on the basis of reason alone that we would have the means to make any decisions whatsoever in the original position in the absence of bias and preference? For example one problem with a purely rational mechanism for decision-making is that there is going to be no motivation for it. Why would we choose to reason unless there was something beyond reason motivating us to do so?

I want to make a further point about the concepts of objectivity and impartiality. Both of these concepts seem important in Rawls's suggestion about how we might imagine correct absolute judgments of laws to be enacted. But here we should ask, is it impartial to view all people and situations from the outside as the objective legislative council of equals would? Judgments above and beyond individual lives and situations would appear to be dehumanised judgments. If we edit out all subjective points of view we have edited out all individual perspectives other than imagined ones. Such objectivity leads us more towards a partial humanity than impartiality. Objective, absolute judgments about ethics, if they exist at all, would appear inaccessible – at least in any strong sense – to the human mind.

A Way of Dialogue

So, if cultural relativism seems deeply problematic, and absolutism and complete objectivity are equally unattainable at least as regards judgments about culture and religion, where does that leave our capacity to make judgments and most especially ethical evaluations of faiths?

Our human capacities for reason and empathy are, I believe, a good place to start in answering this question. 'Reason' as an abstraction may be not a lot more, if anything more, than a set of figments of the imagination, some ancient and some modern, yet human beings are able to reason, and not just about mathematics. Hunter-gatherer communities, today's ethics committees, international negotiators and Ph.D. students in Islamic jurisprudence all use reason because without it we could hardly understand or ethically deliberate. The vast majority of human beings also have a capacity for empathy. We can use what has been sometimes called the 'sympathetic imagination' to think and feel our way into another's situation, dilemma or world-view; by this I mean a determined effort to reconstruct the perspectives and feelings of another, through the use of imagination for the purpose of understanding and with good intent.[11] Key ways in which we find ourselves able to use the sympathetic imagination are through hearing someone else's story and through having a variety of experiences ourselves. Now, importantly, it is not just individuals that have their stories or narratives, it is whole cultures and strands within cultures. Religions too have their stories by which they understand themselves and the world, and these narratives through internal and external dialogue with the wider world continue to be reiterated and reformulated.

I don't think we can get off the starting blocks of understanding and ethically evaluating religion without trying to find out how the lives of individuals and groups within a religion make sense to the people concerned. Religion is a practice of making sense of life, of individual life, human life and the universe beyond human life. The stories concerned are not simply the stories of sacred texts. Rather, they are the stories of how rituals, ethics, sacred objects, places, times, texts and people offer meaning and direction, hope and love. When you talk to religious people about their faith they will often tell you a story about their life or a story about the life of someone they know, they will mention their feelings of peace or community in a Quaker meeting or speak about drama, holiness and mystery at a Catholic Mass or the intimacy of a Passover meal. For some secularists who feel implacably hostile towards religious faith, their focus tends to be on the cold creedal statements of belief, on some of the most gruesome and questionable rituals and practices and on the many moral failings to be found in all faiths. What gets missed is the rich cultural and emotional life that individuals and communities share, the stratospherically glorious aesthetic and spiritual expressions that testify to remarkable religious motivation and vitality.

I am not suggesting at all that the believer's account of meaning, salvation or ethics is the end of the story. But without it we shall neither be able to understand nor judge religion. Without it we shall have fallen into the trap of de-humanising our understanding and judgment in the way that we have seen absolutism does. Whether we are a patient, a tax-payer or a religious believer and practitioner it is important to us that our subjective view is appreciated. Now there have been many perspectives that have taken the opposite view, that the subjective and insider account of religion is a delusion that gets in the way of proper understanding. Some of the godfathers of the social sciences – Ludwig Feuerbach, Karl Marx and Sigmund Freud – all shared this view, and a great deal has been written about their critiques of religion. For that reason and because the nub of my critique of them is the same as my critique of the new atheists, I shall not devote time to consider their judgments of religion. My key point is that dismissing the perspective of religious believers at the outset only makes sense if, as Feuerbach, Marx and Freud claimed, an absolute point of view can be attained that rules out all such perspectives. Yet I have already argued that even if this were so – which is very questionable – we would have no way of knowing that we had reached such an absolute place from which to judge and ethically evaluate religion, no way of checking. Marx and Freud give us two excellent examples of very different, even contradictory, alleged absolute truths about religion. They illustrate well how the contents of supposed absolutisms are so often contradictory, and perennially subject to change.

In our quest to understand and ethically evaluate religion I will therefore take seriously the perspectives of religious believers themselves, their outlooks, hopes and fears. I shall seek to understand something of the meaning that religion offers to people. In this sense the insider perspective needs to be a significant part of the picture. Faiths judge themselves, they are constantly in debate, conserving and reforming, and the judgments that are made at grass roots levels and also at institutional levels need our attention. Such insider perspectives however cannot be the end of the story. We saw that cultural relativism implies an inability to make judgments across cultural and religious divides and how such a relativism is incoherent. People from outside any particular faith must play their part in an evolving, balanced judgment of faiths. Religion and its institutions impact significantly upon those who have no religious belief at all and upon people of other faiths too. Crucially, there are the victims of religion as well as ex-religionists who have converted away from religion, sometimes for ethical reasons. Historians, sociologists, psychologists and philosophers of religion, some religious believers some not, also have a great deal to contribute to an evaluative judgment of faiths and some of these perspectives will often be in the foreground in order to begin to comprehend religious belief and practice on any significant scale. So any judgment of religion or any particular religion that failed to take account of outsiders' views would be very incomplete.

Judgments reached will therefore arise from dialogues within religion, between religions and between religion and those beyond its ken. By dialogue I don't just mean conversations but the whole complex of responses and dynamics that are in evidence between these groups. Ultimately, however, our evaluative dialogue must always remain open to response and be non-coercive. By its nature this on-going dialogue is neither owned nor controlled; this must be so if understanding and judgment are to best get along.

Further Direction

In discussing ethical evaluations of religion I shall focus on the present and recent past, on the twentieth and twenty-first centuries, for the following reasons. First our need for judgment is for most people about making sense of the ever changing present, the bewildering variety of events and situations that crowd the airwaves, the internet and social media. Secondly, the category of religion, as I have just indicated, applies best to the present and the recent past, it is in the widest sense a modern category. Thirdly, we have – by way of encounter, conversation and media – the greatest range of resources available about the last one hundred years or so by which to understand and judge.

Our task is complex but understanding and judging religion is necessary and is happening all the time. The writer Bernhard Schlink in his book *The Reader* suggested that insofar as we seek to judge we cannot understand and insofar as we seek to understand we cannot judge. Judging and understanding are perhaps as cross-currents or like an ebb and flow. Understanding involves a persistent, unceasing listening. Judging involves some element of stasis, of halting, of taking a snapshot view. I will reach tentative conclusions or judgments, we have to, to have a fresh basis from which to move on and to keep seeking further understanding. Equally judging constantly needs to give way to understanding, listening and dialogue and as such there is always an incompleteness about judgment and ethical evaluation.

Bearing in mind this approach, Chapter 2 examines media analyses of religion so as to identify the moral profiles of faiths that are impressed upon us. It considers what we might review from what we are offered and makes clear in some cases this urgent need. In Chapter 3, I consider the ethical profile of religious faiths, within four recent historical contexts that continue to impinge upon our world today: i. the civil rights movement in the US in the 1960s; ii. the rise of Nazism and its accompanying persecutions, especially of Jews, leading to the Holocaust; iii. the practice of, and reactions to, what is known as liberation theology in Latin America in the 1960s, 1970s and 1980s; and iv. the Israeli Palestinian conflict since 1948. Chapter 4 then considers the ethical significance of some central religious practices including, i. prayer; ii. meditation; iii. charity work; iv. mission and evangelising. Chapter 5 considers how religion affects the ethical character of the upbringing and schooling of children.

In chapters 6, 7 and 8, I focus on Islam as a case study, and begin in chapter 6 by examining a variety of understandings and interpretations of the Qur'an and its companion text and guide, the Hadith. Here I seek to bring to light some of the history of how these texts have been read, and the diversity of current interpretations that point us beyond specific pictures of Islam, towards greater plurality. In Chapter 7, I build on understandings brought out in Chapter 6 so as to better appreciate the variety of evaluations being made about women's rights within Islam. Drawing upon the arguments of Muslim feminists, Western critics and conservative Muslim scholars, I seek to construct an ethical appraisal that neither shies away from criticism of Islam, nor accepts without demur condemnations from without or within. A similar evaluative exercise takes place in Chapter 8 as regards the rise and countering of militancy within Islam. Here I bring together a set of historical contexts and factors to be related and understood before analysing the relative significance these have played within cultures of discontent and belligerence.

Chapter 9 turns to look at problems of evil and suffering. This is not distinct from ethical evaluations of faith. After all, for some kinds of atheism, belief in an all-good God is itself a moral outrage. This chapter, though, points beyond the theoretical character of the arguments towards the practical implications of the debate for believer and non-believer alike. In Chapter 10, Beyond Conclusions, I consider how future evaluations of religion are likely to develop, and I look at what are the best prospects for this necessary and inevitable enterprise.

2

Through A Glass Darkly: Religion In The Media Spotlight

In the Introduction I suggested that the process of understanding and ethically evaluating religion was a matter of dialogue, involving the many perspectives of religious believers, of critics and victims of religion, as well as of experts from a variety of disciplines. Yet this process can hardly begin without some indication of which evaluations are, as it were, 'in play' at present. In any culture at any given time, evaluations of many sorts are taking place, never more so than in the media-rich age in which we find ourselves. The media showcases specific evaluations, it also teaches the public, by example, how to reach judgments, often within the timeframe it takes to ingest a soundbite. Before we know it, we find ourselves in mid-stream among these appraisals of all aspects of our culture, including religion.

If we are to judge the ethical character of religion, it is important to understand something about the quality of the judgments that surround us, since they almost inevitably feed into our perspectives and points of view. This chapter will, I hope, offer us the space to reflect critically on our own views about religion, on the views of those around us, as well as on the processes by which they have been reached.

With these goals in mind, we shall focus on the character of the media's presentation of religion. We shall look in particular at UK media coverage of Christianity and Islam today, because these religions are those most reported about and because, as I have mentioned, they are centre-stage within our evaluations more generally.

First, though, I want to make an observation about the relationship between media judgment of religion and public engagement with it. This will indicate something about how our culture is inclined to reach judgments about religion at present.

Active personal involvement in religion on a regular basis is at an all-time low in the UK today and has been on the decline for many decades. Most of the mainstream Christian denominations here have suffered from falling rolls. The Catholic Church, the Church of England, the Methodist Church and the United Reformed Church are clear examples of this. This does not mean that there is not a residual belief in God that is widespread; there is, but this is detached from active religious engagement. So while aspects of Islam are growing, especially in parts of urban Britain; and while on occasion some types of evangelical Christianity buck the trend of institutional religious decline; a large proportion of Britons have negligible direct contact with a religious community, religious leaders or figures. Most people's contact with those who are actively engaged with a faith is through someone they may bump into at work or through friends. This trend means that the sources of information people access today about religion are often second-hand and thus somewhat depersonalised compared with a couple of generations ago.

Concurrent with this tendency, there has been a change within the media in the reporting of religion. In the 1980s and 1990s, quite a number of people who reported for major newspapers about religious affairs were themselves ordained clergy. Richard Chartres, recently retired Bishop of London, was Religious Affairs Correspondent for the Telegraph before his removal by Max Hastings in 1986. Today, very few news reporters are clerics of any persuasion, and the digital revolution, with its interactive dimension, has, in a secular age, further diminished a religious voice within the media crowd. In the 1980s and

1990s, reporting about religion was also considered 'soft news'. However, the course of events in the 2000s changed such perceptions dramatically. Religion came increasingly to take the form of 'hard news', as resurgent Islamism – including 9/11 and 7/7; the new atheism; and the horrors of child abuse at the hands of priests and clergy from a variety of denominations have made clear.

So what emerges is a situation where the public is largely disconnected – even alienated – from religious practice and engagement, and as such cannot easily critique a diet of high profile, hard and sometimes quite negative news about religion. In this situation, in effect the media becomes for many the conduit of what religion is all about. In fact some scholars have gone much further than this, writing about 'the mediatisation of religion'. This means that news about religion is not simply edited according to media design. More radically, the concepts of religion and how it works have become media constructions that operate independently of, and not particularly informed by, academic study or consultation with faith groups. Professor of Media Studies Stewart Hoover cites the reporting of 9/11 both in the US and in the UK as a classic case of this, where 'a priesthood of media reporters and anchors' constructed the meaning and importance of events as they developed.[12]

The receipt of hard, quite often negative news about religion by a highly secularised public is, in the long view, a new phenomenon. Forty years ago things were very different. At the same time, this situation has been around long enough – twenty years or so – to have bedded down as part of our zeitgeist. In these circumstances, an anti-religionism is valourised in some quarters as a newly-received wisdom. More moderately, though, religion is seen as something of an oddity, and to defend it or extol its virtues – whether or not there are any – is somewhat countercultural, in the sense that it goes against the direction of travel. It is all too easy in these circumstances for a confirmation bias to set in, whereby the public imagination expects and seeks out negative images of religion.

Of course the critic will protest first that the media does not invent religious atrocities where they occur and that, second, religion therefore only has itself to blame for its quota of bad press. This book will examine the first of these issues at length. Clearly there are religious atrocities, and we shall seek to understand some aspects of them. This chapter will consider the second question of the fairness and accuracy of reporting about religion, by looking at how news is formulated and produced.

I am contending, for reasons so far merely indicated, that there is a slight disposition to negatively judge religion in the media. This is not evenly spread: for example, as we shall see, negative judgments are much more pronounced as regards Islam compared with Christianity. This is not at all the same as saying that negative judgments about religion are mistaken or unjustified, they may be entirely justified. By negative I simply mean pejorative, rather than unbalanced or inaccurate. However, in the remainder of this chapter we shall try and find out a little more about media representations of religion, and ask three key questions: First, how reasonable is it to claim that in general there is negative treatment of religion in the media? Secondly, do we have good reason to question the accuracy of media portrayals of religion? Thirdly, how should we calibrate our own judgments about religion in view of the evident character of its media portrayal?

In order to consider the first two of these three key questions, I shall investigate two ancillary questions. In the first instance, we must look at who it is that reports on religion. What are their credentials and qualifications for doing a good job? And secondly, we need to understand how media outlets choose what is selected as a story and what gets left out; and how they choose the slant for a story, consciously or not. If we are to gain ground in our judgments of religion, we need to get a handle on these questions if, as I have suggested, the media is so pivotal as a source of information.

Who is it that reports about religion and what are their credentials for doing so?

Tom Butler, ex-Bishop of Southwark, often lamented the domination within the British media of a metropolitan, liberal, secular elite. His implication was that many journalists just don't do religion and that reporting about religion suffers as a consequence. How far journalists, especially those who report about religion, are more or less likely to be religious themselves is a matter of some dispute. All the same, Bishop Butler's objections about the secularist character of media personnel raises the question as to whether a squadron of committed believers would be any less prejudicial than their non-believing counterparts. Of more concern than the religious adherence, or lack thereof, among journalists are comments made by Andrew Brown, Religious Affairs Correspondent for the Guardian. Brown suggests not only that journalists are quite a sceptical lot, but that in the media there is little sense of religion as a lived reality, and that this is especially the case with Islam. This begins to raise deeper questions. Regarding those who report about religion in the media, it would be good to know that they understood a fair amount about religion(s), as they serve up a regular diet of judgments that are sometimes more and sometimes less well-founded on this basis. It would be worth knowing too that they had the time, inclination and skills to get to know religious communities and individuals well, that they had a sense of what a religious faith meant for people so committed. Having such a sense of religion as a lived reality doesn't entail having any religious commitment whatsoever, but it does involve having the time and skill to understand those who do, and to understand too the religious issues and organisations with which they are engaged.

It seems, however, that there is cause for concern on this front. The theologian and media commentator Dr. Christopher Landau writes, 'Religious stories will often be handled by journalists with little or no specialist knowledge of the subject matter, and precious little time to undertake background research on key issues of the day.'[13] He cites the case of an on-screen caption for BBC breakfast news introducing a Canon in the Church of England as a 'Cannon'! He continues that a lack of religious literacy results for example in some poor radio broadcasting, where 'car-crash' interviews featuring vehemently opposing voices produce lively argument and confrontation, while failing to inform.[14] The problem is that some journalists, not knowing the terrain of a religious affairs issue or the different interest groups in any depth, simply opt for well-known extremes, however unrepresentative they are either of the public at large or of religious interest groups in particular. Landau suggests that religious affairs compares badly with other news sectors. He suggests that in reporting say, a Labour government budget, you wouldn't bring on the Conservative grandee and former cabinet minister Norman Tebbit in dialogue with the Socialist Workers Party, even though controversy about the issue might well result. Instead, you would involve people who, while disagreeing, might themselves be closer to the issue. A lack of knowledge about religious organisations, structures and influence means that journalists all too often fail to identify the right representatives so as to shine light on an issue, beyond simply highlighting controversy. Landau cites the case of Christian Voice (not a very representative Christian voice by the standards of the vast majority of Christians in the UK or even in the US) and the National Secular Society both wheeled on to dispute the issue of religious offence caused by *Jerry Springer: The Opera*. Landau's point is that there were many better-informed religious and non-religious voices whose disagreements would have been more enlightening. We might equally consider the interviewing of Anjem Choudary by Channel 4 News and on BBC2's evening news programme *Newsnight* about the murder of Lee Rigby in Woolwich in 2013. Choudary is a sufficiently unrepresentative Muslim voice in the UK that there is good reason to ask why he was given the oxygen of publicity in relation to an audience that is not necessarily aware of how unrepresentative he is. While far more moderate representatives of Islam were there, such as Julie Siddiqi from the Muslim Council of Britain, other moderates from, for example, sections of the Shi'a community, could have been represented as well. Perhaps out of ignorance about who to select, but equally, at least, out of a focus on controversy rather than representation, both Channel 4 and BBC2 wheeled in Choudary probably the most radically belligerent Islamist leader in the UK today.[15]

In terms of who reports about issues, reporting about Islam would seem to be a particular concern. Few Muslims pursue a career within the media and journalism. According to research from City University, less than 0.5% of UK journalists are Muslim, while Muslims constitute about 5% of the country's population.[16] Again, this is not necessarily a problem in its own right – although it is hard to see that this fact is disconnected from Andrew Brown's observation that many reporters about Islam today have a particularly poor sense of that faith as a 'lived reality'.

Beyond the issue of the credentials of journalists and editors to inform or misinform us about religion, there is, it seems, an author-less process well underway in the digital world that is very powerful. Professor of Media Studies and Journalism Lynn Schofield Clark writes about the algorithmic authority of 'consensus based collective evaluation systems', where the number of hits a Youtube page or other website gets forms the basis of its authority. The most popular sources of information are not, for that reason, necessarily the best informed. and in an increasingly secular age, they are often quite critical of religion, thereby recycling somewhat negative perceptions as true.

Questions of research and editorial choice

Christopher Landau makes a crucial point when he writes that 'the ever-present danger is of what one might call "template journalism" – where hard-pressed hacks pick a tired cliché off the shelf and repackage it as a "news" story.'[17] Landau explains; 'so stories about Catholicism will tend to involve paedophile priests; interior shots of Church of England buildings will feature empty pews; and Islam will only feature in a story also featuring the word 'terrorism'.[18] The upshot is that stereotypes are reinforced and themes run and run without respite or deviation. Whatever the merits of such themes, little else gets selected. Landau continues that while deadlines have always been tight, naturally pushing journalists towards this kind of 'template reporting', the digital age has accelerated this trend, with print journalism failing to keep pace. According to media experts at Cardiff University, the amount of copy journalists have had to produce between 1988 and 2006 has trebled. Their reliance on pre-packed news from the public-relations world and wire copy has vastly increased during that time.[19] What strikes me is that the repetition of specific narratives and associations over long periods of time – that is, the consequence of such template journalism – has proven to be a most effective means of conditioning and indoctrination. I am also struck by the fact that for the last decade and a half, most especially after 9/11, religion has become hard news, and subject to a fair amount of negative template treatment. This is especially the case with Islam.

There is much more to say about questions of research and editorial choice, but let's pause to summarise at this point, before we look more specifically at these issues in relation to Christianity and Islam within the media. We are considering two key questions. First, how reasonable is it to claim that in general there is negative treatment about religion in the media? And second, do we have good reason to question the accuracy of media coverage of religion? To assist us with these questions we have been investigating our two ancillary questions, namely, 'Who is it that reports on religion and what are their credentials for doing so?', and, 'What is the quality of journalistic research and editing as regards media coverage about religion?'

We have found that the media framework within which religion is reported about in Britain is one in which we find the following five characteristics. First, there is something of a deficit of religious literacy and academic expertise about religion, Secondly, there is little sense of religion(s) as a lived reality. Thirdly, and subsequently, the most well-placed representatives of religious issues often fail to gain the media attention that might be the case in a more religiously literate environment. Fourthly, when the news is also filtered through the universes of a generally secular social media, 'consensus based evaluation systems' recycle somewhat negative perceptions of religion as true. Lastly, faced with on-line competition, often negative template journalism prevails, and this too feeds back into the consensus-based evaluation systems that reinforce such negativity. So, to answer the first key question about the negativity of reporting about religion, such a framework is not particularly sympathetic to religion. Crucially, this is antecedent to the question as to whether or not it is due our sympathy. The commercial imperative to report controversy all too easily fills in the gaps where understanding and insight are in relatively short supply. As regards our second key question to do with the reliability of media portrayals of religion, there are also reasons for concern. These include questions about the credentials of those reporting, their lack of appreciation of religion as a lived experience, their lack of time to research, including identifying the best representatives about an issue, and the increasing dominance and effects of template journalism over an extended period of time.

I shall now look more directly at editorial coverage of Christianity and Islam within the UK media.

Reporting on Christianity

Complaints about media coverage of religion are most numerous with respect to Christianity, principally because Christians are by far the largest religious constituent within the UK. These complaints invariably take the form of claiming either that Christianity is under-represented within the media and/or that it is overly negatively presented there. A particular charge is that controversy features over-much in media coverage.

As regards the question of the 'under-representation' of Christianity, Christianity seems hardly less represented today than it was in the 1980s, when a significantly larger proportion of the population was Christian. What has changed is that other religions feature more in media coverage. Much of this, though, is negative coverage about Islam, as we shall see, and not the kind of coverage about which another religion has any reason to be envious. The point is also made by media representatives that it is not the job of the media to represent constituencies of people proportionate to the size of those constituencies. Furthermore, it is not at all as if Christian voices are marginal when religion is in the news. In fact, even when speaking about British Muslims, according to one piece of research into UK media coverage, Christian leaders are marginally more frequently a source of information compared with Muslim community leaders.[20]

As regards the second issue – that negative and, most especially, controversial issues feature prominently in media coverage of religion and of Christianity – Ruth Gledhill, Religious Affairs Correspondent for the *Times* until 2015, points out that five specific areas of coverage about religion have been a consistent focus of attention in recent times: 1. As regards Christianity, sexuality and the split between evangelicals and liberals, regarding homosexuality for example. 2. The ordination of women priests and bishops in the Church of England. 3. The new atheism. 4. The rise of Islamism. And 5. Clerical child sex abuse.

Gledhill is in this sense quite happy to affirm that there is a prevalent template of negative reportage of religion in general, and of Christianity in particular, that has been in place for some time. Her point is that nothing is wrong with that and that bleating from the churches cuts no ice. She writes that what makes a religious affairs story work is what makes all other stories work, whether about scientific discovery, local planning, education or NHS reform: all such stories work because they contain controversy and division. The writer and journalist Andrew Brown comments on his work in the *Guardian* and *Church Times*, saying that whenever he gets a good story about religion he writes it as the greatest schism since the Reformation. Gledhill suggests that as far as those within faith communities are concerned who would like them to report on harmony within religion, they must first of all supply it, and then buy the papers that report it. Andrew Brown remarked when I interviewed him that 'everyone is misrepresented in the media, that is how journalism works'.[21] All of this, though, is to admit and not deny that Christianity gets something of a bad press. It's just that it has a lot of company – if for no other reason than that good press makes for poor sales. What is also being emphasised again here is that balance and fairness, accuracy and reliability are not the driving values of media coverage. Such values are, as ever, subservient to commercial imperatives.

There is some evidence that press coverage of Christianity is not entirely negative, and not even focused exclusively on controversy. Professor of Religious Studies at Lancaster University Kim Knott tells us about interviews with newspaper editors and religious correspondents conducted by the journalist Annikka Mutanen (2009).[22] She reports that none of the mainstream papers thought themselves to be anti-religious. The editor of the *Independent* (the most secular paper considered) maintained that the paper was 'opposed to aggressive secularism'.[23] On a pro/anti religious spectrum, the pro-religious newspapers began with *The Daily Telegraph*, followed by *The Daily Express* and *The Daily Mail* and *The Sun*. The *Independent* appears at the anti-religious end of the media spectrum followed by *The Guardian*, *The Daily Star*, *The Daily Mirror* and *The Times* in the middle, numerically. *The Times* and *The Telegraph*, while critical of Islam, are also highly critical of radical atheism. Given that *The Telegraph*, *The Sun* and *The Daily Mail* are the most popular dailies, Knott concludes that 'there is a conservative and pro-Christian emphasis in the British newspapers'.[24] The sociologist Professor Robin Gill reports from his 2011 survey of British newspapers that he 'detected little or no hostility towards mainstream Christianity or the Church of England in particular'.[25]

Yet, these surveys by Knott and Gill are not particularly extensive, and others report indifference and hostility to Christianity. Knott also makes it clear that media coverage beyond the newspapers stereotypes Christianity as out of date and anti-egalitarian, especially about issues of gender and homosexuality.[26] This illustrates once more the kind of negative template journalism that would appear to frame – and therefore overshadow – some specific, positive media coverage of Christianity.

Christianity no longer lives within a media friendly world in the UK It is largely out in the cold. While this puts it on a par with other aspects of public life where controversy is the mainstay of media attention, the widespread disengagement of the public with religion doesn't help its cause. Despite some research evidence to indicate a degree of positive coverage about Christianity, specifically in the mainstream press, more generally negative template treatment prevails – to return to our first key question. I am not claiming that this is necessarily unfair – that remains to be seen from what we will find more generally throughout this book – but, returning the focus on our second key question, we have found reason to question the reliability of media reporting about Christianity too. It should also be emphasised that the somewhat negative coverage of Christianity can so easily set up a confirmation bias, whereby we head off in a critically judgmental direction, irrespective of the evidence; where we come to observe and question in line with a somewhat pejorative predisposition. When that happens, it is unjustified.

Reporting on Islam

Following 9/11 in 2001 and 7/7 in 2005, Islam fell under the media spotlight more than ever in the UK, and a persistent association of Islam with terrorism became normative. A two-week study in 2008, compared with the early 1980s, saw a rise in references to Islam from 38 to 306, making it the largest, single category of reporting on religion in newspapers, and the fourth-largest topic of coverage on TV.

Three researchers into media coverage of religion, Teemu Taira, Elizabeth Poole and Kim Knott, conducted a qualitative analysis of three quarters of newspaper articles on Islam from October 2008.[27] Of the 87 articles analysed, 55 could be said to cover topics relating to terrorism, conflict and extremism. Seven of the articles could be described as broadly positive, the remainder of the articles showed Muslims in a predominantly negative light. Further observations were clear: for example, no political or historical context was provided regarding terrorism, the acts were simply linked to Islamic beliefs. Some of the most detailed research into media coverage of Islam in the UK has been undertaken at Cardiff University,[28] which then fed into written evidence to the All Party Parliamentary Group on Islamophobia given by Dr. Chris Allen in 2012.[29] This revealed a number of issues about UK press coverage of Islam. To quote from Dr. Allen's report:

'Four of the five most common discourses used about Muslims in the British press associate Islam/Muslims with threats, problems or in opposition to dominant British values. So, for example, the idea that Islam is dangerous, backward or irrational is present in 26% of stories. By contrast, only 2% of stories contained the proposition that Muslims supported dominant moral values.'[30]

The most common nouns used in relation to British Muslims in British print media were 'terrorist' (26%), 'extremist' (21%), 'Islamist' (9%), 'suicide bomber' (8%) and 'militant' (5%), compared with more positive epithets e.g. citizen (1%) and scholar (1%). References to 'radical' Muslims outnumbered references to 'moderate' Muslims by a ratio of 17:1. The report goes on to point out that while the majority of coverage about Islam does not compare it to other religions, where comparisons are made, negative comparisons outweigh positive ones by a ratio of 4:1. Of interest too are the sources of information quoted by the media in articles principally about British Muslims. The most popular sources are politicians (23%), the general public (13%) and criminal justice professionals (11%). Christian religious leaders stand at 4% and Muslim religious leaders at 3%. In other words, British Muslims themselves hardly feature as a voice about themselves. The Independent Press Standards Organisation (IPSO) has also had to make many interventions correcting negative misinformation about Islam within the media. According to one estimate, IPSO has needed to intervene twelve times more often with respect to Islam compared with Christianity, notwithstanding that, as we have seen, complaints about the coverage of Christianity far outweigh complaints about the coverage of Islam.[31] Kim Knott goes on to comment:[32]

> 'The frameworks within which Muslims are represented and understood continue to problematise and homogenise a diversity of people. Difference is highlighted [between Muslims and non-Muslims]. Categorising and classifying people in this way divides them along the constructed categories, concealing commonalities and obstructing understanding.'

The European Commission against Racism and Intolerance has also intervened calling for the UK media to 'avoid perpetuating prejudice', remarking that 'fuelling prejudice against Muslims' was 'reckless'. The United Nations human rights chief, Zeid Ra'ad Al Hussein, has similarly urged the UK to 'tackle hate speech', including in the media.[33]

To sum up then as regards our two key questions about negative media treatment, and about reliability of media coverage with respect to Islam, Islam in the UK has been subjected to sustained, heavily negative treatment over a period of almost twenty years. We have every reason to regard such treatment as unfair both in the sense that it is inaccurate – and has been proven to be so on many occasions according to IPSO standards; and also in the sense that it has given rise to deep-seated prejudice, and worse.

So let's now turn to our third key question of the chapter: how should we calibrate our own judgments about religion in view of the evident character of its media portrayal? We have identified something of the character of media judgments about religion, focusing especially on UK coverage of Christianity and Islam. Here we have found reason to call into question the expertise behind such evaluations. We have also found reason to query the quality of research involved, especially as regards the pace with which appraisals are made. None of this is perhaps at all surprising, but at the same time it is easy to feel in a quandary about such a state of affairs, and by default take more seriously than we would ideally choose some form of media diet which so easily feeds our conversations and reflections because it so dominates the public space.

I do not wish to suggest that we should on principle set aside whatever impressions we have gained about religion(s) from media sources, but rather that we should set out in our search to understand and judge religion, aware that what we have gleaned from media impressions about it should at every level be open to critique and revision. Understanding doesn't sell as well as judgment; the headline, strapline and sound bite won't accommodate it so easily. We therefore need to recalibrate the relationship between understanding and evaluation, putting more emphasis on the former. In this way, beyond the media spotlight, we may actually see more clearly. We shall therefore hear more from a wider range of voices about religion than we often do within media coverage. For example, we need to take a longer view of religion, to see it at work in specific situations over decades, as we shall in the next chapter. Understandably, with its inevitable focus on the news of the day, the media tends not to do that. We also need to see more of insider-narratives as well as academic studies of religion, and we'll do this in chapters 3, 4 and 5. Our case study of Islam in Chapters 6, 7 and 8 will engage with a variety of Muslim perspectives as well as academic voices – some Muslim, some non-Muslim. In this way, we shall better appreciate the problems associated with the mediatisation of religion and how making sound judgments about it requires the kind of on-going dialogue involving a wide variety of perspectives and expertise that I referred to at the end of the Introduction.

3

Religion Before The Ethics Tribunal: Four Contexts Of Religious Life And Practice

The next three chapters take forward the ethical appraisal of religion at the heart of this book. In this chapter I've chosen to examine the ethical character of religion within four recent contexts, from different parts of the globe.

Establishing that such an approach is reasonable and fair is dependent in large part upon the contexts and episodes that I select. So, I want to look at a range of situations that at least on first impression seem to reveal a variety of ethical results. This variety is not difficult to find and is crucial to represent if we are to make an attempt, from the outset, of being fair-minded rather than merely polemic.

The following four contexts that we shall consider offer a range of narratives from different parts of the globe about the ethical nature of religion. These are: The significance of Christianity and Judaism for members of those faiths in Nazi Germany and Nazi occupied territories from 1933 until the Holocaust. The role played by the Christian Churches within the civil rights movement in the US in the 1950s and 1960s. The role played by liberation theology and evangelical Christianity within the Churches in South America where, from the 1960s until the millennium, the Churches found themselves in many cases living among dictatorial regimes. And finally, the role of religion in the Israeli-Palestinian conflict since 1948.

I've chosen these narratives because they present religion in a variety of ethical lights as they have responded to a range of large-scale ethical challenges. The four contexts I describe also help to make clear the very varied ways in which religion engages with, and is engaged by, wider political and cultural influences that give it, as we shall see, a complex set of ethical profiles. It might well be objected that here I am being unfair in focusing on how religion responds in challenging ethical circumstances. Why don't we look instead at how religion operates more routinely? I will in effect do this in the next chapter when we consider the ethical significance of some routine religious practices. For now, though, it seems to me reasonable to ask how religion responds when the going gets ethically tough, and how far it makes the going tougher itself when it comes to ethics.

The moral significance of Christianity and Judaism in Nazi Germany and occupied Europe

When a delegation of Catholic bishops asked Hitler in 1933, shortly after his assuming power, what he was going to do about the Jews, he replied that he would do exactly what the churches had advocated and practised over the past 2,000 years.[34] While we can pick up a situation in which religion is involved in the present, the past is always relevant and the fact is that Churches – Protestant, Catholic and Orthodox alike – have been thoroughly anti-Semitic through significant parts of their history. To the credit of the Christians who made the film '*Shadow on the Cross*'[35], this is brought out clearly. From the fulminations of the early influential Christian thinkers known as the Church Fathers, such as St. Augustine, John Chrysostom, Tertullian and Origen; to the persecutions of Jews across Europe during the Crusades; to the visceral religious bile of reformist Martin Luther, significant aspects of church teaching had inspired vicious anti-Semitism throughout its history. This paved the way for the Holocaust, so that at the Nuremberg trials, Nazi leaders could accurately claim, as they did, that their crimes were following in the footsteps of Luther.[36] The following set of excerpts from Luther's *The Jews and Their Lies* makes this connection alarmingly clear.[37]

> 'What shall we Christians do with this rejected and condemned people, the Jews? Since they live among us, we dare not tolerate their conduct, now that we are aware of their lying and reviling and blaspheming. [ ] I shall give you my sincere advice: First, to set fire to their synagogues or schools and to bury and cover with dirt whatever will not burn, so that no man will ever again see a stone or cinder of them. This is to be done in honor of our Lord and of Christendom, so that God might see that we are Christians, and do not condone or knowingly tolerate such public lying, cursing, and blaspheming of his Son and of his Christians. [ ] Second, I advise that their houses also be razed and destroyed. For they pursue in them the same aims as in their synagogues.'

For all of the very distinct and direct links between the writings of Luther – alongside other Christian anti-Semites – and the Holocaust we cannot go so far as to say that Christian anti-Semitism was its chief cause. To understand more we need to look at how the churches acted and reacted before and during the 1930s and 1940s while Hitler was in power.

Many Christians who formed the German Christian movement saw Nazism and Christianity as essentially one religion – contrary to Hitler's perspective. The 'German Christians', as they were known during the 1930s and '40s, were mainly Protestant. They formed a movement of over half a million members, with branches throughout Germany. They praised both Jesus and Hitler in church services. African and Asian Christians had to be kept apart from German Christians.[38] In 1932, even before Hitler's dictates were made, German Christians excluded Jews from churches under their influence. This movement represented about a third of Christians in Germany. We get more of a sense of the continuity of Christian anti-Semitism when we look at some Protestant theology of the nineteenth and early twentieth centuries. The idea that Christianity might become Judaised, or in some sense polluted, seems to be a central fear. For the hugely influential Protestant theologian, Friedrich Schlieremacher, Judaism was a dead religion, redundant following the time of Christ, since the Jews should have been expected to convert, but didn't. Given what he described as their 'pathological state of mind', Schlieremacher was even against the conversion of Jews to Christianity, for fear they would Judaise the faith. Similarly, the Lutheran theologian, Adolf von Harnack rejected the Old Testament as not part of the canon of scripture, and the New Testament scholar Gerhard Kittel exhibited a series of anti-Semitic biases in his *Theological Dictionary of the New Testament*. The theologian Professor Diamaid MacCulloch who, having been a deacon in the Church of England, now describes himself as a 'candid friend of Christianity', comments that for a number of Christians in Germany at the time, this gave some superficial plausibility to setting up an anti-Semitic German church aimed at eliminating Jewish influence on all ecclesiastical institutions.[39]

There were also Christians directly involved in atrocities, for example army chaplains who witnessed mass killings. MacCulloch points out some notable individuals. 'Presiding over the German atrocities in Ukraine as its chief administrator was Erich Koch, among the most long-standing members of the Nazi Party, but also a devout Protestant who was sometime President of the Provincial Synod of the Lutheran Church in East Prussia.'[40]

A little background to the Catholic Church's situation in Germany in the 1930s will help set the scene. Describing the removal of the democratic apparatus within the Nazi state once Hitler had assumed power in April 1933, McCulloch writes as follows:

> 'The final barrier to [Hitler's] abolition of those same institutions was removed by the over-trusting agreement of Germany's Catholic Party, the Centre (Zentrum), who in March 1933 decided to vote for an Enabling Act in the Reichstag, giving Hitler supreme power and suspending democracy. ...Rome's chief envoy in Germany, the future Pope Pius XII, Eugenio Pacelli, negotiated a concordat with Hitler which promised to preserve freedoms for the Catholic Church [...] the price was the dissolution of the Zentrum and Catholic trade unions, and a ban on any political activity on the part of the Church's clergy.'[41]

McCulloch paints a picture of Papal naivety, explaining that from there on Pius XI 'did what he could', issuing an encyclical that was read out in German in all German Catholic churches on Palm Sunday in 1937 entitled 'With Burning Anxiety'. The text condemned the harassment of the Church and criticised Nazi racism.[42]

All the same, significantly affected by the anti-clericalism of the communists and anarchists in Spain, the Pope regarded communism as a far greater threat to the Church than fascism. He made no complaint when Hitler marched into Czechoslovakia. The puppet regime Hitler installed was led during World War II by Monsignor Jozef Tiso, who continued to act as a Catholic parish priest during his presidency. He was directly responsible for implementing the deportations of Jews and Roma at the Nazis' request. In Croatia, Ante Paveli led a self-styled Catholic regime, devoted to ridding a multi-ethnic state of Jews, Roma and Orthodox Serbs. Even the Nazis thought his methods sadistic. Pope Pius XII also gave at best a very muted critique of the Nazi treatment of Jews. The most that can be said is that in 1942, in his Christmas speech, he referred to those killed by the Nazis; but he failed to mention the Jews. Pope Pius XII's near silence about the subject continued for thirteen years after the war.

There was, nonetheless, some very brave and concerted opposition to Nazism and anti-Semitism on the part of the churches. While the Catholic Church and the Pope initially welcomed the Vichy regime in France, with its traditionalist slogan 'Work, Family, Country', as time passed, more clergy and laity came to oppose the regime and the deportation of Jews, many hiding Jews in their homes. Ethicist and author of *Humanity: A Moral History of the Twentieth Century*, Jonathan Glover explains that in Holland, where there was widespread resistance to Nazism from the beginning of the occupation, opposition to the persecution of Jews took place early. This is consistent with the psychological point that initial, slight collaboration or passivity tends to significantly weaken resistance. Dutch historian, Professor Louis de Jong estimates that about 25,000 Jews were hidden in people's homes in Holland.[43] Christians have made much of people like the Dutch woman Corrie ten Boom and her family who sheltered Jews, clearly motivated by a Christian ethic. However, there were many who sheltered or made provision for those persecuted who were not particularly religious or whose religious affiliation was merely official. Oscar Schindler, the real man behind the hero of the film *Schindler's List*, was officially Catholic, although Catholicism can hardly take credit for his list. As explained by Thomas Keneally, who wrote the book Schindler's Ark upon which the Spielberg film is based, it was out of a basic, human gut instinct, that Schindler was repelled by the sight of innocent people being brutally bullied, mistreated and killed.

The case of the Protestant Confessing Church is interesting. Motivated by a concern that Nazism looked like Hitler worship, and that it sought to take over the organisation and guidance of the church for nationalist purposes, leading figures like Karl Barth and Martin Niemoller came together in 1934 to write the Barmen Declaration. This sounds like a timely and promising development in Germany, and in many ways it was. The writings and activism of Confessing Church pastors such as Dietrich Bonhoeffer further illustrates Christian resistance to Nazism. Bonhoeffer was initially a pacifist, doing everything to persuade Protestant clergy to refuse the draft. He had every opportunity to spend the war in the US when he visited in the summer of 1939. Instead, he committed 'to [being] with his own people in its darkest hour' and returned to Germany, ultimately turning away from his pacifism in support of a plot to assassinate Hitler in which his brother-in-law Hans von Donanyi was involved. Following Hitler's orders to annihilate all resisters Bonhoeffer was ultimately executed at Flossenburg concentration camp just days before its liberation in April 1945. Yet for all of the courage displayed by many members of the Confessing Church, the Church as an institution, as well as the vast majority of individuals within it, do not seem to have particularly spoken out specifically about anti-Semitism. We have seen why theologically the Confessing Church might have failed to do this, or failed to see the need to do it. Very sadly, this seems to fit some of the facts. Karl Barth, who like Bonhoeffer did speak out against anti-Semitism at times, also observed of the Barmen Declaration that in the early 1930s, no text that had condemned anti-Semitism would have been acceptable, even to the Confessing Church, given the atmosphere that there was then.

One question to consider is, compared with the various groups of Christians, whether or not non-religious people would have behaved any better towards those who were persecuted in the Holocaust.

This is not at all easy to answer, and is just one reason why our judgments must always be provisional. Still, anti-Semitism as a basic thread throughout much of the Churches' histories would seem to have some role in assisting the Holocaust, and to have done little to stand in its way. There were a minority of brave Christians who stood out and sought to protect Jews and other victims of Nazism. Christian opposition to Nazism within the hierarchies of the Confessing Church, however, was not focused on anti-Semitism, and the theological weakness of Protestantism is starkly apparent here.

Many Christians today are not particularly aware of the vast history of anti-Semitism within their faith. Some who are, are actively engaged in countering it.[44] Nevertheless, there is also a lack of awareness that it persists in some Churches today.[45] Such a lack of self knowledge is a key moral weakness. Not forgetting the Holocaust is not enough. The various factors that parented it, including Christian anti-Semitism, must also not be forgotten.

Nazi persecution, of course, had been unlike all forms of Christian anti-Semitism hitherto, and focused on ethnicity, not on religion. Whereas the victims of the Spanish Inquisition could convert to Christianity (and then annul their Christian vows) through the Jewish rite of Kol Nidre designed for the purpose, with Nazism conversion was irrelevant. A rather sad aside in relation to this is the story of Edith Stein. Born in 1891, Edith Stein converted from Judaism to Catholicism in 1922 and ultimately became a Carmelite nun. The Nazis still executed her but, after the war the Catholic Church and the Jewish authorities have failed and still fail to agree about whether she was a Jewish or a Catholic martyr. It seems to me that in this rather hideous retrospect the Catholic Church has wanted more than its pound of flesh.

One consequence of the Holocaust as an ethnic rather than religious 'genocide' is of course that there were Jews in the concentration and death camps, in the transports and the ghettos who had faith, and there were those who did not. How did the faith of the victims help them? Or did it make things worse? What does seem to be the case is that those who found the psychological stamina to survive have been said to fit largely into two categories, those who had or thought they had families outside the camps; and those who had a deep religious faith. Insofar as this points to religious faith as an extraordinary psychological and spiritual resource, this seems to me to be a good and a moral good. The writer, Brian Close relates the following account from the Holocaust:

> 'An inmate of Buchenwald, Eugene Heimler, found himself responsible for a group of children who had been separated from their families. As he shared his faith with them he discovered hidden resources within himself: "I felt I was praising the Infinite power which had granted me the opportunity of playing a positive role in this inferno. I felt that I had strength only because He was present in my blood and in my senses, and that so long as I realised this force within me, the Germans would be unable to touch me."[46]

A further interesting example of religion as a source of strength relates to an incident in Auschwitz. Yossel Rosensaft testified that in December 1944, he and a group of inmates calculated when Hanukkah would occur. They went out of their block and found a piece of wood lying in the snow. With their spoons, they carved out eight holes and put pieces of carton in them. Then they lit these and sang the Hanukkah song 'Ma Oz Tsur Yeshuati'. None of the people who did this were religious, but on the threshold of death they demonstrated that contrary to Nazi lore, they were human and that Jewish tradition, history and values had a meaning for them. So, even those who were not particularly religious could and did draw strength from their religious affiliations and culture. When all else is gone, religion seems to have been for some – at least in the worst conceivable circumstances – a remaining strength, and of moral worth.

To summarise: within the Christian Era, until the Holocaust, the various Churches have been at the heart of the development and sustenance of anti-Semitism. This is still the case in some instances now, while anti-Semitism is firmly rejected in most Church institutions today. Through acts of commission and omission, and often through a desire for self-preservation, the Churches thus enabled anti-Semitic cultures to flourish, which Nazism then co-opted, with genocidal intent. The Confessing Church in Germany opposed Nazism for its adoration of Hitler rather than for its anti-Semitic practices. A limited number of Christians did on occasion oppose anti-Semitism, but those with firm religious conviction do not particularly stand out in relation to those with less of, or without, such a conviction. Religious devotions and practice offered something of spiritual worth to those suffering the worst forms of persecution, especially within Judaism, even in cases where some such victims were not routinely religious. So in these very varied examples we see therefore how religion can be at once devastatingly vicious; extremely malleable; and also a profound source of strength, giving glimpses of transcendence in the worst of circumstances. This multifaceted character of religion is at the heart of our moral dialogue about it.

Christianity and the American civil rights movement in the 1950s and 1960s

In this section I shall look briefly at Christopher Hitchens's critique of the view that Christianity made a significant ethical contribution towards the civil rights movement in the US in the 1950s and 1960s. This approach both grounds this aspect of an ethical evaluation of religion within dialogue, and also gives us a glimpse of the calibre of a specific, new-atheist perspective within this. In his critique of Christianity and his account of civil rights reforms, Hitchens goes to some lengths to dissociate the American civil rights movement, led by Martin Luther King, Jr., from Christian inspiration and influence. He makes three suggestions to support this view. Firstly, that unlike the warnings about hellfire for the unbeliever to be found in Judaism, and the teachings of both John the Baptist and Jesus, Martin Luther King on the other hand never suggested that there would be divine revenge against anyone, either now or after death. Therefore 'in no real, as opposed to a nominal sense, was [King] a Christian.'[47] Secondly, that many within King's inner circle were communists and socialists who had been 'manuring the ground for a civil rights movement' and had helped train volunteers. So that, by implication, the dominant role of Christianity in the civil rights movement has been much exaggerated. Thirdly, that the Churches, having historically been so involved in slavery in America, appear in the 1950s and 1960s to have been more for than against racial segregation.[48]

Let's take these points in turn. The first argument here is a candidate for absurdity and religious illiteracy if ever there was one. Many Biblical scholars (unlike Hitchens) who are also self-confessed Christians, do not believe in hell and if they do, many do not believe in eternal hell.[49] Hitchens starts from the premise that all Christians either do or should take a fairly literalist view of their scriptures, because this is the only type of sense that Hitchens, rather than Christians, can make of the Bible. Therefore anyone who fails to live up to Hitchens's interpretation of the Bible cannot be judged a Christian. Second, if Hitchens read the Gospels at all closely, he would see that forgiveness features rather more than hell as a teaching. King who, I dare say, knew the Bible rather better than Hitchens, was conscious of this. King is being utterly consistent with the Sermon on the Mount – to turn the other cheek, to repay evil with good; and with the Parable of the Good Samaritan – to treat those who may most hate you with love and kindness. His views are consistent with Jesus's alleged utterance during crucifixion, 'Father forgive them, they know not what they do,' and with I Corinthians 13, that love 'keeps no score of wrongs'. Unlike Hitchens, King knew his Koine Greek and Hebrew, and unlike Hitchens, King did not keep to literalist interpretations of the Bible. I doubt there is anyone who knew King who thought he wasn't a Christian. What this first point of Hitchens demonstrates is his desperation, when faced with Christianity seeming to do good, to force the facts to say the opposite.

King, of course, is both a product of Christianity and a forger of it. Like everyone he had his faults, but he and others within the movement drew upon Christianity very effectively to achieve desegregation. They were inspired by its teaching, its worship and its prayer. Early in campaigning, after many threats, including to his life, a phone call one night made him want to give up. King prayed to the effect that he could not face intimidation any more. He wrote,

> 'At that moment I experienced the presence of the Divine as I had never experienced Him before. It seemed as though I could hear the quiet assurance of an inner voice saying: "Stand up for righteousness, stand up for truth; and God will be at your side forever." Almost at once my fears began to go. My uncertainty disappeared. I was ready to face anything.'[50]

From the outset, it is clear that without his Christian context and experience King would not have been the person he was, to do what he did. At crucial points his Christian faith was at the heart of his motivation, inspiration, courage and mission.

Three nights later, King's house was firebombed with his family inside. A crowd of about a thousand gathered outside, keen to find and deal with the culprits. King told them, 'We must love our white brothers no matter what they do to us. We must make them know that we love them. Jesus still cries out in words that echo across the centuries: "Love your enemies, bless them that curse you, pray for them that despitefully use you." This is what we must live by. We must meet hate with love. Remember, if I am stopped, this movement will not stop, because God is with the movement. Go home with this glowing faith and this radiant assurance.'[51]

The Gandhian philosophy of satyagraha combined with Christian worship were at the heart of civil rights campaigns.[52] A good example of this is the campaign in Birmingham, Alabama. King teamed up with the Rev. James Lawson who, like him, had been to India and had studied satyagraha. Richard Deats, in his biography of King, writes about the preparations in Birmingham:

> 'Nightly mass meetings brought the community together for inspiration and education, mental, and spiritual preparation. Prayers and singing undergirded the message of the preachers. Regular church-goers were well accustomed to 'altar calls' in which sinners were called to come to the front and pledge their lives to Christ. Similarly, altar calls were given to those who were ready to give their lives to serving Christ through the non-violent campaign.'[53]

So a religious ritual of commitment was being augmented to create and sustain pacifist solidarity in the civil rights cause. Volunteers signed a commitment card that read as follows:[54]

Name
The Birmingham Campaign

I HEREBY PLEDGE MYSELF -- MY PERSON AND BODY -- TO THE NONVIOLENT MOVEMENT. THEREFORE I WILL KEEP THE FOLLOWING TEN COMMANDMENTS:

1. MEDITATE daily on the teachings and life of Jesus.
2. REMEMBER always that the nonviolent movement in Birmingham seeks justice and reconciliation -- not victory.
3. WALK and TALK in the manner of love, for God is love.
4. PRAY daily to be used by God in order that all men might be free.
5. SACRIFICE personal wishes in order that all men might be free.
6. OBSERVE with both friend and foe the ordinary rules of courtesy.
7. SEEK to perform regular service for others and for the world.
8. REFRAIN from the violence of fist, tongue, or heart.
9. STRIVE to be in good spiritual and bodily health.
10. FOLLOW the directions of the movement and of the captain of a demonstration.

I sign this pledge, having seriously considered what I do and with the determination and will to persevere.

Address Phone

Nearest relative

Address

Besides demonstrations, I could also help the movement by:

(Circle the proper items) ,

Run errands, Drive my car, Fix food for volunteers, Clerical work, Make phone calls, answer phones, mimeograph, Type, Print Signs, Distribute leaflets.

ALABAMA CHRISTIAN MOVEMENT
FOR HUMAN RIGHTS
Birmingham Affiliate of S.C.L.C.
505 1/2 North 17th Street,
F. L. Shuttlesworth, President

The whole philosophy of non-violence was predicated on a combination of Biblically-based pacifism and Gandhian satyagraha. The campaigns were also object lessons in Christian living, as the above pledge card from the Southern Christian Leadership Council makes clear.

There is something else indelibly Christian that gave the civil rights movement its non-violent force, and that was the power of martyrdom. Explaining the commitment for which he and others gave their lives, he wrote 'If someone has not found a cause for which to die, he has not found a cause for which to live.' Martyrdom has become a dirty word in our time, sullied through the history of Islamism, and of political and secularist polemic. However, I want to suggest that martyrdom can be a supreme moral act. To be clear, for the likes of King, Lawson and other Christians within the movement, it involved an absolute rejection of killing others but an affirmation that the lives of others and the lives of those in the future were something that one's own life should serve. It was a reversal of the consumerist ethic whereby those who come after us will pay the environmental cost of our consumption. So there is very good reason to think of the civil rights movement as Christian in its roots, in its inspiration and in its ethics.

What of Hitchens's second point, that the civil rights movement was significantly inspired and supported by communists and other primarily political elements, and that the contribution of Christianity has therefore been much exaggerated? It would have been odd if such communist elements had been absent from the movement, because it stood in opposition to establishment capitalist concerns and structures that entrenched poverty, as well as racism. It should be clear though that King spoke out specifically against communism, and pointed out its incompatibility with Christianity in his eyes[55] – not the kind of thing to do if you had been trying to maintain good relations with a significant element of your powerbase. Rather like in many protest marches in the UK and elsewhere, the communists and their acolytes were hangers-on.

The view that the civil rights movement and the effectiveness of Martin Luther King are due in large part to his communist and socialist backers has no basis in what Hitchens writes nor anywhere else that I can find. Hitchens moves effortlessly from the fact that King had some such backers (all he can find evidence for), to the conclusion that by implication they were responsible for the success of the movement. It is interesting, despite the evidence, that Hitchens is keener to credit communism (with all its virtues?) than Christianity, a further example of ideological desperation.

Hitchens' third claim, that in the America of the 1950s and 1960s, the Churches appear more for than against segregation is by far his strongest point.

Much of US Christianity at this time was quite opposed to the civil rights movement. King is himself deeply critical of the Churches in this respect. He also opposes those who on paper agree with the justice of the civil rights campaign, while in practice advocating delay. His *Letter From Birmingham City Jail*, as Hitchens points out, is icily polite, while making clear to the white clerical recipients of the letter that a policy of 'be patient' will not do when it comes to justice and equal rights. In his *Strength to Love*, King writes,

> 'One of the chief defenders of the vicious system of apartheid in South Africa today is the Dutch Reformed Protestant Church. In America slavery could not have existed for almost two hundred and fifty years if the church had not sanctioned it, nor could segregation and discrimination exist today if the Christian Church were not a silent and often vocal partner. We must face the shameful fact that the church is the most segregated major institution in American society, and the most segregated hour of the week is…eleven o'clock on Sunday morning.'[56]

King's accusation here against the Christian Church goes to the core of its ethics. We should be clear that the vast majority of those who were implacably opposed to the civil rights movement, who hounded and physically attacked members of the civil rights movement, were self-confessed, church-attending Christians who, in support of their racism, cited the Bible, church history and anything else they could dream up. There were of course other versions of Christian theology at large. The fundamentalist evangelical Billy Graham, hidebound with a specific type of Protestantism, viewed salvation as very much an individual matter, and not to do with societal and institutional change. For this reason, while criticising racism, Graham would not associate with the civil rights movement, and dissuaded other evangelicals from doing so. On the other hand, the National Committee of Negro Churchmen declared that God had chosen black humanity to resist the powers of racism, capitalism and imperialism. Adopting the slogan 'Black Power', it affirmed a special covenant between God and black humanity to ultimately work for the liberation of all human beings.[57]

Hitchens concludes from the fact that different Christian groups espouse different theologies, and from the fact that there were and are millions of secular anti-racists, that King's life, example and teaching had little to do with his professed theology. King devoted a good deal of time to explaining exactly why the civil rights movement had everything to do with his professed theology. *Strength to Love, Stride Toward Freedom, The Trumpet of Conscience,* and the *Letter from Birmingham City Jail* are all good examples of this. However, Hitchens fails to engage in any theological argument, and as such makes no case for his claim.

One thing that must strike any reader, from what we have seen very briefly here, is the plurality and plasticity of Christian ethical responses, of their theologies and institutions – even within the specifically Protestant context we have observed – with respect to a single set of issues. The more we look, the more we shall find of this. We see extraordinary moral and spiritual courage in fighting racial hatred and discrimination rooted firmly in a Christian faith, alongside other forms of that faith that display racism of every stripe. Such diametrically opposed positions are worth identifying as aspects of the ethical dialogue this book is about.

Liberation theology and Protestant conversions since the 1960s in Latin America

My third choice of narrative about the ethical roles and responses of religion in challenging circumstances focuses on Latin America since the 1960s. I shall look especially at the role of the Catholic Church as it has engaged with, and been engaged by, oppressive dictatorial regimes there. I shall also consider the ethical character of US evangelical Protestantism and its rapid missionary expansion throughout the region.

For over three hundred years following the Spanish and Portuguese conquests in Latin America, the Catholic Church had played a pivotal role in maintaining the semi-feudal structures of the old colonial order. 'It became locked in a symbiotic relationship with the civil authorities, who granted it status, wealth and influence, particularly through the education system, in return for the Church's unequivocal support.'[58]

The sociologist of religion Professor Steve Bruce argues that this courting of oppressive, often right-wing political regimes is a familiar theme within

Catholicism in recent times. From Franco's Spain and Mussolini's Italy to the Latin American dictatorships of the late twentieth century, the Catholic Church, he claims, has more than occasionally bolstered its institutional interests through less than savoury means.[59] Speaking specifically about Nicaragua Bruce explains:

> 'Bishop Canuto Reyes y Balladres blessed the weapons of US marines before they went into battle against the leftist guerrilla forces led by Augusto Sandino, leader of the 'Sandinistas'. When Somoza Garcia was murdered in 1956, Archbishop Gonzalez offered 200 days' indulgence to those Catholics who assisted with prayers for the departed dictator.'[60]

However things were to change. Bruce continues:

> 'By 1979 the attitude of the Catholic Church in Nicaragua had shifted sufficiently for the ousting of the Somoza regime to be accepted. The previous two decades had seen Latin American politics become increasingly polarized. Half the states already had military dictatorships; the other half acquired them. Opposition became increasingly radical.'[61]

These changes were built upon, while at the same time they also inspired, what the Peruvian priest Gustavo Gutierrez christened 'liberation theology', a movement within Catholicism that grew out of this oppression and gained traction across Latin America in the 1960s and 1970s. Liberation theology has had to a varying extent a Marxist pedigree – more so in its relation, for example, to the Christians for Socialism movement – but for all of this it has been very much Christian.

It took as its paradigm the story of the exodus of the Israelites from slavery, a pointer that enjoined the Church to liberate all humanity from bonds of poverty and injustice. Jesus's first sermon in Nazareth in Luke 4: 18, where he claims to have come 'to bring good news to the poor' and 'to liberate those who are oppressed', is set alongside prophetic condemnations of those who fail to live up to these demands (Amos 2: 6). This 'preferential option for the poor', as it became known, drew upon recent Catholic teaching and theology at the time. For example, the second ecumenical council of the Catholic Church known as Vatican II in the early 1960s called on the church to 'remove the immense economic inequalities on the planet', and mandated that the 'poor and afflicted' should be the special focus of its mission.[62] A conference of Latin American bishops in Medellín, Colombia in 1968 built on this, and liberation theologians such as Gutiérrez, Leonardo Boff and Jon Sobrino went further, suggesting that theology should be derived from the circumstances and needs of the poor. For example, the meaning of concepts such as salvation, crucifixion and resurrection were to derive from, and speak to, the material and the spiritual needs of those at the bottom of society. Sin was also to be understood as just as much to do with the systems within society as to do with the motives, dispositions and deeds of individuals. Legal frameworks, financial structures and government bureaucracy, when they operated as part of systems that maintained or exacerbated the plight of the poor, were ripe for transformation. In this way in his *Theology of Liberation*, Gutiérrez made clear that the political and the spiritual were indissoluble.

Liberation theology was never one thing. Sometimes guerrilla warfare and militant opposition was advocated against repressive regimes by members of the Church, especially early on. Camillo Torres, a former chaplain at the National University in Bogotá, joined a guerrilla group in 1966 and was killed in action by the Columbian military. Others saw liberation theology as quite incompatible with violence, even in the face of oppression. It also, to a lesser or greater extent, took a dim view of 'imposed' theology sent down through Church hierarchy, preferring community-based theology that evolved through the practical needs that were encountered.

Oscar Romero, archbishop of San Salvador, was appointed because the Catholic Church believed he could temper the radical, and at times militant, aspects of liberation theology tying it more firmly to conservative and official elements within the Church. Romero consistently spoke out against violent opposition to the state, both from members of the Church and from anyone else. But he also condemned state violence and its oppression of the poor. He was nominated for the Nobel Peace Prize for his campaigns about human rights. Despite the close association of his predecessors with the president and governments of the day, he refused to appear in public with any army or government officials until the government investigated the assassination of his friend and colleague Father Grande by an El Salvadoran National Guard commando shortly before Romero's appointment as archbishop. For his pains, and after many threats and warnings, Romero was himself assassinated by four masked members of the state militia in 1980. While this essential moral courage is perhaps most visible in public figures like Romero, liberation theology would not have gained ground as it did without that same courage being very widespread, a motif that we have already observed in the American civil rights movement.

In the 1980s liberation theology in Latin America began to decline, but not before it had helped spawn more democratic forms of government and a greater political engagement of ordinary people, including the indigenous peoples, in many countries. The story of this movement in Latin America also intersects with other religious developments. Concerned by its Marxist inheritance, the Vatican became more critical of the movement in the 1980s. It also saw it as too horizontal, forging cohesions across communities based on grassroots suffering and 'on the hoof' theology. This was at odds with its institutional needs: that the Catholic masses consistently rely for their guidance and theology on the hierarchy of the Church. It imported many priests from abroad, including from Europe, but failed to recruit enough and lost its local grip on many communities, paving the way for US evangelical missionary activity with its own right-wing agenda.[63]

Often Pentecostal, this US-backed missionary activity was very organised and well financed. Its campaigning was a further effective antidote to the moral and political agendas of liberation theology, and in the 1980s this US-based Christian fundamentalism was converting the Latin American population on a grand scale. Luis Palau and US television evangelist Jimmy Swaggart preached to packed city stadiums of tens of thousands, aggressively criticising Catholicism. A Catholic survey in the 1980s indicated that every hour, 400 Latin Americans converted to some form of evangelical church – especially Pentecostalism. One-eighth of the region's 481 million people came to be fundamentalists or evangelicals at this time. The Catholic bishops registered such conversions as one of their three top concerns, along with foreign debt and guerrilla violence. According to a study by the Brazilian Institute of Geography and Statistics at that time, nearly 10% of the country's 140 million people had come to belong to 4,077 evangelical churches.[64]

In Chile these became known as Reagan cults by their Catholic critics, due to their close ties with the US administration of then-President Ronald Reagan, and their evangelical celebrities in the field such as Swaggart, Pat Robertson and Jerry Falwell.[65] Despite their success in converting about 10% of the Chilean population in the 1980s, they also met moral resistance from ordinary Catholics. When Swaggart visited Santiago in early 1987, praising the regime of then president and dictator Augusto Pinochet and its expulsion of 'the devil' – that is, the Left – in its 1973 coup, Chilean Catholics, tired of the regime's brutality, took umbrage. The Protestant evangelicals also preached a political conservatism akin to Billy Graham's disengagement from the American civil rights movement, and reflective of St. Paul's dictum of obedience to state authorities[66] – a recurring theological vulnerability that contrasted starkly with liberation theology's political radicalism. Much of this US-inspired Pentecostalism was nonetheless very much politically engaged, but in the opposite direction, supporting right wing dictatorships throughout the region, not just in Chile.

Guatemala has become perhaps the most Protestant country in Latin America. Following a devastating earthquake in 1976, protestant evangelical missionaries poured across the border, so that by the 1980s, perhaps a third of the country's population was Protestant. Left-wing guerrillas had been actively resisting a succession of right-wing governments in Guatemala since a US-backed coup in 1954. By the early 1960s, this had developed into a full scale civil war, which only ended in 1996. The government's wholly inadequate response to the havoc wreaked by the 1976 earthquake provoked a renewed upsurge in public unrest and guerrilla attacks. In 1982, the four main insurgent groups merged to form the much stronger Unidad Revolucionaria Nacional Guatemalteca (URNG). The Guatemalan regime responded to all this with increasingly brutal counter-insurgency measures, culminating in those meted out under General Efrain Rios Montt, who was president and dictator from 1982-83.

Telling us a little more about Guatemala, the professor of international politics and religion Paul Freston explained at a conference entitled 'Christianity and Conflict in Latin America' in 2006:

> 'When Ríos Montt took power in 1982, he oversaw the scorched earth campaign in the largely indigenous highlands that virtually eliminated the URNG guerrillas. He also oversaw the destruction of 450 indigenous villages and may have killed as many as 100,000 people in 18 months.'[67] Ríos Montt, a born-again Christian, appeared on TV every Sunday night offering 'the Sunday sermon', an evangelical anti-communist message, designed to impress his faith and his Christian credentials on the population. Rios Montt's rule also received the moral and financial support of American evangelical Christians, including the televangelist Pat Robertson.

More recently in Guatemala, extremes of violence have been associated with what might be called Christian evangelical extremism. In around 2004-5, a group of Christian leaders initiated a policy of what they called 'social cleansing' in a series of events in the community of San Lucas Toliman, a Mayan town of about 17,000 in the highland region of Lake Atitlan. A group of evangelical vigilantes closed down bars and exacted sin taxes from businesses they considered to be immoral. They sent Bible verses and threats out to 'sinners' in the community. Beginning in July 2005, they began to go onto buses with lists of people they considered to be sinful and who needed to be called out for it. They would get on the buses and pull people off, either roughing them up or, in some cases, killing them. In July 2005, there was a case where a group of vigilantes got on a bus and pulled off a serial adulterer and executed him in full view of everybody on the bus. Seven of the vigilantes of this group were arrested in February 2006, but many have continued with these activities.[68]

Continuing to bring us more up to date on a wider scale, Paul Freston went on to make the following comments:

> 'In some countries, notably in Brazil, in the last fifteen years there has been a shift towards the left – or at least towards the centre-left – on the part of evangelicals (...) This I think has many causes. There

has been a growing evangelical social discourse with an emphasis on justice, partly resulting from an increased participation in social projects. Also, there have been many left-wing politicians who have converted to evangelical churches and have continued their left-wing militancy in their new religious identity (...) There has been considerable Pentecostal support for Hugo Chavez in Venezuela.'[69]

Freston also mentions how the development of Pentecostalism among some of the poorest in society has been significant in the story of its more left-wing trajectory. It would seem that in the favelas of São Paulo and Rio de Janeiro, faith healing among Pentecostals has become very attractive. In these urban areas, where state policing is absent, Pentecostalism has offered a point of moral and social stability in desperate circumstances. It has trained local, often uneducated, people as pastors. It has used the music of the streets, and become indigenised.

The Professor of Political Science Anne Hallum distinguishes between what she sees as this type of Pentecostalism and the more US-inspired Neo-Pentecostalism of Swaggart, Robertson and Falwell that we have already noted. Neo-Pentecostalism has often appealed more to the middle classes and elites, and a significant feature of it is what has become known as 'prosperity theology'. This is a persistent theme within US evangelical Christianity, and it has spread far and wide, to Latin America, sub-Saharan Africa and beyond. Still, it should be said that prosperity theology is also a key feature of the indigenous Brazilian church Assemblies of God, and this in turn begins to blur the distinction Hallum makes. Prosperity theology's central claim is that God rewards the faithful with material success. If you keep to Bible teaching as defined in fundamentalist terms, and keep to God's commands as defined in associated puritanical terms, then God will reward you abundantly. Liberation from evil spirits, cures and wealth can all be 'claimed'. The sincere believer just has to ask. Of course, if you ask and don't receive, then obviously you're still too attached to sin, or you're not praying hard enough: because in a relationship with God, only you can get it wrong. Your lack of fortune and, by implication, any misfortune suffered, are also your own fault. Such a prosperity theology, unlike liberation theology, is a theology written by the wealthy with a preferential option for the wealthy. Forms of this kind of Christianity, exported first to Latin America, have been further transformed and now find themselves re-exported to the UK for example, in mission churches such as the Universal Church of the Kingdom of God (UCKG)[70].

This thumbnail sketch of late twentieth century Christian history in Latin America gives rise to a number of ethical observations.

We can't say that evangelical Protestantism consistently eschews left-wing politics, or fails to stand up for the poor. While these forms of Christianity in their US incarnations from the 1980s have been generally on the right of politics, when the context changed and Pentecostals and evangelicals found themselves in the favelas of São Paulo and Rio de Janeiro, their politics – alongside their ethical mandate – changed too. Whatever the ulterior motives, some of their work would seem to have helped alleviate poverty and stabilise some families and communities in some of the most poverty-stricken, crime-ridden neighbourhoods. The journalist Linda Green is similarly positive about the effect of Pentecostalism in Mayan villages in Guatemala, where many of the men had been killed in the civil war.[71] She speaks about Pentecostalism here as 'a religion of survival'. 'In these churches women pooled their meagre resources, shared child-care needs and supported each other financially and emotionally during emergencies.'[72] The anthropologist Sheldon Annis also reports how the practice of Pentecostal and evangelical religion in Guatemala correlates with an upwardly mobile trajectory from a very low base. Compared with Catholics, evangelicals and Pentecostals in Guatemala were more likely to own their own business and to send their children to school.[73]

Neo-Pentecostalism as Hallum describes it has remained on the right however, and its prosperity theology has received sharp critiques from many theologians and church leaders as idolatrously replacing God with mammon.[74] Its supporters will maintain that prosperity theology inspires a work ethic in line with the kind of upward mobility I have just mentioned in Guatemala, but there is not compelling evidence for this specific point. Prosperity theology does though preach that the poor and oppressed, in whatever way, have earned their misfortune, unlike the rich, who are divinely blessed. It places a premium on this worldly fortune not as something to be shared, but rather as a badge of divine grace. In fact, the poor often have to pay to belong to these churches, when they can hardly afford to eat.[75]

Liberation theology, rooted in what became known as 'base communities', offered moral and spiritual fibre, alongside dignity and hope, to those at the bottom of society who came to believe in it. Through it they realised that they could stand up for themselves against oppression, which in turn played its part in the democratisation of a continent. While in its early days, in the time of Camilo Torres, it was involved in violence, that involvement significantly decreased due in part to moral pressure from the grassroots and from leaders like Romero.

Liberation theology has also achieved some valuable moral results in a far wider range of situations than in Latin America. In his book *World Religions and Human Liberation*, the rabbi and professor of Judaism Dan Cohn-Sherbok charts the meaning and effect of a theology with a preferential option for the poor across a wide range of religions. He also makes clear how this type of theology can be, and is already, a means of religions working more co-operatively together.

We can understand the Catholic Church's desire to hold onto power in the face of an ideological battle with a potentially militant, Marxist-inspired form of theology at a time when, globally, Marxism was, as Martin Luther King remarked, the key ideological force that Christianity had to reckon with. All the same, the Catholic hierarchy once again sought to protect and advance its own power to the detriment of millions of ordinary people suffering under the dictatorships of the 1960s, '70s and '80s. Similarly, seeing Communism as the 'Great Satan', Protestant support of oppression in Pinochet's Chile shows how politically ideological the evangelism of Swaggart, Falwell and Robertson was. Its focus on salvation as an individual thing eschewed social movements for justice and societal structural change. This was a gift for dictators. Perhaps there is an allied moral weakness within much official Catholicism and within forms of evangelical Protestantism as we have briefly observed them in Latin America. The Catholic Church often seems to be motivated by a desire to maintain a grip on power. The forms of evangelical Protestantism we have looked into here seem very much engaged with the saving of individual souls for the hereafter. What happens and what is sacrificed to achieve these ends seems to be morally problematic; the foreground gets lost. If a totalitarian state will give the Catholic Church more power than it would have otherwise, and if Church power trumps all other objectives, then moral compromise to achieve the required end becomes acceptable. Protestant whole-hearted support , like that of Swaggart to Pinochet's regime, is subject to a similar critique.

A further feature that is apparent is a kind of George W. Bush mentality that: 'You're either with us or against us.' – as far as many conservative strands of religious adherence are concerned. This tends to obliterate the subtlety and complexity of morality as we find it in life. Human beings agonise about moral issues exactly because they are so often unclear. The Catholic Church, as part of its discipline, has formulated things in this way, and the sharp lines dividing truth from falsehood are central within the architecture of Protestant fundamentalism too.

We see again how deeply religion is affected by both politics and wider cultural forces. Pentecostalism, within this US missionary context, initially right wing if anywhere on the political spectrum, became at times left-leaning when rooted within cultural and political contexts of the kind encountered here. Conversely, liberation theology, quasi-Marxist in the 1960s is far more centre ground by the twenty-first century, following significant democratization. With the election of the Argentinian Pope Francis, liberation theology has also gained genuine recognition within Vatican circles.[76] Catholicism has also since the 1970s and 1980s assimilated – and been influenced by – certain styles of charismatic worship from Pentecostalism. This malleability of religion that we keep encountering is both a source of danger and of hope. Religion, as we shall keep observing, is so often a political target for use as a mechanism for manipulation and control. It is equally less impervious than one might think to the conscience of those without, most especially in its more liberal forms – as we have seen in the increased concern for social justice in Latin American Pentecostalism. Further examples of this kind of moral osmosis from without are the extent to which churches have taken a greater interest in environmental issues in recent decades, following rather than leading wider environmental activism, the extent to which some church views have become more liberal about divorce and the degree to which a limited number of churches have come to accept LGBT sexual relationships following the moral lead of the wider society.

The rivalry between different forms of faith also deserves comment. Protestants and Catholics in recent times have very rarely killed each other in Latin America, unlike in the Europe of old. Still, we have noted at the extremes of each faith a religiosity with lethal capacity. Psychologically, an institution that believes it has exclusive access to truth is as problematic and challenged in relationships as are individuals who have this perspective. The rivalries and rhetoric of Churches with exclusivist views bears this out, as Gary Potter, President of Catholics for Christian Political Action, illustrated all too well when he announced that when the Christian majority comes to power, there will be no more rights for homosexuals and no Hindus or Muslims… the state would no longer allow it.[77] These very many and varied dynamics within religion, and between religions and the wider world, are constitutive of the moral dialogue I wish to bring to light. Some of these dynamics are antagonistic, even violent, some co-opt ethics from beyond the faith, and a variety of theories of salvation put different emphases on alleviating poverty on the one hand and otherworldly goals on the other.

The role of religion in the Israeli-Palestinian conflict since 1948

It is a common assumption that religion is and always has been the key engine of conflict in the Israeli-Palestinian issue since Israel's founding in 1948. Christopher Hitchens writes, referring to the two-state solution to the Israeli-Palestinian conflict;

> 'and so it would have been, decades ago, if the messianic rabbis and mullahs and priests could have been kept out of it. But the exclusive claims to god-given authority, made by hysterical clerics on both sides and further stoked by Armageddon-minded Christians who hope to bring on the Apocalypse (…)have made the situation insufferable, and put the whole of humanity in the position of hostage to a quarrel that now features the threat of nuclear war. *Religion poisons everything.*'[78]

The Professor of comparative politics of the Middle East and North Africa Robert Lee, in his *Religion and Politics in the Middle East*, suggests that we can put too much emphasis on the role of religion as opposed to politics and the state in the case of Israel. He writes,

> 'politics, not religion, drove the Jews towards independence, and politics dictated forgoing a constitution opposed by the forces of religion. David Ben-Gurion [the first Israeli Prime Minister], a socialist who led the Jewish community in Palestine to independence, shunned the separation of religion and state because he wanted to

control religion. Twenty years later, it was politics, not religion, that pushed Israel to victory in 1967 and to domination of the West Bank and the Gaza Strip areas.'[79]

Lee adds, though, regarding the Israeli victory in the Six Day War of 1967 'The conquest, however, triggered an outburst of religious enthusiasm that fostered pressures for settlement and long-term retention of the conquered territories.'[80]

Zionism from its origins was a nationalist movement, and as such political rather than religious. In the early days of Zionism, thought was given to the establishment of a Jewish state in Eastern Europe. It was socialist, not religious in outlook. In keeping with this, the initial Declaration of the State of Israel allowed full citizenship for all, including non-Jews, irrespective of creed for all that it was a Jewish state, in the ethnic rather than religious sense of the word. To quote from the Declaration,

> 'The State of Israel…will ensure complete equality of social and political rights to all its inhabitant irrespective of religion, race or sex; it will guarantee freedom of religion, conscience, language, education and culture.'[81]

From the state's establishment in 1948, until the Six Day War in 1967, the dominant Mapai Party that merged with other parties to become the Labour Party in 1968 sought to remove religious ritual and rabbinic law from the core of Jewish identity and mark that identity by national affiliation. 'The "New Jew" would be the product of collective political and social [rather than religious] endeavour.'[82] Ben Gurion, himself an atheist, expressed this view clearly when he wrote,

> 'For this generation, this land is more holy than for the tens of generations of Jews who believed in its historical and religious sanctity; for it has been sanctified by our sweat, our work and our blood.'[83]

However, during these first twenty years of the state of Israel, many Mizrahi Jews (from North Africa and the Middle East) migrated to Israel. Many were more religious than the secularised Ashkenazi Jews from Europe. The Mizrahi also suffered discrimination at the hands of the Israeli Labour government during these years. They therefore became attracted to, and supportive of, the more right-wing and religiously sympathetic Likud party, which came to prominence later in the decade, after its founding in 1973. In the coalition politics of 1970s Israel, religious groups gained significant influence in the country.

Individuals were also key to the ideological change that took hold following the Six Day War. A highly influential religious academy, Merkaz Harav, was founded by Rabbi Abraham Isaac Kook. He began articulating religious arguments for what his irredentist cause has called a 'Greater Israel' advocating Jewish settlement of the Occupied Territories. Lee writes,

> 'While the senior Kook had argued that redemption of the land was a precursor to the spiritual redemption of the Jewish people and the world, [it was his son] Zvi Yehuda Kook who portrayed the conquest of the land as a holy endeavour in and of itself.'[84]

Zvi Kook became the spiritual inspiration of the settlement movement of the West Bank. He also had significant political influence on Likud. When Menachem Begin was elected to power as leader of Likud in 1977, he instructed that Biblical names be used for places in the Occupied Territories where, over time, more and more land was being annexed by Israel. As Ilan Pappe, Professor of history and director of the European Centre for Palestinian Studies at Exeter University reports, Israel had confiscated 28% of the West Bank by 1972, by 2000 this had risen to 42%.[85]

The fact that international law forbade the building of settlements in the West Bank did not matter to hard-liners of a religious bent. Significantly, they took a parallel approach to Martin Luther King's rejection of human law as outlined in his *Letter From Birmingham City Jail*. Yet here the rejection of human law was for a different (non-pacifist) end. Justifying settlements in the West Bank, the militant Zionist group Gush Emunim wrote,

> 'We are commanded by the Torah, according to the will of God…and therefore we cannot be subject to the standard laws of democracy.'[86]

Another champion of belligerent Zionism was Rabbi Meir Kahane who moved from the US to Israel in 1971. He claimed that militant conquest of Gaza, the West Bank and all of Biblical Israel was the primary, divinely inspired purpose of the whole state of Israel. Kahane advocated the suspension of democracy, the imposition of halakhic laws – including dietary laws, dress codes and the teaching of halakhah (the collective body of Jewish religious law and tradition) in all schools. He pressed for the imposition of censorship laws, and proposed that non-Jews should be stripped of all political rights and of the right to work.[87] Kahane gained a seat in the Knesset, and in the 1977 coalition with Likud gained the government's increased support for religious institutions and religious schools. In 1980, in keeping with his claim that 'no trait is more justified than revenge in the right place and at the right time', he attempted to blow up the Dome of the Rock, (one of the world's most sacred sites for Muslims) situated on Temple Mount in Jerusalem. Following his arrest he received a five-year suspended sentence.

Still, some religious Zionist militants were more successful in their endeavours. The seeds planted in some of the extremist schools and yeshivas (a Jewish institution set up for the study of Talmud and Torah) bore an ugly fruit. In June 1992, Labour returned to power with Yitzak Rabin as prime minister. Under Rabin, Labour was somewhat less sympathetic to aspects of the settler movement, though settlements continued apace on their watch. In 1993, Rabin signed the first of the Oslo Peace Accords with Yasser Arafat, recognizing his Palestine Liberation Organisation as a legitimate representative of the Palestinian people. Considering Rabin a traitor to the Zionist cause, a religious extremist from an Orthodox background named Yigal Amir assassinated him in 1995. Amir had studied in a West Bank yeshiva that had propounded militant Zionism. Lee writes that a quarter of Israeli Orthodox teenagers condoned the assassination![88] Some religious schools and yeshivas that had been supported by the state had become an effective investment in belligerent extremism against it.

Having said all this, it is important to be clear that Orthodox Judaism, especially outside of Israel, is very much opposed to the behaviour of characters like Amir. Militant Zionism is also very much out of the question for the Haredi – ultra-orthodox Jews. For them the state of Israel will only be properly achieved through a miracle, not through human intervention. They do not see the current state of Israel (in its institutions) as divinely ordained, but see it instead as a secular political entity. Accordingly, they do not view it as a vehicle (by violence or otherwise) for the full establishment of Israel according to Torah.[89] When the time comes, God will achieve that. The Haredi will leave this up to God. As such, they are quite 'other-worldly', eschewing politics while demanding their political concessions in terms of an exemption from the otherwise compulsory military service as well as for religious schooling. Such schools, though, are for the Haredi to be in keeping with halakhah,[90] and not an induction into Zionist religious militancy at all.

All this is just one side of the story. What about the role of Islam among the Palestinians? Has Islam been the main motivator and inspirer of violence there? The Palestinians are an ethno-national group – ethnically almost entirely Arab. They constitute about 49% of all inhabitants of Israel, the Gaza Strip and the West Bank combined.[91] 90% of Palestinians are Sunni Muslims, perhaps 6% are Christians. The Druze and Samaritans constitute smaller minorities.

Ilan Pappe, when writing about Palestinian identity between 1948 and 1967, comments that religious identity never became an influential factor as regards Palestinian attitudes towards Israel, despite Israeli attempts to divide the Palestinian Muslims from the Palestinian Christians by treating the Christians more favourably so as to rule both more effectively.[92]

When we look at the fida'iyyun (the precursor to the Palestine Liberation Organisation) and the PLO in the 1960s, it is clearly influenced by Marxist ideology rather than Islamic militancy of any sort. This and other Palestinian groups were of their time. The PLO was influenced by the Communists of North Vietnam and their guerrilla tactics against the US in South Vietnam. Ilan Pappe tells the story in more detail. In around 1970, Pappe explains, disputes about the alternatives of Trotskyism and Marxist-Leninism led Yasser Arafat and two leading PLO figures to form different groups, the PDFLP (Popular Democratic Front for the Liberation of Palestine) and the PFLP (Popular Front for the Liberation of Palestine). This was of a piece with the USSR being the PLO's chief arms supplier at this time. Other communist regimes such as North Korea, China and Cuba provided training for the PLO and in return everyone from the IRA, the Baader Meinhof Gang and the Viet Cong sent soldiers to train in southern Lebanon in the 1970s. By contrast specific Islamic militancy does not appear to be part of the PLO's worldview at this time. There is no mention of Islam. There is no mention of religion of any kind within the 1964 Palestinian National Charter – the founding statement of the objectives of the PLO. It is a movement instead for national liberation and self-determination. Article 10 of the charter reads,

> 'Palestinians have three mottos: National Unity, National Mobilization, and Liberation. Once liberation is completed, the people of Palestine shall choose for its public life whatever political, economic, or social system they want.'[93]

We can conclude that in the 1960s and early 1970s Islam was not the key ideological force behind the PLO, the PDFLP and the PFLP, but rather that communist influences and nationalist aspirations dominated.

Reinforcing this picture, Ilan Pappe points out that initially (in the 1960s) the Israeli government actually supported political Islam as something that was anti-nationalist and as such opposed to the PLO. It calculated that a stronger political Islam would divide the opposition.[94]

But things were to change. Since the Palestinians' defeat in the Six Day War in 1967, the PLO had lost its hold on the hearts and minds of some Palestinian communities. This created space for more religiously-inspired groups. As time passed, the failure of the PLO to afford protection to Palestinian civilians left them looking for alternatives, and a more religiously-based militancy emerged as the most promising means of resistance to settlement of the West Bank. Pappe notes that clashing religious identities led to a more extreme, uncompromising confrontation with the 'other'.[95]

Moving into the 1980s, events pushed Palestinian opposition further towards religious affiliation, justification and support. Professor of Middle Eastern Politics Laleh Khalili explains:

> 'Internationally, the failure of the Soviet Union (1989) resulted in the termination of ideological and financial support for Marxist insurrectionary groups, among them Palestinian organisations, leading to shifts in the ideological underpinning of many such groups, and the receding

of secularist notions of armed resistance; to be replaced in the Middle East with the Islamist version which had proved triumphant during the Iranian revolution of 1978/1979. Logistically and practically, mosques could act as safe havens and foci of meetings and gatherings under the watchful eyes of the Lebanese army and hostile militants, and Friday prayers were useful as starting points for demonstrations, both contributing to the increasing predominance of Islam-centred narratives in Palestinian commemorations.'[96]

Iran's Islamic revolution of 1979 gave rise to the regime of Ayatollah Khomeini. Iran and its Shi'a clerics conceived of Hezbollah (meaning 'Party of Allah') and inspired it to resist the Israeli occupation of Lebanon from 1982. Iran also supported Hezbollah militarily. Shi'a Islam has the ideal of martyrdom – of dying for one's faith as opposed to killing for one's faith – at its core.[97] But in the hands of Hezbollah in the mid-1980s, suicide bombing in Lebanon became their chosen expression of this ideal. Islamic Jihad[98] was the first to call such actions acts of 'martyrdom', and Hamas[99] followed suit. By the time of the second Intifada (or 'Uprising', 2000-2004/5), suicide bombing had become the preferred method of protest against occupation,[100] because Hamas had declared the whole of Palestine to be a holy endowment, or *waqf*.

Without religion, there would still have been conflict following the takeover of Palestine in 1948 – what Palestinians call the *nakbah* (catastrophe) – and at several points since then. We don't need to rerun history in some counterfactual way to see this, we simply need to observe, as I have noted, the non-religious factors that have thus far played out. Nationalist agendas ensured that conflict would continue to flare up, as have the economic and social deprivations experienced most especially by the Palestinians. Time and again, Ilan Pappe emphasises these economic factors, and goes on to suggest that by 2000, with 50% unemployment in the Occupied Palestinian Territories; with constant Israeli blockading of the West Bank cities, and the electric fence around the Gaza Strip; and no hope for a political solution, there was only need for a constant supply of explosives and grenades to keep the conflict alive.[101]

However Pappe also makes clear that at times when the peace process has shown some signs of success (1996) the Islamist militant groups have resorted to suicide bombing thereby undermining the process. Pappe is emphatic that suicide bombing and extremist violence is not justified in Islam either textually (in terms of the Qur'an and Hadith) nor legally (in terms of the law schools). He concludes that extremist violence has been more closely associated with religious justification from the Israeli side than it has been from the Palestinian side.[102] It seems to me however that Pappe is treading on thin ice here in his interpretation of religion and I shall say more about this in Chapter 6 about the Qur'an and Hadith. For the time being though it will suffice to say that sacred texts are interpreted by their adherents in contradictory ways even within very specific religious traditions. There are fundamentalist Christians who are pacifists and others who are militant. Whatever a text does or doesn't justify is an insufficient condition whereby to judge that a practice is true to that faith, not least because the reading and interpretation of a text is not an agreed matter either within or beyond any religious tradition. For example, as is relevant here, many Palestinian Muslim militants see what is known as the lesser Jihad, the struggle to rid society of evil by force if necessary, as the sixth pillar of Islam. By contrast for some other Muslims this is blasphemy because it simply doesn't follow the text as far as they are concerned.[103] Religions are simply far too malleable and easily influenced by other factors as to be circumscribed in the way that Pappe recommends. We also run the risk of white-washing a faith by distinguishing between 'true' Islam or 'true' Christianity or Judaism and 'false' versions. There will be as many such versions as there are religious adherents. If as they do, members of Hamas and Hezbollah regard what they do as a worthy Islamic cause, we must take that very seriously. There is every reason to think of religions as how they play out in the world, not as some idealized fiction whether past or present.

Pappe is perhaps right that religiosity has been more consistently at the heart of Israeli belligerence than Islam has been at the heart of Palestinian militancy but both religions have played their part in decades of civilian carnage.[104] At the very least we can say that contextualised versions of Judaism and Islam and individuals and groups inspired by such versions of these religions have intensified and made almost irrevocable the violence that is centre stage in Israel and Palestine today.

A key problem is the sacred character of the causes at the heart of the conflict. That the sacred cannot be negotiated seems to be a key sense in the case of Israel and Palestine as well as in many other settings where religion is at the root of trouble and a real source of moral catastrophe. In the case of Islamist Hamas and militant Zionism the sacred claims could hardly conflict more. Militant Zionism regards all land between the Mediterranean and the Jordan River including Gaza as the land of Israel, for the Jews. By contrast Hamas regards the land as sacred land too, not just land for the Palestinians. The Director of Research in Anthropology at the National Centre for Scientific Research in Paris, Professor Scott Atran interviewed Sheikh Hamed al-Betawi, a spiritual leader of Hamas in the West Bank and head of the Palestine Ulema (Scholars League). He asked why Hamas militants were so willing to die in their suicide bombing attacks. Betawi responded 'Because this is sacred land, the holiest land in the world. That is why Palestine is the 'Mother of the World's Problems.'[105] Betawi explained how some of the brightest most promising youngsters go on to be suicide bombers, how they as much as anyone see the point of putting sacred values above self-motivation.

Atran points out the special difficulties that surround any attempt at negotiations about sacred territory. He makes clear that the usual 'trade off' strategies can actually be one's worst enemy! Suggest that a piece of sacred land might conceivably be an object of negotiation and the very suggestion is an insult of the highest order, an invasion of the profane into sacred conceptual space. This religious aspect of intransigence then, linked to the sacred, especially sacred land is a real barrier to peace and even mutual co-existence. Turn rivalry over territory into rivalry about sacred territory and solutions and strategies for negotiation rapidly disappear.

We can often explain some aspects of religion too by reference to further non-religious factors. However the sacred and sacred land are irreducibly religious. It seems to me that moral blame lies firmly with this aspect of religion in the form of militant religious Zionism, and the political Islam of Hamas, Hezbollah and Islamic Jihad to name only some of the key contenders. The often more distant, and excessively ignorant Christian Zionism peddled in the Christian fundamentalisms of the US and also sadly in the UK helps to both stoke and financially fuel militant Zionism on the ground. Rivalry about sacred space is toxic. Making Hitchens' wild accusation a little more specific, rivalry about sacred space does poison everything.

A Brief Recent Chronology Of Israel / Palestine

14th May 1948   Declaration of the Establishment of the State of Israel

1948   **First Arab-Israeli War** ending in ceasefire and armistice deals signed being with each surrounding Arab state individually. Most of the British Mandate territories came to be ruled by Israel from then on.

1956   The second Arab-Israeli War or the Suez War.

1964   **The Palestine Liberation Organisation** (PLO) is established by Yasser Arafat.

1967   **The Six Day War or third Arab-Israeli War** sees Israel win control of the West Bank from Jordan and the Gaza Strip from Egypt. Israel achieves some victories in the Golan Heights on Israel's northern border with Lebanon. PLO therefore moves its headquarters to Jordan.

1970   The **Jordanian-Palestinian civil war** leads to the defeat of the PLO that subsequently relocates to southern Lebanon.

October 1973   **Yom Kippur War** or fourth Arab-Israeli War sees initial advances for Egypt. But Israel takes the offensive both against Egypt and Syria to achieve territorial gains.

1977   The right wing **Likud** party, under Menachem Begin, comes to power in Israeli as a coalition with more religiously-minded militant Zionist groups, who consequently gain further political influence.

1978   **The Camp David Accords are signed between Egypt and Israel** and lead to the return of the Sinai to Egypt and to the two countries signing a peace treaty in 1979, the first such treaty between Israel and one of its Arab neighbours.

1982   Israel invades southern Lebanon and gets fully involved in the Lebanese Civil War supporting the right-wing Christian Phalange Party. Many Jews in Israel protest against Israeli involvement in this war which involves the death of many civilians. Following the capture of Beirut by Israel, Yasser Arafat relocates the PLO's HQ to Tunisia.

1985 - 1990	Iran supports Shi'a militants in Lebanon. They come to form **Hezbollah** in 1985 and continue to benefit from Iranian military and financial assistance.
1987	**The first Palestinian Uprising or Intifada** against Israel, following increased occupation of the West Bank.
1993	**The Oslo Accords** allow the PLO to establish itself in West Bank and the Palestinian Authority is created.
1995	**Yitzak Rabin** assassinated by a religious Zionist militant.
2000	Israel withdraws from southern Lebanon.
2000 - 2004/5	**The second Intifada** follows Ariel Sharon walking around the Temple Mount.
2002	The Israeli West Bank barrier or wall begins to be built.
2002/2003	President George W. Bush announces the 'road map' peace proposals.
November 2004	Following being besieged by the Israelis, Yasser Arafat falls ill and is taken to France where he dies in hospital.
2005 - 2007	Israel withdraws from Gaza Strip in 2005. Following the election of Hamas in Gaza and the West Bank in 2006 Israel imposes a naval blockade on Gaza.
2008/2009	Israel attacks Gaza following hostilities from inside the territory. Ceasefire declared in February 2009.
2011 /2012	The Palestinian Authority gains increasing recognition. In 2012, Palestine is recognised as a non-member state by the UN and is granted observer status.

Conclusion

We have seen religion, in a wide variety of forms, at the root of psychological survival. It has sustained and nurtured individuals and groups – whether in the favelas of São Paulo, in the 1960s American civil rights movement or in the horrors of the death camps. In places like Auschwitz, Jewish religious ritual also offered strength to those who were not at all religious. Religion also persistently offers values that extend beyond the individual towards wider and deeper meaning, that at the most profound and extreme, find expression in martyrdom. Bonhoeffer, King and Romero all exemplify a kind of spiritual and moral courage that led to such ends. Still, we are also aware that the moral and the spiritual are not at all in sync in many situations. We have seen religion not simply cave in to the worst of political pressures, but also ally with them – especially at an institutional level – in order to maintain power and influence. A particular religion can also of course stand for diametrically opposed ethical values. This may be to do with different denominational orientations, it may be to do with differing cultural contexts, it may be to do with the course of history. Post-Holocaust Christianity is, in the West at least, significantly less anti-Semitic than it was both in its theology and its practice before the Holocaust. The divergent denominational and cultural contexts of prosperity theology and liberation theology have oriented their respective faith and practice, again, towards very different values and ethics. The southern Baptist Church of Martin Luther King's civil rights movement, set over and against some of the white supremacist Churches that dominated that time; as well as the pro-apartheid Dutch Reformed Church in South Africa of that era, offer further startling contrasts between the variety of ethics being espoused all within the extremely broad umbrella of Protestant Christianity. This fits too with how much we have seen that religion can be effect as much as cause. Contrary to a stereotype that religions live by unyielding principles and that this is their moral Achilles heel, we have seen on a number of occasions a pragmatic means-ends rationalisation at play in order to achieve power and influence. We have also seen that the demonising of 'the other', including within one's own faith, is a particularly close bedfellow of exclusivist forms of faith. Couched within evangelical and missionary polemic, this never makes for the best of community relations, with tension and, occasionally, violence appearing as a result.

Concepts of sacred territory take the matter of exclusivism to a new level. This stands out within the pantheon of religious values towards the ethically problematic end of the spectrum. It doesn't simply resist efforts at negotiation, it closes them down – while often raising the stakes within negotiations in lethal ways. Concepts of sacred territory are also irreducibly religious in nature for all that political, cultural and economic forces may have played a part in how such territory comes to be perceived. In this sense it is hard to deflect criticism away from this aspect of religiosity. It is also essential to emphasise that religions are within themselves not at all in agreement about sacred territory. Not all practising Jews nor all practising Muslims regard the Temple Mount in Jerusalem as their sacred space, and those that do vary considerably as to what follows from this – as we saw for example in the case of the Haredi.[106] Part of why religions are sometimes so divided is that aspects of them hold the keys to peace, while other aspects have conflict written into their raison d'être.

None of this involves drawing hard and fast conclusions. These observations offer a few pointers in the kind of open-ended dialogue that is at the heart of this book – to which I have referred in the Introduction. I shall develop this dialogue in later chapters, and in the conclusion take further some of the issues mentioned here.

4

Religion Before The Ethics Tribunal: Four Elements Of Religious Life

A key problem in so many assessments of religious life is that the focus is put on caricatures of abstract beliefs, on the high politics of religion and of course, for those who are its detractors, on wars, schisms and rivalries. Yet every day the ordinary religious practice of billions of people goes on, beyond the radar of media interest. Muslims rise early for prayer, Buddhists for meditation, grace is said before meals in many Christian homes. From rites of passage, to pilgrimage, to the rich and exotic festivals of communal religious life, the planet is alive with displays of religious adherence. Secularisation in Europe is the exception to this rule. Are there moral outputs from all this activity? Let's try and find out.

I shall begin with some introductory remarks about the alleged relationship between religiosity and mental health, Today among health service professionals, within education, among parents as regards their children, there is deep moral concern about mental health. If then there is some significant evidence to show that religious practice benefits mental health then it is hard to see, without prejudice, why this should not be understood as religion making something of, if not a very significant moral contribution. Following on from this question I shall look more specifically at two extremely widespread religious practices and consider their ethical import more generally. The first major practice is prayer. Prayer is central to the three key world monotheisms of Christianity, Islam and Judaism, but it is also to be found in the many expressions of Hinduism and even in some aspects of Buddhism such as Pure Land in China and Japan. The second central practice I shall consider is meditation. Meditation is the engine of spiritual development and awareness in Buddhism and much of Indian religion. It also plays a key role in the contemplative and mystical traditions within Christianity, Islam and Judaism. I shall consider how far such practices are of benefit to people. How do people use them? Do they have a morally dubious side, at times, in the way they are practised? While prayer and meditation are in many respects to do with the ordinary life of religions in themselves, religions also engage more obviously with the wider world. I will therefore consider the ethics of two further features of religious life and commitment: first, mission and evangelism and second charity work. What is the ethical character of these practices? Let's begin then by considering what relationship there may be between mental health and the practice of religion.

Mental health and the practice of religion

Despite problems of definition and measurement, some clear statements have been made about the relationship between religiosity and mental health in recent years. For example, in 1998 Professor of Psychiatry and behavioural sciences, H. G. Koenig writes 'the mental health influence of religious belief and practices – particularly when imbedded within a long-standing, well integrated faith tradition – is largely a positive one.'[107] Psychiatrist and social anthropologist Professor Simon Dein gives us further detail: 'By now several thousand studies have been conducted demonstrating positive associations between the various dimensions of religiosity and mental health.'[108] Dein continues to claim that, on balance, religiosity correlates with more hope, optimism and life satisfaction, less depression and faster relief from depression, lower rates of suicide, reduced prevalence of drug and alcohol abuse and delinquency.[109] He refers to a meta-analysis of studies investigating correlations between religious involvement and depression, and finds a reasonably strong inverse correlation. Referring to Koenig's research he writes, 'Of 93 observational studies, two-thirds found lower rates of depressive disorder with fewer depressive symptoms in persons who were more religious. In 34 studies that did not find a similar relationship, only 4 found that being religious was associated with more depression. Of 22 longitudinal studies, 15 found that greater religiousness predicted mild symptoms and faster remission at follow-up.'[110] Professor of epidemiology and population health, Jeffrey Levin refers to the 'protective effect' of religious participation:

> 'Within the gerontological literature, especially, features of institutional religious involvement (attendance at worship services) and non-institutional involvement (e.g. private prayer, embeddedness in religious support networks) have been associated with positive mental health outcomes and high scores on scales and indices assessing psychosocial constructs such as self-esteem, mastery (self-efficacy), optimism, hope and dimensions of well-being. The overall finding has been replicated across age cohorts, in both sexes, and regardless of social class, race or ethnicity, religious affiliation, and specific diagnosis or outcome measure.'[111]

However, Levin is circumspect in his analysis of these findings. He claims that there would seem to be a relationship between religious affiliation and mental health that is worth further analysis. But the findings as stated thus far cannot be interpreted without a theoretical framework from within modern psychology, such as psychodynamic theory, humanism or transpersonalism. Only within such sub-disciplines do clear explanations begin to come to light. We can't, for example, say straightforwardly that religion has a healing effect.

It seems to me that what we can say is that based on the limited research done so far – and contrary to the views of Freud – religion may well have a beneficial psychological effect and there is less evidence, other things being equal, that it has a negative psychological effect. The innumerable victims of religion, though, cannot go unmentioned here. There are very many different kinds of victim, many of whom have now ceased to practice or believe in any religion whatsoever, and so would not feature in the statistics just mentioned. Let's suppose, for example, in keeping with what we have just seen, that overall religious affiliation correlates with mental health. This needs to be seen over against the devastating effects, for example, of the systematic sexual abuse of children in the Catholic Church in Ireland, the US, Australia and elsewhere, to say nothing of similar behaviour among clerics and officials in other denominations and religions. It is arguably obscene to seek to 'measure' such suffering so as to reach some overall credit/deficit bottom line on a moral balance sheet. But it is certain that the research results we have offered can't simply bypass the voices of victims, who speak with moral authority.

So, while religious affiliation would seem to tend, more than not, to correlate with mental health, and while we need far more data about this across religions and locations, it is also at times a real moral hazard.

I shall now briefly look at prayer as a more specific, but very widely practised, aspect of Western theistic religion. Does the practice of prayer have moral significance?

Prayer

William James's *The Varieties of Religious Experience* published in 1902 is still often regarded as the key text on the subject of religious experience in the Western tradition.[112] James writes that prayer is 'the essence of religion'.[113] Research into prayer has gone on since James's time. Even before James, there were those interested in scientifically investigating prayer. Sir Francis Galton, nineteenth century anthropologist and eugenicist, was intrigued by the longevity of the clergy and, thinking of them as 'praying people', wondered if there was any connection between their prayfulness and long life.

Prayer comes in all shapes and sizes. The purpose of prayer can also vary; it may be petitionary prayer; or praise; it may be prayer of intercession. It may be highly liturgical, following a set pattern where the priest and congregation speak in response to each other; or simply set out as with the Lord's Prayer for Christians. On the other hand, it may be extempory or spontaneous, as in the case of much Pentecostal prayer. The contexts may be congregational, in the home, at a birth, as part of a prayer cell on the Internet, through a prayer app., on the battlefield, on the Hajj, in a monastery or in an anchorite's cell. Prayer may be highly ritualised, as in the series of movement or *rakahs* in Islamic prayer or *salah*, it may involve a fair amount of preparation such as the washing or *wudu* that precedes Islamic prayer. Prayer may be a state of mind – as portrayed in Lee Hall's film, *Spoonface Steinberg*, where the script reads 'and there's another type of prayer when everything you do is a prayer, as the Rabbis said'.

Some years ago, a new fundamentalist church opened up in what used to be a local cinema. The church distributed a newspaper about their activities and people's stories. On the front page was an account of how someone down on their luck had been prayed for and had their problems solved. My instant reaction was one of cynicism. Richard Dawkins is quite right to point out that in experiments about the effectiveness of petitionary prayer there is no particular evidence for its effectiveness.[114] The Christian theologian Maurice Wiles has, however, made an ethical point in relation to petitionary prayer and divine intervention more generally. He sees a God who intervenes to help a student pass exams or even to put someone's cancer into remission as a morally arbitrary God. As a Christian, Wiles cannot begin to come to terms with such a God, one who has not granted so many identical requests in the past; who has allowed the Holocaust to happen; and the 'Great Leap Forward' in 1950s China, in which as many as 38 million people starved to death. The point being made is that to petition such a God is to collude with unjust intervention, to believe and hope for a God who will regard your petition as more pressing, for whatever unfathomable reason, than all those whose petitions were in vain. Such prayer would seem to be predicated on the idea that God is willing to fulfil our desires rather than those whose petitions failed. Or perhaps it sees God as a whimsical God in relation to whom we might as well try our luck. Either way, for Wiles, both the God that is believed in, and the petitions in his name, are morally suspect. In my view we should of course, be more than sympathetic towards someone who prays for a close relative to be cured of a terminal illness, but at some other, less fraught time in their lives, such a person might consider whether or not the kind of God implied by such prayer is either good or worthy of worship. This is what Wiles *as* a religious believer, has done and he has found such a God ethically wanting. There are, after all, very many gods, within the minds of those who believe in God, so many of which can and should be dismissed, as Freud suggested, as childish wish-fulfilments. This specific point is very much in keeping with some of the strongest theological traditions within Judaism, Christianity and Islam, which regard such gods – within their own traditions – as idols and, as such, view belief in them as not a belief in God at all.[115]

Quite a lot of intercessionary prayer is not necessarily petitionary as such. For example, 'In our prayers we think of so and so...', intentionally allows for a congregation to focus attention in a wide variety of ways on people far and near, and a key aspect of this clearly expresses good will and love towards others. It is hard to see, without prejudice, that this is not a moral good.

Petitionary prayer is the target for assault by many secularists. Both Dawkins and Hitchens cherry-pick this easy target, but they fail to consider any other form of prayer. It should also be clear that in a great deal of liturgical prayer, petition is not the focus. For example, within the liturgy of the Eucharist, where the bread and wine are consecrated, prayer is about thanksgiving. In *salah* prayers in Islam, that are said five times a day, petition is not part of these prayers at all. They are mainly prayers of praise. The questions we might ask from a purely humanist ethical point of view is 'what is the effect of prayer on the individual doing the praying, and on a community that prays?' Does prayer do them any good?

There is much less specific research on the mental health benefit of prayer than on the mental health benefits of religious adherence more generally, but there is some evidence. In summarising a number of research findings British academics, John Maltby, Christopher Lewis and Liza Day write the 'frequency of prayer or meditative prayer has been shown to be related to better mental health' and 'in terms of health variables, prayer is associated with fewer self-reported health symptoms.'[116] Among the various measures regarding prayer, they also report that frequency of personal prayer was found to be the best predictor of better mental health. Based on a cognitive behavioural framework, Maltby, Lewis and Day give evidence that prayer helps provide an interpretative framework in peoples' lives that helps them make sense of their existence.[117] Prayer would also seem – in its reflective, meditative form, for example as 'listening to God', 'thinking about God' – to 'help provide the self-regulation by which individuals are able to reduce their self-focus, worry and stress.'[118] These writers conclude that, according to standardised measures of subjective well-being (reduction in depression, anxiety, somatic symptoms and social dysfunction), frequency of prayer, meditative prayer and prayer experience seem to lead to better mental well-being. Two theologians, Professor Leslie Francis and Thomas Evans examine a range of research on a number of aspects of prayer. They looked at how people report the effects of prayer on themselves and found that people reported an associated well-being with the practice of prayer. Francis and Evans emphasise that we cannot deduce from this that prayer has any spiritual efficacy, the research is about psychology not metaphysics.[119] Markus Shafer's research from Toronto University suggests similar findings.[120]

Not all research, on the other hand, gives such positive results about prayer: 'prayer is inversely associated with symptoms of anxiety-related disorders among individuals who have a secure attachment to God, but positively associated with these outcomes among those who have a more insecure or avoidant attachment to God.'[121] In other words (and this correlates too with the research of Simon Dein[122]), those who seem to regard God more as someone to be feared, as a stern and distant God – and who as such feel insecure about God – fare less well in terms of mental health than those who see their relationship with God as more secure.

Dawkins would of course remark, 'But you'd be better off without your prayer crutch altogether if you could manage it – and wouldn't that be better?'. But this argument doesn't work for a number of reasons. Contrary to the views of Dawkins and Nietzsche, not all religious adherents are, to understate the case, the weak and the desperate. Very many are strong, psychologically very well-adjusted members of society. But where this is not the case, perhaps in some ways religion offers something to such people, besides morally questionable petitionary prayer. Other forms of prayer and worship may be a valuable crutch for some and perhaps, with this, there is actually a moral contribution that is being made. Anaesthetic is a drug that takes away the reality of pain and is a moral contribution to life because it hides that reality. Rephrasing Voltaire, if there were no religion it would be necessary to invent it.[123] Some religious people would regard what is said at humanist funerals as essentially prayers, in that the words express sentiments of goodwill and love about those who have died and for those who are bereaved.

For many liberal and conservative religious believers, prayer is the most intimate way of being communal, a way of embracing the individual and the whole in a repeated style of love. When and insofar as prayer is about compassionate intent and motivation, or the celebration of life, it seems to me there is something very good about prayer. It is of course one of the cords that binds people to religious institutions, with their powerful longings and their longings for power. Prayers can also petition for terrible things, it may, and does, at times involve the blessing of armies and the blessing of weapons, on opposing sides, but no human endeavour is untarnished and prayer is no exception. In the daily lives of millions of Christians, Muslims, Jews and so many others, prayer, as research supports, adds something to the value of human life and experience.

In summary, we should ask some straightforward moral questions regarding petitionary prayer. It seems morally dubious. The effect of prayer is worthy of moral consideration, irrespective of the existence of a God. Insofar as we can understand the effects of prayer, it seems quite often to benefit its practitioners, at least according to their own account of things. We should take this fact seriously. In limited ways but to a widespread extent, much prayer seems to make a moral contribution to life.

Meditation

Dawkins and Hitchens, in their key critiques of religion, make not one reference between them to meditation. To be fair, Dawkins makes clear that he is focusing very much on Western religion, although meditation certainly features there too in a variety of mystical traditions. Hitchens manages to write four and a half pages about Buddhism referring only to some of the worst atrocities with which it has been involved, without once mentioning its central practice of meditation.[124] I shall argue that forms of meditation, principally the Buddhist practice of mindfulness (*sati* in Pali), would appear to have some beneficial effects on people's state of mind, and that Buddhism deserves some credit for this. Mindfulness is a key factor on the path to enlightenment for Buddhists, but as we shall see, it has also travelled widely and today is part of much mainstream mental health practice in the West.

Buddhist meditation, as it developed historically, and is practised today most especially by monks and nuns, takes the form of either *vipassana* (insight) or *samatha* (calming) meditation. Essentially, these forms of meditation are techniques for spiritual development and in fact are often combined, leading ultimately to the Buddhist goal of enlightenment. They fit with some remarkable insights into the human mind. Key amongst these is that the human mind generally runs around desiring things it doesn't possess or doesn't think it possesses. Such craving may equally take the form of fear, or a desire for escape. We will perhaps re-run a recent incident in our lives with regret or pride, or pre-run a possible future event with apprehension or triumphalism. Our mind is so often not satisfied with where we are, where it is. This is the wandering mind that can take us over. Buddhism is not saying that we shouldn't plan. It is saying that the degree of fear and desire that accompanies the life of the mind are symptomatic of an attachment. Due to its cravings and its ignorance of these processes as a whole, such a mind is out of tune with how things are, and therefore suffers. The mind does not see things aright and is therefore constantly self-correcting, trying again and again to get things, events and people in focus but this will always fail since all is impermanent – most of all ourselves. For Buddhism, we are simply a series of changes that give rise to each other.

Most Buddhists are of course lay people, not monastics. For the laity, meditation is not about achieving enlightenment at the end of this life but rather about coming to terms with one's situation and becoming less attached and more compassionate. What has always struck me about the Buddhist diagnosis of the human mind is that it is onto something. Like the picture of the mind as a raging bull that can't be tamed in Jonathan Haidt's book *The Happiness Hypothesis*, our minds, as complexes of desires and impulses, seem so often to run our lives. The possibility that the mind could be more directed, focused and honed is perhaps of real value both for people generally, but especially for those who suffer from depression and mental illness, where self-recrimination and a sense of worthlessness can seem to take over. Key to Buddhist meditation, especially insight or *vipassana* meditation, is the practice of mindfulness (*sati*), or awareness. It is the seventh factor in the eightfold path leading to *nirvana* in Buddhism. The Sri Lankan Buddhist monk and scholar Walpola Rahula describes it as follows. 'Right mindfulness is to be diligently aware, mindful and attentive with regard to 1. the activities of the body 2. sensations or feelings 3. the activities of the mind and 4. ideas, thoughts, conceptions and things.'[125]

This process of awareness and alertness, of being able to register what is going on in one's mind, can be a crucial tool in helping to control the mind, or so we are told. Let's look at the alleged mental health benefits of mindfulness.

Various studies testify to the beneficial effects of mindfulness practice, especially as regards stress reduction.[126][127][128][129] An Oxford University study has concluded that relapse rates into depression can be reduced by up to 44%[130] and the Oxford Mindfulness Centre, led by Professor Mark Williams, continues to produce research publications supportive of this view. The National Institute for Health and Clinical Excellence (NICE) has also endorsed mindfulness treatments. Harvard neuroscientist Sara Lazar has looked at the brain images of meditators and non-meditators and found by comparison that the cortical areas in the brains of meditators were significantly thicker than the same areas in non-meditators. 'The cortex atrophies with age; in Lazar's meditating subjects, however, these enlarged areas were the same thickness as what was measured in non-practitioners twenty years younger.'[131] Looking at the issue of the longer term effects of mindfulness, Dr. John J. Miller and colleagues concluded, in a three-year follow up study of patients who had suffered from anxiety disorders, that 'an intensive but time-limited group stress reduction intervention based on mindfulness meditation can have long-term beneficial effects in the treatment of people diagnosed with anxiety disorders.'[132] A meta-analysis of mindfulness based stress reduction therapy (MBSR) reached similar, tentatively positive conclusions: that a broad range of individuals may be helped to 'cope with their clinical and non-clinical problems.'[133]

A key criticism of MBSR and Mindfulness Based Cognitive Therapy (MBCT) from a Buddhist point of view is that it is an appropriation of Buddhist practice by mental health experts in a clinical setting. Estranged from its spiritual home in this way some Buddhists have alleged that MBSR and MBCT have very little to do with Buddhism. In this sense, it might be argued that any beneficial effects of MBSR and MBCT are irrelevant for my argument that in mindfulness we find a beneficial effect of religion, since the benefits of mindfulness – as they have been measured in a clinical setting – can be seen as the benefits of a practice that lies largely outside the realm of religion. This view, however, is extremely dubious, for several reasons. First, while some trainers in MBCT, especially the eight-week initial course, emphasise its secularist credentials as a selling technique within highly secular societies like the UK, there are many links with Buddhist practice in much MBCT. The techniques are drawn directly from Buddhist practice. The pioneers of MBCT and MBSR Jon Kabat-Zinn in the US and Mark Williams in the UK, have no problem admitting this. If mindfulness is therefore having a positive effect on people's lives then the initial insights, practices and influences of religion – specifically Buddhism in this instance – should be given some credit.[134]

A further key point is that research has been done among Buddhist practitioners about the effect that meditation has on them and their physical and mental well-being, and has indicated positive results in terms of mental health. One such piece of research was undertaken by Dr. Heidi Wayment and colleagues from Northern Arizona University in *'Doing and Being: Mindfulness, Health, and Quiet Ego Characteristics among Buddhist Practitioners'*,[135] Here Wayment identifies a number of ways in which mindfulness training facilitates physical and mental health among Buddhists. The benefits mentioned include: i. a strengthening of the immune system, ii. improved social relationships with family and strangers, iii. reduced stress, depression and anxiety, and increased well-being and happiness and iv. increased openness to experience, conscientiousness and agreeableness. A further study, specifically among Buddhist monks and nuns, has concluded 'that monks and nuns who are more advanced in practising meditation show fewer signs of psychological distress than monks and nuns who are less advanced in the art of meditation.'[136] So here we have direct evidence that religion – specifically Buddhism – has some beneficial effect on its practitioners.

It should also be mentioned that in Thailand, monasteries have in recent decades been of significant help as drug rehabilitation centres, due in part to the meditation techniques on offer, along with the watchfulness and care of a community.

The new atheist and author of *The End of Faith*, Sam Harris regards mindfulness as hugely beneficial, while making clear that, in his view, it needs decoupling from its Buddhist roots since all religions are, as far as he is concerned, sectarian and divisive. He is also keen to extract what he sees to be a beneficial humanistic practice from its metaphysical baggage. Here Harris is simply misunderstanding religion and, certainly, Buddhism. Meditation and mindfulness are at the core of Buddhism. The truth, for Buddhists, is also ultimately beyond language, and all metaphysical claims are, as such, provisional – they are therefore not necessarily what Harris imagines. Buddhism, in this respect, emphasises its empiricism and practicality. Many Buddhists would be delighted that the benefits of Buddhism are being reaped by a radical secularist like Harris.

Buddhism is of course extremely diverse, and its recent history of meditative practice is extremely disturbing at times. Buddhist scholar and practitioner Dr. Brian Victoria in his *Zen at War* criticises both Nicheren and Zen Buddhism – both significant forms of Japanese Buddhism – for their role in support of the Japanese imperial cause during the Sino-Japanese War of 1937-45 and its continuation throughout World War II. Attempts at genocide and war crimes against Chinese citizens were committed in the first of these conflicts, and the brutal mistreatment of prisoners of war during World War II is well known. These behaviours do have something to do with meditation. Within Zen Buddhism, there is the concept of *'mushin'*, or no-mind, that was inherited from the samurai and from the confluence of Buddhism and Taoism. Without emotion, attachment or reflection (the interfering, conceptual, dualistic mind), one was to just act spontaneously, 'to flow' without fear or inhibition. To be in such a state of 'no-mindedness' is to have meditation as a way of life, an ultimately effortless and natural practice.[137] *Mushin* was crucial for the bravery required by the samurai in keeping to the *bushido* code – a code of honour that governed the samurai way of life. It would also prove indispensable in unleashing the savagery of imperial Japan in the mid-twentieth century, where, in many instances, conceptual inhibitions had no traction. *Mushin* is perhaps best understood in terms of Freud's analysis of World War I where, for him, the 'id', the part of the mind representing instinct and inherent needs, was loosed upon the world without inhibition, without the critical mind available to interfere.

Morally, two points stand out for me here. First, as is becoming a theme, religion is often in moral peril when it serves a political regime. When the psychological depths and strengths of spirituality are harnessed for militant ends, the road to hell shines bright. Civil religion[138] tends to hallow the tank more than the ploughshare. Secondly, in order to gain self-understanding, religion(s) should always actively seek sociological and psychological critique, rather than defend itself against this.

More generally though, it would appear that Buddhist mindfulness meditation has been, and today is being, put to some good effect, both within and beyond Buddhism.

Mission and evangelising

Reaching out to the world beyond the faithful is to many religious groups – within, for example, Christianity and Islam – like the necessity of breathing as far as the life of that group is concerned. As such, I don't think religious groups can be criticised for simply doing this. For the sake of brevity, I'm going to offer some evaluation of Christian attempts to evangelise. This will include how Christians work with other types of Christian, and how in other ways they come to terms with the world and faiths beyond their own.

To begin with, what people are being converted to or persuaded about, or the lifestyle that a group espouses is pivotal, and there is clearly huge variation here. Liberal types of believers are often criticised by the more evangelical for their lack of evangelistic zeal and perceived moral laxity. Liberals in turn critique fundamentalism and exclusivism (where groups claim to have the whole truth, and others none of it) for intolerance towards other religions, and for their moral strictures – for example against homosexuality. So, moral evaluations about mission begin from different places within religion.[139] With this in mind, I decided to interview a range of Christian leaders and figures engaged in mission who represent a variety of views about it. To my surprise, when asked, participants seemed to offer up a fairly agreed list of ethical criteria against which mission and evangelism were to be evaluated. These criteria include: a) How those doing the evangelising are treated by the denomination or church they represent. b) What methods and techniques are involved in mission? c) Who are the target audience of mission and why? d) How evangelising responds when it encounters other religions: does it help generate animosity, or respect and dialogue? And e) How mission and evangelising proceed outside of the media spotlight, especially in the developing world? I will keep referring back to some of these means of evaluation in my discussion.

It is as ever hard to work one's way through the spin, the media messages and websites that religious groups and their opponents become ever-more adept at constructing. Nonetheless, today in Christianity even distinctly evangelical forms of faith increasingly talk the language of tolerance and respect for others, including other religions. Gary Gibbs, in charge of Reach (the outreach programme for the Elim Pentecostals), was keen to emphasise the importance of friendship between people of different faiths, while making clear that for him, for example, Muslims were mistaken in their faith.

This respectful voice is centre-stage when one looks at bodies like the World Council of Churches (WCC), at the heart of the worldwide co-ordination of Christianity. For example, the WCC, the Pontifical Council for Interreligious Dialogue and the World Evangelical Alliance jointly published a document entitled: '*Christian Witness in a Multi-Religious World: recommendations for conduct*'. These include building 'relationships of respect and trust with people of all religions…inter-religious dialogue [that] can provide new opportunities for resolving conflicts, restoring justice, healing memories, reconciliation and peace-building.'[140]

Fitting well with this are communities for reconciliation and social justice like the Corrymeela Community in Northern Ireland, committed to bringing together those whose lives were torn apart by the divides between Protestants and Catholics there. There is, of course, an entire inter-faith movement across the world[141], in which a moderate proportion of Christians are involved, that really does seek to bring together people of various faiths for the purposes of mutual understanding and the development of inter-religious co-operation. I have been to a number of inter-faith meetings and events over the years, and would argue they are morally well-intentioned, focused often on building better multi-religious and multi-cultural relations between different groups in society, with goals of mutual understanding, cooperation, co-ordination, tolerance and openness.[142] Of course, for those at the fundamentalist/exclusivist end of the mission spectrum, this is exactly where inter-faith cooperation is theologically and morally adrift.

There is also much inclusiveness in many religions, where the view that other religions have none of the truth is rejected. A thoroughgoing pluralism goes further, suggesting that all faiths have access to the truth – if not equal access – therefore removing the missionary imperative. The Dalai Lama's sentiment that non-Buddhists should continue in their own faiths, if they have them, and not convert to Buddhism; and his feeling that in this way complementary insights can be shared, reflect this kind of pluralism.[143] Richard Harries, the ex-Bishop of Oxford, made it clear he did not think it was the job of the Church to seek to convert people from other faiths, but rather to convert those of no faith. Recent Papal statements from Pope Francis have been inclusive of other faiths, eschewing the view that they are denied salvation.[144] In many public statements and collaborative operations, Christianity fares quite well when it comes to our criterion of how it encounters other faiths.

All the same, the *practice* of a wide variety of Christianity can impede developing the trust and cooperation needed and recommended by the WCC document as we have seen, for example, in Chapter 3, between the missionary activities of evangelical Protestantism and Catholicism in Latin America. Voices of bigotry, intolerance and exclusivism are also not hard to find. Besides those pronouncements of American Christian fundamentalists, more central figures like Cardinal Ratzinger (soon to be Pope Benedict XVI) wrote in 2000, in *Dominus Iesus* (an official statement of Catholic doctrine, ratified by the then pontiff Pope John Paul II) that members of other religions were 'gravely deficient' relative to members of the Church of Christ who already have 'the fullness of the means of salvation.'[145] Reflecting this kind of disparaging perspective Pope John Paul II in speaking about Buddhism, described its spiritual goal, nirvana as a state of absolute indifference towards the world, lacking all compassion.[146] This is both aggressively polemical and false. Clearly this kind of claim does not fare well as regards our criterion (d) of meeting other religions and generating respect rather than animosity.

For many within a particular religion, there is a narrative about 'other' faiths, what they believe and what they are like, and those other religions have an internal narrative about how they view themselves. These accounts of how a religion perceives itself and how others perceive it rarely coincide. What I have noticed in teaching children is how those from the strongest religious backgrounds have, in effect, to unlearn some of the prejudices about other faiths. For many believers across the world, other religions are not well known to them,[147] and sources of information, if there are any, come from within their own faith. At best they may hear friendly overtures, but do they believe them? People will listen to events, to what happens, more than to rhetoric.

A central difficulty to do with the encounter of religions and their respective missions is where they see themselves and each other as making exclusivist and competing truth-claims. Some religions too like Christianity and Islam do, by and large, for all the respect we have heard espoused, seek to convert those of other faiths. Hinduism, by contrast is less conversionary.[148] So long as faiths see themselves in opposition to each other, tension will arise from such competition, and the narratives about other religions are likely to come off the worse. The Christian theologian Stanley Hauerwas reaches a significant point along this trajectory when he claims 'Christians are people who believe that any compassion that is not formed by the truthful worship of the true God cannot help but be accursed.'[149] Polemic reaches fever pitch of course on the internet, as a website like www.christianaggression.org.violence.php testifies – whatever we make of the veracity of its content. Sometimes such tension is seen, within some forms of fundamentalist Christianity or some versions of Shi'a Islam, as a good thing, a sign of Armageddon, when 'the Rapture' will end it all, or the Mahdi return. Evangelical activity on the part of such groups can actually seek to spark tension, and under our test as regards how religions behave when they encounter others, this kind of faith scores particularly badly.

I want to look at a popular and mild form of exclusivism, the Alpha course. Their press secretary, Mark Edison-Dew, told me when I interviewed him that 1.2 million people have taken the course in the UK, making it the most popular evangelical project in the country. It was developed, to be what it is today in the 1990s, by Nicky Gumbel, who is the vicar at Holy Trinity Church, Brompton, in central London. There is now Youth Alpha, Alpha in prisons, as well as chapters in 169 countries across the world. The Alpha course is evangelical – though it eschews such pigeonholing – and is charismatic, with its Holy Spirit weekend at the heart of the course. In considering the second measure I mentioned, that is, to morally interrogate mission about the character of techniques used, the Alpha course doesn't fare particularly well. One participant described the technique of drawing people in as 'bait and switch'. In the first couple of sessions people ask their questions, are listened to and encouraged to feel comfortable. However, in the weeks that follow, a fairly hard line is plugged. Regarding other faiths, Alpha respects them, according to Mark Edison-Dew. Is it interested in converting people of other faiths? Not necessarily, according to him. Yet Nicky Gumbel states that while there may be truth in religions other than Christianity, it is only through Jesus Christ that there is assurance of salvation and life after death.[150] Gumbel clearly believes in the imperative to seek to convert all those who are not currently Christian to that faith. The author and journalist Jon Ronson left the course with the distinct impression that, as far as Alpha is concerned; members of other religions are ultimately 'going to hell' and as such need to be converted, not a message to build a great deal of trust and respect between faiths. What bothers me perhaps most about the course is the glossing over of any engagement with Biblical criticism. The reasonableness of the historical claims of Christianity, such as the resurrection of Jesus, or his Virgin birth, stand or fall on the basis of that text. When one digs deeper and reads what Nicky Gumbel writes about the Bible, it becomes clear that a good A-level student in Biblical studies could tell you how very misleading Gumbel is. For example, there is no mention of types of Biblical criticism, such as source criticism or redaction criticism.[151] One gets the distinct impression that the intention is to convert people before they realise the paucity of Biblical support for a number of key doctrinal claims. The best theology departments in the world and in the UK are not filled, not even sprinkled, with conservative or fundamentalist Christians, because an open academic study of the text is just too hard to square with such views. Returning to the 'techniques' criterion for evaluating mission, the Alpha course does not fare well with respect to questions about intellectual honesty.

Let's be clear: the Alpha course does not advocate violence or coercion towards those of other faiths or to those of no faith in any way. Quite the contrary, it advocates friendly relations. Yet given that some other faiths take a similar stance, some degree of tension is likely, and grows depending on the degree of conviction and the urgency of the sense of mission. Demonstrating both of those qualities, a more radical, exclusivist Christian, well known for his missionary activities, namely the late Ulster Unionist Ian Paisley, condemned Alpha as sinister, and other exclusivist Christian fundamentalists have been similarly vitriolic. We can see a story here, the ratcheting up of tension. When groups start saying that the other is of the Devil, the internal narratives about the other have well and truly grown horns. When (unlike with Alpha), both join in this, so that whole communities become demonised, one is half way down the road to violence, because this rhetoric beds down the idea of mutual existential threat. At this point, all the ecumenism in the world is so much hot air. When people are fearful, and sense loathing and hostility from the 'other', it just takes a further hostile remark, an abusive or misinterpreted gesture, a paranoid interpretation of events, and the fuse for violence is lit. The story of how religions track such downward spirals is, however, not the story of religions in themselves. They are never so isolated – as we have seen. The Internet and social media; as well as economic, political and historical forces, mould religions and mould relations between them, as we have noted already and will continue to observe throughout this book. All the same, religions and those within them are responsible for how exclusivist and conversionary they are. The extent and character of such tendencies causes tension, and possible violence, despite the fact that many exclusivists explicitly speak out against violence. It seems to me hardly surprising that Hindu nationalists, defensive of their cultures, prohibit by law some of the conversionary activity of Christianity and Islam. Indian religion, after all being a family of ethno-religions is not, generally speaking, engaged in converting non-Hindus. Many Hindus therefore see themselves as 'on the back foot' in relation to the universalist religions of Islam and Christianity. Mission-oriented faiths such as these can also often fail to appreciate the political and geo-political ramifications of their activity.[152] Sometimes, on the other hand, they appreciate them all too well.[153] I do not seek to defend Hindu nationalism – it has a morally dubious track record to say the least – but what exclusivists with conversionary intent need to do to morally defend their missionary activities, is to argue in ways that convince those of other faiths and of no faith that their missionary behaviour is reasonable, and here they often fail.

Charity

The ways religions most engage and relate to those not so affiliated cannot be properly considered without reference to the charities and philanthropy to which many religions would appear committed. This is perhaps where the voice of religion is most morally persuasive.

As with so much about religion, polemic abounds as to the relative contribution they make to the general good of society through charitable and philanthropic work. In attempting the briefest of assessments of this vast area I shall look mostly at Christianity in the UK.

I shall consider four issues: First, the extent to which religious people volunteer for philanthropic causes that are not directly associated with the religion concerned, and not associated with proselytising as such. Second, the extent to which the more religious are involved in giving to charitable causes beyond their specific churches, mosques and other places of worship. Third, the extent to which charities that are broadly philanthropic have religious associations. And, finally, the philanthropic outcomes that are reasonably associated with religious charitable work.

All of this is open and will be subject to critique throughout. Some definitions may help to begin. In keeping with what I have mentioned in the Introduction, being religious should be taken to mean that this is someone's account of themselves, unless there is particular reason to question that account. A narrower definition runs the risk of imposing an agenda on members of a faith.

When considering the philanthropic work of religious institutions, credit is, perhaps, especially due where the recipients are not associated with such institutions or religions. Terry Sanderson, of the National Secular Society, understandably protested that a BBC poll alleging that religious people give more to charity than non-religious people, omitted to mention that such 'giving to charity' included giving to churches, which begs the question as to what counts as charity.[154] All the same, there is a great deal of what we might call 'outreach charitable work' to those of other faiths or none, and religions surely deserve credit when we consider the many charitable ways they engage with issues of homelessness, alcoholism and make provisions such as food banks, prison visiting, and overseas aid, notwithstanding that proselytising is often a part of the picture. Where proselytising is absent, as is sometimes the case, particular credit is due.

i. Volunteering

Ingrid Storm, in analysing data sets from the European Values Study (1999-2008) and the Ethnic Minority British Election Survey (2010), concluded that in Britain 'religion increases volunteering primarily through bonding rather than bridging social networks.'[155] She continues 'people who are involved in religious volunteering are almost 3.6 times as likely to volunteer for non-religious causes.'[156] This of course does not tell us what proportion of those who consider themselves religious are involved in religious volunteering but that if they are, this is often correlated with wider voluntary commitments. Storm finds that 'religiosity is positively associated with both religious and non-religious civic engagement...even when controlling for education, socioeconomic factors, values, and attitudes'[157] based on the European Values Study. She speculates that many people get into the habit of volunteering within a faith community and that this has the 'spill over' effect that such people volunteer more generally.

This would appear very creditable to religious adherents who, in addition to volunteering within their own religious contexts, seem to also offer their services elsewhere.

Statistically speaking, though, this is a very complex issue. In his research about the UK, Senior Research Fellow at the Centre for Institutional Studies at East London University, Greg Smith concludes that the people most likely to engage in formal volunteering within an organisational setting are white, middle-aged, affluent, educated, and settled in a local community.'[158] Within this context, there is some evidence that such people, who have an active faith and involvement in a Christian or Jewish congregation, are more likely than non-believers or people of other minority faiths to be volunteers. Nevertheless, this research does not distinguish between those religious people volunteering within a religious context and those volunteering beyond it. Neither does it make clear how far the same people volunteer within either context. As such some critics of religion will be unconvinced about the moral character of voluntary contributions being made suggesting that they are, all too often, self serving. Such judgments seem to me rather harsh.

What is also hidden in this research, as Smith admits, is that as regards Muslim, Hindu and Sikh volunteering (rated at 27%, 31%, and 29% respectively – below data for non-religious people (39%), Christians (50%) and Jews (63%)) there is a great deal of informal volunteering in such communities that is, in his words, 'below the radar' of many surveys.

It strikes me that we need to handle the limited amount of data we have in this field carefully. Crass conclusions that religious people are more or less altruistic than others seem unjustified and unhelpful. Nonetheless, there is much evidence that members of religious faiths, especially when these are well established in the wider community, contribute to that wider community, and sometimes in ways that have no direct association with their faith. As such, the idea that religion is detrimental to society more generally seems odd in this respect.

ii. Giving

Data from the Charities Aid Foundation for the UK for 2012 showed 'that people who are religious in the widest sense donate almost twice as much money to charity as those without a faith. The average amount that religious people gave to charity was £576 over the previous 12 months, compared to £235 contributed by those of no faith.'[159] Professor Cathy Pharoah, co-director of the Centre for Charitable Giving and Philanthropy at the Cass Business School of City University in London, and Tom McKenzie, then a research fellow at its Faculty of Management,[160] both reported in a study published in 2010 a significant variation in giving across the UK, where 'households from Northern Ireland and north west London – both areas with a strong religious tradition – were found to be generous donors relative to income.'[161] Especially in Northern Ireland, the study speaks about a 'historically strong culture of giving'. Pharoah makes the point that a high level of church attendance in Northern Ireland 'provides an impetus and framework for giving.'[162] In north-west London, compared with elsewhere in the UK, average donation is both high in absolute terms at £11.55 per week, and also high as a percentage of total household spending (2.17%).

Pharoah ascribes this to a relatively large Jewish community in the area, as well as higher-than-average income levels. As quoted, the report continues, 'Britons who consider religion to be very important in their lives were found to be nine percentage points more likely to give than those who do not consider religion to be important at all. Those for whom religion is "quite important" are four percentage points more likely to give, according to previous research by Professor Pharoah.'[163] The *Huffington Post* also reported about the UK that Muslims are giving especially highly to charity (£371 per annum), followed by Jews (£270) and Christians (£178), with the non-religious giving least at £116.[164]

Critics might again respond that if the giving is to religious institutions, we should raise questions about how philanthropic it is. There is in fact more significant evidence that deals with this question. Jonathan Haidt (an atheist psychologist) writes about the US: 'religious believers give more money than [the non-religious] to secular charities, and to their neighbours. They give more of their time too, and of their blood.'[165] This trend seems to be followed too in the UK, Richard Harrison, director of research at the Charities Aid Foundation in 2012, writes 'those of faith are more generous to charity in general, [and] their giving is not uniquely focused on their own religious activities.'[166] According to the Charities Aid Foundation's 2011 Market Tracker Report, 'only 31% of religious donors had supported religious activities in their giving as against 68% donating to medical charities and 48% to overseas aid.'[167]

In some respects, none of this should surprise the reader. In Islam, in addition to the mandatory *zakah*, calculated at 2.5% of disposable income, there is also the concept of *sadaqah*, which is voluntary giving. In Judaism, *tzedekah*, which involves giving 10% of disposable income, is to be given as a duty and the Christian practice of tithing derives from the same Biblical sources. In Hinduism, Jainism and Buddhism, '*dana*' – generosity and giving – is a key virtue. In Buddhism it is one of five principal virtues that mirror five precepts to be kept by all lay Buddhists. Many would emphasise the golden rule, 'to do unto others as you would have them do unto you', as a moral benchmark expressed in sacred texts across all major faiths in one way or another, however much they all often significantly deviate from that ideal.

As regards giving, it is hard to avoid the view that in the UK religion is not simply self-serving, at least not as far as the giving of ordinary religious believers is concerned. We should not conclude that the religious are better people than the non-religious. This cannot be deduced. Pharoah makes clear that religion sets up mechanisms, opportunities and motivations for giving. There are also socioeconomic factors that are hard to exclude from calculations. Still, when it comes to giving, religious believers in the UK would appear to be generous.

iii. The Contribution of Religious Charities

If we look at the largest UK charities by both income and expenditure, religiously-based charities that focus on issues of poverty and overseas aid are towards the top of the list – including Christian Aid and the Tear Fund – along with non-religious charities like Oxfam.[168] David Ainsworth, now group online editor, but then deputy editor of charity finance at Civil Society Media, told me that of the 161,000 charities in the UK, somewhere between 80,000-100,000 of them have religious associations, depending on how charities are categorised.[169] If we look at the Disasters Emergency Committee, which co-ordinates responses to urgent appeals, religiously-based charities like Christian Aid, the Catholic Agency For Overseas Development (CAFOD), Islamic Relief, World Vision International and the Tear Fund are among the thirteen major UK charities that make up that committee.

Another way to view religious involvement in charity work is to look at new needs that arise, and see who perceives those first and responds most promptly. For example, over the last ten or so years, the growing need for food banks has been met in part by the religious charity the Trussell Trust. Churches have also played a key role at a local level. Another perspective is to consider those causes that, however important they may be, do not garner sympathy from much of the general public. Who responds there? Taking the example of the rehabilitation of sex offenders, I remember a local Quaker meeting getting involved with this kind of work. Once again, a picture is created that religion makes an important philanthropic contribution to society.

My point in all this is not that 'religion does better than its secular counterparts' but rather that religion makes a very significant, positive contribution.

iv. Outcomes

It is far from easy to measure the specific philanthropic outcomes of faith-based charitable work. Nonetheless, from what we have seen so far, we might judge it not insignificant. We could take examples from many religion-based charities: for example, Christian Aid spent over £73m on long term development projects and emergency aid in 2012-3. Its development work is done irrespective of the religious belief or practice of the people they are helping. CAFOD, the Tear Fund and the Salvation Army, as other examples of Christian based charities, have also spent large sums of money in similar ways. In its foreign aid work, the current UK government has understandably found it efficient to work with existing religious charities and organisations on the ground across the globe, because their charitable networks and local knowledge are so valuable, and in many cases unrivalled. According to the 2007 World Health Organisation report *'Towards Primary Health Care: renewing partnerships with faith-based communities and services'*, 'approximately 40% of health services in sub-Saharan Africa (rising to 70% in various countries) are provided by faith groups.'[170]

Some critics of what I have been suggesting would argue that the contributions of volunteering, giving and charitable work with religious origins may be significant, but they are largely harmful. Accusations take various forms.

Firstly, that religious, charitable and humanitarian involvement is mainly instrumental to proselytising. Secondly, that religious charities all too often impose their own questionable moral agendas on those with whom they work. And lastly, that religious charities are disproportionately corrupt, seeking to make money for their own religious causes rather than for philanthropic ends.

Let's look at the first two claims together.

Caspar Melville, in the *Guardian*,[171] quotes the founder of the Nigerian Humanist Movement, Leo Igwe, as saying, 'No doubt religions have executed many humanitarian projects on the continent that have impacted positively on the lives of Africans. But these projects, as helpful as they may appear, are Trojan horses. They are evangelising weapons which missionaries use to get Africans to embrace Christianity. Missionary schools are religious indoctrination centres.'[172] He continues, 'It is true that missionary hospitals heal the sick. They also kill by denying women their rights to abortion and to reproductive health services. Missionary hospitals in Nigeria carry out forced baptism on infants and forced conversion on death beds.'[173] Melville notes that, 'Many Catholic aid agencies, especially those involved with AIDS, continue to suppress or deny the importance of condom use in the fight to prevent the spread of HIV.'[174] This last point is surely significant. The Catholic Church, both in Africa and also in a Catholic country like the Philippines, has actively discouraged the use of condoms, which has in turn increased the spread of HIV. This has done untold harm in terms of mortality rates and all the attendant health problems associated with HIV.

At times, there are different moral complexions as regards secular and religious charitable and philanthropic contributions. Ingrid Storm's research indicates that values of individual autonomy feature highly within the ethos of secular civic engagement.[175] An interest in gay rights, gender equality, opposition to capital punishment and the blasphemy laws in some states are examples of secular moral concerns. Clearly, there are clashes as regards some of these issues with some religious interest groups and churches. All the same, these tensions can be seen as too centre-stage as well. For example, even from a moderate secularist point of view, while the work of the Catholic Church as regards abortion and contraception is extremely harmful, it would be quite illogical to say that it erases all the philanthropy even of all Catholic charities. We should also be clear that many religious charities neither seek to proselytise nor to impose specific religious strictures on those whom they serve. Let us think counterfactually for a moment. If there were no Christian Aid, no Trussell Trust, no Red Cross, if local churches did nothing philanthropic within their communities in the UK, and if people were not religiously motivated to work for non-religious charities like Oxfam, would the world be a better or worse place? Any sense of proportion tells us that without such contributions we would be worse off.

Melville's *Guardian* article raises the issue of proselytising. Let's suppose the points about forced baptisms in Christian hospitals in Nigeria are true. Again, the points raised by counterfactual argumentation are interesting. Let's suppose we shut down all Christian hospitals in Nigeria, would Nigeria be the better or the worse for that? Even with forced baptisms and sacraments, I'm not sure it would be better without these facilities. The tribalisms of religions in Nigeria, especially as regards Christianity and Islam, are clearly powerful, violent imperatives and ones that concern Christians and Muslims as much as anyone. Ian Linden, writing in the *Guardian* about a wide range of faiths involved in health care in Africa, and about his own considerable experience, remarked, 'I cannot recall any of them [religions] who understood their primary purpose in caring for the sick as their conversion.'[176] To take another example, the World Bank has recently been looking at the educational effectiveness of faith-based schools in sub-Saharan Africa. So far as it could tell, sometimes they do better than government schools, sometimes they do worse. Sometimes they reach inaccessible rural areas the government doesn't reach. We should, as I suggest in Chapter 5. about faith schools, be concerned about proselytising, but where it is a choice between a faith school and no school, unless one has already reached the conclusion there is something innately, ineradicably harmful about being religious that far outweighs any good produced, faith schools are surely better than no schools.

The other key element of concern about religious charities is that of corruption. In some individual cases it is not easy to know what to conclude, whatever one suspects. I remember walking along High St. Kensington in central London one Christmas. Every fifty yards or so in fluorescent yellow, two or three larger than life figures, noisily shook tubs of change collecting for a children's charity – or so it appeared at the time. I asked one of them more about their charity and saw their UCKG badges. The United Church of the Kingdom of God is a relatively new, evangelical, charismatic church, with a membership of about 8 million worldwide. We came across it in Chapter 3 when investigating Christianity in Latin America. Their leader, Edir Macedo in 2015 was estimated to have a personal fortune estimated at $1.1bn,[177] some allege on the back of takings from the Church, but such charges have not been proven, though various controversies abound about the Church, one of which is the opacity of their fundraising campaigns.[178][179] So, does corruption feature especially in religious charities? David Ainsworth told me that in the UK, about a third of those charities under investigation for corruption are religiously-based charities. Small Christian evangelical charities, Muslim charities and Jewish charities seem to feature most prominently among these. We should be clear, however, as we have seen, that religious charities constitute considerably more than a third of all UK charities: using Ainsworth's figures, they represent roughly 50 – 62% of all UK charities. By these calculations, religious charities are therefore doing better on the corruption front than their secular counterparts. Editor of the Ecclesiastical Law Journal and Secretary of the Churches' Legislation Advisory Council, Frank Cranmer also points out that 'if only 23 religious charities in England and Wales were the subject of statutory inquiries in 2013-14, it is difficult to understand in what way religious charities represent a particular problem to the regulator.'[180]

We should engage our critical faculties when it comes to religion, just as we do when considering other human ventures, irrespective of whether we consider religion or forms of it to be more than a merely human endeavour. There will always be those on the make, who seek to hide from scrutiny, and religion can act as a convenient cover. It is hard to know why some Muslim, Jewish and small Christian evangelical charities should feature prominently among those religious charities that are susceptible to corruption, according to Ainsworth's figures. I suspect there is no simple answer, but it would be a valuable piece of research to discover more. In the meantime, as regards giving and the work of many mainstream religious charities, it appears the world would be poorer, missing some expressions of kindness, generosity and benevolence in their absence, and in the absence of their grassroots, local community work. This does not entail the view that religious people are more philanthropic than the non-religious. In a world without religion, all the people who are currently religious might be equally philanthropic or even more so, although evidence does not particularly support this latter view. Once again, the point is that, religious charities, carry out a fair amount of philanthropy – whatever would be the case otherwise – and this moves us away from the most outright, wholesale condemnations of religion to say the least..

Conclusion

In this chapter, we have switched from considering religion in terms of the high politics of challenging situations, to reflecting on how some of its basic practices affect the lives of ordinary believers and the society around them. I have also moved away from narrative accounts of events and towards social science, in terms of the evidence and arguments presented. Varying perspective and focus in this way indicates something of what is needed if we are to begin to grapple with understanding and judging religion.

To summarise, from the evidence presented in this chapter, religious practice and belief would appear to be more associated with mental health than with mental harm notwithstanding that it has done enormous mental harm to individuals and whole communities in many ways, the examples of systematic child sexual abuse in the Catholic Church, other churches and religions being a headline example of this. Prayer in many forms seems to be an example of a practice with associated benefits. Meditation, especially in forms of mindfulness, where much research has been focused, appears to have favourable effects too. The fact that in its clinical setting mindfulness has been somewhat appropriated from Buddhism does not detract from the credit to and benefit of that religious legacy. The fact that meditation brings mental health benefits also strikes me as being of moral worth, and therefore in terms of the effects that prayer and meditation have on believers themselves, there is some real moral value to be found there. That said, forms of petitionary prayer raise moral, philosophical and psychological questions that religious communities, leaders and institutions would do better to face than avoid. And we have also found that Buddhist meditative practices in mid-twentieth century Japan were put to the service of civil religion, with terrible consequences.

When we consider the moral complexion of how religion affects others, and look specifically at mission and evangelising, its ethical profile is less appealing, with the more exclusivist types of faith being the most problematic. Despite overtures of friendship and co-operation in many official statements from organisations such as the World Council of Churches, and despite much excellent interfaith work on the ground, evangelism and mission on the part of any particular religion are, unsurprisingly, not a locus of inter-religious harmony. The encounter of religions with each other when both are exclusivist and universalist – as is the case with significant forms of Islam and Christianity – is one dynamic of tension, while actual violence is exceptional and not the rule. Another type of tension arises when such forms of religion encounter more ethnocentric religions, such as Hinduism, which feel their cultural and political space to be under threat, and sense neo-imperialism and neo-colonialism coming in by the back door. The Alpha Course is decidedly not fundamentalist, while being disingenuous in not making its theological and ethical conservatism clear from the outset.

A consideration of recent charitable work in the UK indicates that religious organisations and individuals play a positive role, to say the least. Religious institutions offer contexts for charitable volunteering and giving and those in receipt of their work and charity often stand outside the religions themselves. Among the range of charities that operate in the UK, those that have some form of religious association are in the majority. Religious charities seem to respond well when new issues and crises arise. Charitable work on the part of religions can of course be harmful. Catholic charitable work that has discouraged the use of condoms, and as such assisted the spread of HIV in the Philippines, for example, is just one case in point. Proselytising in hospitals and schools abroad would also seem morally questionable, as in the Nigerian case we considered, but where there are no alternatives, and where such institutions are doing their job of curing the sick and genuinely educating pupils, then better them than no hospitals or schools at all.

In the last chapter we saw examples of some political and historical contexts within which religion has struggled and been morally tested. By contrast, in this chapter we have found out more about how religions are experienced from within in some of their everyday practices. The polemics that exist between some of the most zealous of atheists and the most ardent of believers is in part due to the fact that they are seeing very different realities. The transformative and ecstatic experiences of prayer or meditation are not generally accessed by the passionate atheist, who may, all the same be genned-up about the questionable character of evangelising and religious mission. The believer, on the other hand is very often neither inducted into a history of the atrocities of their faith, nor shown the questionable history of their religious texts, while at the same time their community and charitable contribution is integral to their philanthropic life and soul.

5

Within The Faiths: The Upbringing And Schooling Of Children

If religion were generally morally harmful in its effect on people – and its absence therefore morally beneficial, we might be forgiven for thinking that the best place to seek evidence for this would be in the effects that a religious upbringing and schooling had on children. After all, there are hundreds of thousands of children in the UK alone that are brought up in decidedly religious circumstances and who, if not home-schooled along these lines, are sent to religious schools of one form or another. On the other hand, there are millions of children brought up in very secular homes who, while they may, in our traditional consumerist fashion, celebrate Christmas, are brought up to have no particular religious belief or association.[181]

The facts of such contrasting situations have been so for decades now. This should enable us to look at the kinds of people who have developed from such differing circumstances and ask: "Is there any noticeable moral difference between these groups or between how the individuals within them develop as children?" We might imagine that this would be quite telling, since there are many children who do have fairly exclusive religious influences – many of whom in adulthood keep very much to their religious group and tradition. There are also many secular members of society who rarely meet people of decidedly religious conviction. The question of how such disparate groups of people 'weigh morally' may sound presumptuous, but it is hardly irrelevant if we are to have an empirical approach to the moral effect of religion on people. As the philosopher Anthony Grayling disparagingly remarks about religion, quoting the Bible, 'by their fruits ye shall know them'.[182]

Interestingly, this approach is not as straightforward as one might suppose. A report from the Joseph Rowntree Foundation in 2007 concluded that 'religion remains an understudied component of family life. Religiosity has been associated with protective factors that strengthen families, but little information is currently available on the beneficial or harmful roles that religion plays in the home.'[183] Since then, some further research has been done. In 2015 the scientific journal *Current Biology* published a report entitled *The Negative Association between Religiousness and Children's Altruism across the World*[184] that indicated that children from specifically Christian and Muslim households were less altruistic than children from non-religious households.[185] Other researchers have, however, strongly indicated that religious upbringings do offer children positive moral resources – for example of resilience under stress.[186] Alongside this inconclusive situation, diverse interest groups jump on their respective bandwagons and polemic reigns.

This very generic type of research also suffers from methodological problems. Establishing the meaning of categories, distinguishing between correlation and causation, and isolating independent from dependent variables are just some of the challenges to be faced.[187] For example, following the adage 'by their fruits ye shall know them', I decided to look at government statistics for the percentage of prisoners who were broadly affiliated to faith groups compared with those not so affiliated in the UK. In 1997, Anglicans constituted 45%, compared with under 30% in 2008. Roman Catholic inmates had declined slightly from about 17% to 15%. Muslims had increased from about 6% to 11%, and those of no religion had increased from 28% to 36%. Unsurprisingly, these changes roughly reflect broader demographic trends in UK society.[188] Anglicanism is in decline, those who regard themselves as members of no religion are on the increase. Islam bucks the general trend of secularisation in the UK as being on the increase. So we should not be surprised that these trends are reflected in the prison population. We should also be clear that how people are designated does not tell us very much. People 'affiliated' to Anglicanism tells us nothing particularly about their home background nor about whether they went to an Anglican school. So I'm not convinced that this kind of very generic statistical approach can get us very far.

Instead, I'm going to begin assessing the moral import of religious upbringing and schooling on children by looking at specific moral criticisms that have been levelled against them. A discussion of these arguments will then follow.

Moral Critiques

An initial objection to some forms of religious upbringing and schooling is that they may instil an authoritarianism that may lead to some very immoral results.[189] Philosopher of religion Dr. Stephen Law, in his book *The War for Children's Minds* maintains that a religious upbringing and education is fine so long as it upholds rationality and leaves beliefs and lifestyles up for critical debate.[190] Where it fails to do this, though, this can give rise to authoritarian types, who are inclined to both obey orders and pass them on through a chain of command rather than to think for themselves. This is a significant moral weakness and is, potentially, morally catastrophic. Holocaust survivor Professor Samuel Oliner and Dr. Pearl Oliner have noted through extensive research that those who sheltered Jews during the Holocaust tended to be those brought up in non-authoritarian ways, and that religious affiliation was only weakly related to those who chose to be rescuers.[191] Law, for his part, is as concerned with what an authoritarian upbringing and schooling inhibits as with what it produces. The inhibition of a critical, rational approach to the world impedes the tendency to reflect, negotiate and compromise, while the cultivation and encouragement to think for yourself is associated with accelerated personal and social development.[192]

It seems to me we do need to call into question authoritarian types of school, where children are discouraged from having their own ideas and their own arguments, whether about sex, religion or anything else. I am not suggesting that this is the norm among religious schools, but many such schools are authoritarian in this way.[193] Quite a number don't want pupils to deviate too far from set views say, about abortion – in the case of Catholic schools, or the infallibility of a sacred text – in the case of Muslim schools and Christian fundamentalist schools. Here, values of independence and intellectual autonomy are overshadowed by higher demands to conform to authority. This does not at all mean that codes of conduct should not be clear and enforced where necessary. Discipline in schools needs to be clear, and can be all the clearer through reasoned explanation and discussion.

A second criticism of religious upbringing and schooling that involves indoctrination and coercive techniques is made by Richard Dawkins. He regards as abusive the labelling of children from a young age as Jewish, Christian, Buddhist or Muslim. This, he maintains, takes away their autonomy and deprives them of choice about themselves. Yet parents should have a very great deal of choice about how they bring up their children. This is surely right. But a key moral question for our time is: Where does parental choice give rise to greater moral problems than it solves? Stephen Law maintains that if foot-binding is morally questionable then surely mind-binding is as well.

Teaching against human evolution is a standard example of a piece of indoctrination at work in a minority of religious schools in the UK today. As Dawkins identified in his documentary *'Religion –The Root of All Evil?'*, the 'Accelerated Christian Education' programme in place in a number of fundamentalist Christian schools which results in pupils not believing in human evolution has hardly accelerated education. To have people dismissing human evolution given its established place at the heart of the life sciences across all academic institutions of higher education in the UK and elsewhere is surely an educational travesty.[194] It also reflects an utter lack of education about the Bible (in the case of Christianity and Judaism) to think that Genesis teaches against evolution, as nearly all Biblical scholars in universities across the globe who are not specifically affiliated to conservative forms of faith will point out.

A third problem allegedly associated with religious upbringings and schooling is an associated tribalism, the establishment and reinforcement of an in-group/out-group mentality. I remember a conversation with the religious education advisor for Northern Ireland in the time of the Troubles. He said that the problems of Northern Ireland would not be properly resolved so long as they had Catholic and Protestant schools. In Israel, tragically, with more and more Jewish children being schooled in hard-line Zionist contexts, prejudice is most potent and combustible among young people. Evolutionary psychologist, Professor John Teehan observes that the in-group/out-group mindset has been of particular significance for the evolving human mind, in helping us gauge who to trust and who not to trust. He continues, 'Religion, however, serves as an amplification device for this mental tool. By connecting the in-group with a divine judge and enforcer, and by raising the stakes for being on the right side of that divide, religion – at least monotheistic religion – has imbued this divide with deadly power.'[195]

Professor of Global Studies at the University of California at Santa Barbara, Mark Juergensmeyer, in his study *Terror in the Mind of God: The Global Rise of Religious Violence*, writes that in all the incidents of religious violence that he has studied 'the script of cosmic war is central'.[196] When an in-group/out-group division or 'struggle becomes sacralised, incidents that might previously have been considered minor skirmishes...are elevated to monumental proportions. The use of violence becomes legitimised...What had been simple opponents become cosmic foes...The process of satanisation can transform a worldly struggle into a contest between martyrs and demons.'[197]

Epithets such as kaffir/infidel/heretic/barbarian/witch can be toxic and further examples of such divisive language are not difficult to find. When I asked the Muslim cleric Dr. Haitham al-Haddad about the Muslim feminist scholar Amina Wadud, he described her as an 'innovator'. This phrase is a clear rebuke – coming from a very conservative Muslim scholar. To use it of Wadud is to cast her out from Islam, a decisively hostile gesture. Insofar as such designations – with their derogatory connotations assault the ears of children in upbringing and schooling, and sacralise in-group/out-group mentalities, they hinder the individual and the human community in coming to terms with itself.

The economist, philosopher and Nobel laureate Professor Amartya Sen is interested in examining what can best be done if an in-group/out-group mentality is evolutionarily so hard-wired; and if, contrary to the secularisation thesis, religion continues to show no sign of global retreat. Ensuring that we keep and grow plural identities is crucial for Sen. The danger comes when particular identities – and religious ones are prime candidates here – exclude all others. Sen's point is that a range of identities and associated belongings help to build in flexibility to a person's mentality, and to their relations with others who in some ways may be quite different from themselves. If Sen is right, and his reasoning seems to me to make good sense, then upbringings and schoolings that emphasise specific types of belonging, to the exclusion or significant diminution of all others, seem once again harmful.

The example of a journalist who visited the Islamic Darul Uloom London School in Chislehurst, in Kent, makes the point well. In conversation, the headteacher made the following remarks, 'As Muslims we're not interested in an education that is simply about getting a job. We're not on Earth for this reason. We live on Earth merely with a view to the next life.'[198] Sadly, and significantly, this type of setting oneself apart seems to be found in a number of Muslim schools.[199]

A fourth point of criticism that relates specifically to the involvement of the Church – most especially the Catholic Church – in the schooling and upbringing of children, is the issue of child abuse, both physical and sexual, suffered by very many thousands of children in Ireland, the US, Australia and elsewhere.[200] One recent report indicates in fact that at least ten thousand children were abused in Australia alone.[201] The fact that it was organised among Catholic priests in Ireland and in the US and that the abuse took place throughout most of the twentieth century and into this century and went on unchecked, raises grave concerns about unquestioned authority and the dangers of such authority. It indicates that we should be highly sceptical about the view that religious institutions be considered moral guardians in any reliable sense at all. We have compelling reasons to be morally suspicious of all closed systems of authority. It is disquieting how easy it is for a society, whose representatives are always adults, to forget the persecution and abuse of children. Children are invariably the most transient aspect of a population and those among them who have been mistreated are unlikely to have risen beyond such mistreatment as adults enough to speak out, be noticed and heard. While social services systems continue to creak and groan under the weight of cost-saving imperatives, it is all-too-easy for a stream of silent victims to continue to pass by largely unnoticed.

One issue I find especially disturbing is an inclination to defend institutions. Discussing child abuse cases in Rotherham and Manchester in 2014, politicians seemed keen to emphasise that children's homes, for which the government is ultimately responsible, have not been so much at the centre of the problem as the media has made out. Similarly on the defensive, a report allegedly sponsored by the Manchester Metropolitan Police is said to de-emphasise police failings. Defending institutions seems to be what so many officials do, whether in a religious or a secular context. Nonetheless some encounters are alarming. I had a telephone interview with a senior Catholic cleric in 2014. I raised the issue of the physical and sexual abuse of children in Ireland and the US as a reason for the general public, at least, no longer trusting religions any more than any other sort of institution regarding the care of children. The first response was to talk about the book and film *Angela's Ashes* by Frank McCourt. The message was that Ireland was a mess following World War I. I didn't follow this argument and replied, 'Why didn't the Catholic Church try to help by simply not abusing children for many decades throughout the twentieth century?' I had to persist with this question, and eventually gained the response, 'We didn't put our best people in charge of certain institutions.' I asked the cleric if he condemned what had happened, and he said he did. It should be noted that I did have to prompt him to elicit this reproof. His first inclination had been to defend the institution of the Church. When institutions are sacralised as the in-group, what is not to be sacrificed for the sake of their reputation?

Response and debate

In looking at these various charges against religious upbringing and religious schooling, a number of points have been made in response. First that authoritarianism should not be avoided, especially in the early development of childhood. Children cannot start off by reasoning about what is right and wrong for themselves. Religious traditions give children the context, ideas, beliefs and lifestyles within which they can begin to reason. The former chief rabbi, Jonathan Sacks, cites the philosopher Alasdair MacIntyre's claim that reason is rooted in tradition, that it cannot be applied independently of it. Stephen Law advocates children employing their rational faculties at every opportunity and as soon as they are able, which is fairly early on. By contrast, Sacks suggests that critical questioning, while it has its place, should be left to a later stage. But why repress questions, what is good about such an upbringing or such schooling? If reason is, as McIntyre and Sacks suggest, rooted in tradition – as I also indicated in the Introduction – one can hardly be departing from tradition by using it at the earliest opportunity.

A further defence of an authoritarian style of religious upbringing and schooling has been to maintain that, without a set of beliefs and lifestyle that is imposed and made clear, a child grows up unscripted, and lacking confidence in what they think and who they are. However, to think out your own ideas freely alongside parents, family and friends is in fact precisely how to grow in confidence. I have seen this with scores of pupils I have taught. In fact, to give a child a rigid script of belief from which they should not depart is precisely to make them vulnerable. It is to engender in them a sense of being in something like a fortress that must be defended against a hostile, unsafe world. Such an inflexible, brittle mentality may tie people closely to the in-group by equally reinforcing the menace of an unfamiliar and imagined out-group, where there is darkness and gnashing of teeth. It is symbolised for example in the covering of a small Jewish child within some Chassidic communities whenever they go out of their community into the wider world. I have seen it too in fundamentalist Christians I have known, a nervousness, a lack of trust and confidence in people and institutions beyond the 'safety' of the faith.

A more substantive defence of authoritarian religious upbringings is a communitarian argument. It claims that all the criticisms of religious upbringing outlined have been focused on the harm done to individuals and that the community dimension is largely neglected. So this communitarian defence of religious upbringing and schooling goes, we cannot simply evaluate the morality of religious upbringings and schooling by reference to their effect on individuals..

In this way the Amish won a court battle to withdraw their children from school, beyond the eighth grade (13 – 14 years of age), in the State of Wisconsin so as to bring them up according to their traditional way of life. The point was that without absenting their children from school the Amish community was faced with an existential threat. They would struggle to work the land especially at harvest time. Passing on their traditions effectively would also be less assured with the persistence of external school culture that was not consonant with their way of life. To counter this threat the Amish invoked the First Ammendment, about freedom of religion and religious expression. And so, in the case of Wisconsin vs. Yoder (1972) the US Supreme Court ruled that the Amish community in this dispute had a valid claim and Amish children were allowed leave of absence from school.[202]

The case is put most dramatically and also, most questionably, by saying that if we deprive a religious community of the right to school its children in their faith tradition, we cut off the life-blood of the on-going community, and in effect commit cultural genocide.[203] Let's accept that we cannot fully evaluate the moral significance of a religious upbringing and schooling by merely looking at its effect on individuals, because the impact of such upbringing and schooling on the community is also morally salient. Still, the question remains as to how much of a moral claim specific religious communities should have over their members, especially when individuals within such communities have their lives and choices determined by such claims. In the chapters about Islam, I broadly agree with Will Kymlicka that community rights should be protected from external (for example government) infringement, but that individual rights should be equally protected from community infringement. We have seen that authoritarian, exclusivist, in-group faiths are damaging both to communities and to the individuals within them, and so the communitarian argument, insofar as it has force, depends largely on the type of community concerned.

Religious communities and denominations are often defined precisely by the slightest of doctrinal and historical disputes. Sigmund Freud coined the phrase 'the narcissism of minor difference' to describe what he took to be the neurotic focus on exactitude in belief and ritual, whether for example, with the creed or the Mass. I remember visiting Sergiyev Posad (Zagorsk during the Soviet era), near Moscow, with an ex-Catholic friend. Sergiyev Posad is a collection of Russian Orthodox churches and monasteries. The rather prim Russian Orthodox woman chaperoning us, having taken my hands out of my pockets, entered into a barrage of insults against Catholicism and the Pope, just in case my friend might lapse back into his old religious ways instead of being the atheist he presently was.

We could be talking about Catholicism and Protestantism in Northern Ireland, the tribalisms of Bosnian Islam, Serbian Orthodoxy and Croatian Catholicism. There is no doubt that there, as in so many instances, we have admixtures of nationalist politics and religious adherence that have been violently fused through war, invasion and territorial rivalry. In-group/out-group mentalities are potent – and potentially violent – among mainstream Christian denominations like Catholicism and the Eastern Orthodoxies in some places, even today. Exclusivist religious schools that cater very much, if not entirely, for children of a specific faith background, and that teach a particular faith as being true (in the kind of authoritarian way criticised above), are thereby vehicles for the establishment of in-group/out-group mentalities. It seems hard to see why the state, in the interests of building a cohesive but non-homogenous society, should fund such types of religious school. In response to those who would object to this line of argument, that it is discriminatory to withdraw state funding for schools that cater more or less exclusively for children of their faith, two points should be made. First, why are the rights of such specific communities more important than the rights of the individual children within them, for example to be able to openly question, or in the case of some fundamentalist schools, to be taught accurately about human evolution? And second, why are the rights of these specific communities more important than the need for cohesion within the wider society that such schools in effect continue to divide?

There is the argument, of course, that the very concept of 'group/community rights' is debatable because surely all important rights are covered by reference to individual rights. Communitarians would regard this as reductionistic: the whole, they would say, is more than the sum of its parts. My point is that the communitarian argument at this juncture pushes in the other direction to imply that the wider community has the right not to be threatened by conflict within and between exclusivist, in-group mentalities. The communitarian can't have their cake and eat it. It makes no sense to say we can have exclusive control of the schooling and upbringing of children within our community so that these children maintain our community while also saying that the wider community can have no particular say about how our community affects or contributes to it.

A final objection by some religionists to the arguments against authoritarian, exclusivist education and upbringing is that without the assured continuance of faiths – which can only be assured by authoritarian means – we would not have the religious diversity and plurality of traditions so celebrated by many of a liberal persuasion. Applied to proselytising types of exclusivist and authoritarian forms of faith such as some versions of Salafi and, more especially, Wahhabi Islam – as well as forms of fundamentalist Protestantism – to take two broad examples, this kind of argument is deeply hypocritical. If some such groups could make the world by their own design, there would be little diversity. To reiterate Gary Potter's claim that I mentioned in Chapter 3.

> "When the Christian majority takes over this country, there will be no satanic churches, no more free distribution of pornography, no more abortion on demand, and no more talk of rights for homosexuals. After the Christian majority takes control, pluralism will be seen as immoral and evil and the state will not permit anybody the right to practice evil."[204]

To be clear about what is meant by pluralism here, this includes the practice of any religion other than Christianity, as defined by the Christian majority. It also includes the mere support or even tolerance of such other religions. All such practices are to be judged immoral and banned by the state. Authoritarian, exclusivist faiths ultimately seek to crush diversity, not serve it.

At this point though, we need to be clear that some religious schools are very much more liberal than others. Some such schools place no requirement upon staff to hold specific religious beliefs. They are often very positive and welcoming both on paper and in practice of pupils from a wide range of religious backgrounds as well as from secular ones. In such schools, in religious education classes, lively, open critical discussion often takes place about a range of religions, beliefs and practices. Stephen Law regards such schools as positive, so long as they encourage that kind of critical, rational discussion where a wide range of views are accepted as contributing to the discursive process. Law is though keen to point out that such a culture does not have to assume relativism, whereby all ideas are equally valid. Nor does such an open-ended type of rational pursuit imply laxity of behaviour. I would again agree with Law that it implies the opposite. The very possibility of open, critical debate in the classroom requires a mature level of behaviour, of listening and reflection. Also, relativism is in fact being rejected in the process of rational discussion, for the reasons offered in Chapter 1: that for rational thinking to be worthwhile, it must make a difference, but relativism suggests the opposite, that sets of beliefs should remain untouched, and be unaffected by external critique.

However, there are secularists like Anthony Grayling who are adamantly critical of all forms of religious schooling, including liberal forms of religious schooling. He concludes from his questionable understanding of Biblical and Qur'anic exegesis that faiths are by their nature, and from their origins and founding texts, mutually exclusive and antithetical towards each other.[205] He writes:

> 'This is the chief reason why allowing the major religions to jostle against one another in the public domain is dangerous. The solution is to make the public domain wholly secular, leaving religion to the personal sphere, as a matter of private observance only (...) To secularise society, in Western democracies at least, requires withholding public funding for, or removing the privileging (for example, by withdrawing charitable status) of, faith schools and related organisations and activities.'[206]

Religions can certainly be read as placing in the out-group all who do not narrowly subscribe to something very precise. Yet quite often religious groups in the UK are more open-minded than this. They don't follow the script Grayling suggests for them. Similarly, many liberal religious schools actually seek to bring together pupils from a wide variety of faiths and of none because they seek such interactions as part of the maturing of faith rather than part of its dismantling. The closure of all religious schools within the state system of education is not foreseeable and also not desirable. A plethora of more unregulated home-schools with an associated ghettoisation would almost certainly ensue. By contrast, policing religiously affiliated schools to ensure that they are not authoritarian and exclusivist, and insisting that this be so, would seem to be a much better option. For example, it would be important to check that such schools taught human evolution properly as the backbone of the life sciences.

In terms of the moral impact of religious upbringings and education on children, we must finally consider the counterfactual arguments: what would the world be like if no one were brought up in a religion, and if no one went to a religious school? For secularists like Dawkins, Hitchens, Grayling and Harris, the answer is obvious, far safer and morally secure. Teehan on the other hand suggests that if religion is a reflection of, and an evolutionary growth of, a basic in-group/out-group instinct, then even if we could get rid of religious upbringings, education and thereby religion itself, we would only have got rid of a particular set of symptoms. The in-group/out-group mentality would simply find different expression – as of course it does in any case. It can be objected, as we noted, that the cosmic significance to believers of *some* religious in-group/out-group identities can push them towards militancy, but as we have also remarked elsewhere, nation-state in-group/out-group mentalities seem to have been significantly more violent than religious ones, looking across the past century.[207] There is therefore no good reason to think that a non-religious manifestation of a 'them and us' perspective in the future would be any less violent than a religious manifestation. Neither evidence nor logic points in this direction. One gets the impression too in Grayling's remark that 'we are to *make* the public domain wholly secular' that his secularism outweighs his liberalism. What if the public don't generally want the public domain to be made entirely secular? Does his secularism also outflank his love of democracy?

We can of course look at education systems built entirely on secular lines. They vary considerably, not least because secularism is extremely diverse.[208] Some in Sweden and Finland seem very good and are held in high esteem by other countries. During my teacher training I studied the education system in the then Soviet Union…not so enlightening. Every child, in every class, in every school in a given year group was to read the same page of every politicised textbook on the same day of the year, every year. Neither of course did such schooling make people immune to religious intolerance and prejudice. Decades of Soviet schooling has not exactly expunged anti-Semitism from the country. Stalinism, neo-Marxism and, even some forms of rationalist secularism, are forms of in-group/out-group intolerance.

Religionists, as we have already seen, are of course often at odds with secularists about exactly what being moral amounts to. British journalist and political commentator, Melanie Phillips, Rabbi Jonathan Sacks and perhaps Jacob Rees-Mogg MP will bemoan rises in divorce rates, abortion and single parent families. Stephen Law, on the other hand, maintains that morality has improved since the 1960s, with declines in racism, homophobia, along with an increase in tolerance and respect for different lifestyles. A good education is one that keeps a dialogue open about such diverse goods. It shares these discussions among adults with children. Being liberal, a good education may be within a secular or a non-authoritarian religious context, where the ground rules are clear about respecting others, however bad their arguments, and about respecting good arguments, whoever offers them. These practices help to grow that crucial ingredient in the moral life: empathy. Those educational practices that widen our empathy circles are to be promoted and those that diminish them, reduced.

Of course there is at least one problem with what I am saying. I seem to have created my own 'out-group' of those advocating authoritarian religious education and parenting. This is of course hard to avoid. This book, however, advocates engaging with, and not ostracising, those with whom one most disagrees and, in agreement with some within such an 'out-group', it regards such engagement as morally important.

Conclusion

There is not at this point a sound statistical basis for measuring the moral significance of religious schooling and upbringing, not least because of the sheer diversity of what is at issue. Among Church of England schools, for example, there are those that do seek to inculcate specific religious beliefs in a quite authoritarian way; and those that actively seek to engage children in critical open-ended debate while at the same time remaining clear that the school as an institution does stand for particular beliefs and values. Authoritarian education that discourages questioning and open-ended discussion deserves moral scrutiny, and it is hard to see how it can withstand this. Communitarian arguments in favour of indoctrination also appear weak. Religious in-group/out-group mentalities can also be problematic, where they forge a distinctiveness that emphasises division and marginalises commonalities and consonant identities. A pupil's self-perception and their understanding of others and the world around them can all too easily become defensive within such a context, which is of a piece with our critique of mission and evangelising – especially of an exclusivist kind.

Nevertheless, we should be clear that more liberal religious schooling moves in the opposite direction, being inclusive of those of other faiths and of none. The alternative to religious schooling, secular schooling, may appear impartial, but this is clearly not always the case, and a great variety of religious parents would, with good reason, not see things this way. Where secularism seeks to eradicate all forms of religious schooling against the wishes of even the most liberal of religious parents, it is not easy to see what remains of its liberal and democratic credentials so lauded within secularist circles. The moral claims of parental choice would seem ascendant here, though these claims in themselves also have their limits.

In Chapter 3, we saw reason to look with a critical moral eye at institutional, hierarchical religion, which can all too easily ally itself with dubious political bedfellows when the chips are down. Once again in this chapter, we saw this type of religion – when not thoroughly accountable beyond itself to the wider society in an open and transparent way – be more than capable of committing alarming crimes, as the recent and historic abuse of children and vulnerable adults in the Catholic church makes plain for example. Still, we also need to ask how the moral profiles of hierarchical religious institutions compare with those of hierarchical non-religious institutions – such as local authority care homes for children – if we are to understand more about the specific character of religion. Once again, more research is needed here.

Ironically, authoritarian religious schools and institutions would do well to have more faith in both reason and in the strength of community that often surrounds them so as not to default in the direction of being defensive and dogmatic. There is no evidence to suggest that pushing a religious faith at children who do not already adhere strongly to that faith has the desired effect, and if anything there is reason to think the opposite. A caring community that happens to be religious will almost certainly by psychological osmosis be more persuasive about its faith than a thousand arguments; and arguments freely discussed may well offer a place for religious faith that a grasping defensiveness will occlude.

6

Islam From The Foundations: Qur'an And Hadith

In the following three chapters we shall consider Islam as a case study of a religion that is persistently in the limelight, perennially judged and about which everyone would seem to have an opinion. As was made clear in Chapter 2, about media evaluations of religion, readers can hardly be unfamiliar with critical appraisals of Islam, and so because this is such familiar territory I shall engage with classical criticisms of Islam beginning in this chapter with the foundational texts of that faith starting with the Qur'an. This largely circumvents the problem that here we have an amalgam of religion and politics because at this point we have reached religious bedrock. If this text is not the pure unadulterated religion of Islam then nothing is. To explain, just about all Muslims regard the Qur'an as the word of Allah, dictated to Muhammad by the angel Gabriel (Jibril) in sections over a period of twenty three years beginning in 610AD. Muslims believe that these dictations in Arabic were perfectly preserved before being written down by Muhammad's secretary Zayd. Muslims also believe that the text of the Qur'an that we have today is word for word what was dictated to Muhammad all those years ago. While Allah had communicated with humanity before the time of Muhammad through figures like Moses (Musa) and Jesus (Isa), those messages are believed to have been distorted following their revelations so as to require a pristine 'reissue' in the form of the Qur'an. So if the source of ethical difficulties is the Qur'an, then Islam, in its purest sense, is a source of ethical difficulties.

Towards the end of this chapter I shall look at the other foundational texts within Islam, collectively known as Hadith, what Muslims take to be a written account of the *sunnah* or the sayings and actions of the Prophet Muhammad. The importance of Hadith can hardly be over-estimated and is more or less universal across all forms of Sunni Islam. For the vast majority of Muslims, Hadith is vital for understanding the Qur'an. Very few Muslims are not guided by it and guided in their understanding of the Qur'an by it.[209]

For now though, beginning with the Qur'an, the kind of ethical critique I wish to consider is expressed in typical ebullient style by outspoken atheist Sam Harris. He writes: 'The truth is that most Muslims appear to be fundamentalists in the Western sense of the word – in that even "moderate" approaches to Islam generally consider the Qur'an to be the literal and inerrant word of the one true God.'[210] He proceeds to quote from the Qur'an about a variety of issues and writes 'on almost every page, the Qur'an prepares the ground for religious conflict. Anyone who reads the Qur'an and fails to see the link between Muslim faith and Muslim violence should probably consult a neurologist.'[211]

My ethical evaluation of Islam will focus on two key questions that are at the heart of much public debate; first the treatment of women, and second militancy and terrorism. It is not that there are not other crucial ethical issues as regards Islam but space dictates that I focus in this way. As such the kind of argument Harris proposes can be précised as follows:

1. Muslims almost universally regard the Qur'an as inerrant and the literal word of God from cover to cover. 2. The Qur'an instructs and inspires violence against unbelievers. 3. The Qur'an is also sexist and misogynist. 4. Therefore since Muslims regard the Qur'an as the literal word of God, at the heart of Islam, militancy and misogyny are part of the essence of Islam.

As regards Hadith a similar argument shall be considered. 1. Hadith is regarded universally within Islam as an authoritative guide to the life of Muhammad who is thought to have lived a sinless life and is therefore to be emulated. 2. As such Hadith are foundational texts at the heart of Islam and key guides to life and to the Qur'an. 3. Hadith is demeaning and discriminatory in its attitudes towards women. 4. Hadith has further encouraged militancy. 5. Therefore misogyny and militancy come from the heart of Islam and are part of its essence.

I want to draw attention to the conclusions of both arguments that speak about essences. Sam Harris and other evangelical atheists reject the view that, for example, militancy is a tiny fringe activity within Islam to be distinguished from moderate Islam. He mocks this notion with his phrase 'A fringe without a centre' asking, 'Where are the moderates anyway?' We shall meet plenty in this and the following chapters. But the central argument to be taken seriously is that Islam is permanently anchored in core texts that are militant and misogynist and these characteristics are therefore part of an Islamic DNA, a thread that has persisted from the time of Muhammad until the present.

I put these arguments this starkly because they properly represent Harris's thinking as well as the murmurings of much casual conversation and speculation. By making plain the assumptions of these arguments they can best be analysed and evaluated.

An initial objection to my whole approach here, that immediately brings in my concept of dialogue, is one that the Muslim scholar and cleric Sheik Abdal Hakim Murad raised when I spoke to him about Qur'anic interpretation. He suggested that Western outlooks were morally dubious, constantly changing, condemning of homosexuality yesterday, asserting the equal status of gay marriage today and who knows what tomorrow. As such the shifting goal posts of modern Western sensibility that bill ancient sacred texts as misogynist or belligerent have no grounds on which to stand, leaving aside the rank hypocrisy of condemning Islamic militancy while bombing Iraq and some of its civilian population to oblivion.

In response, it seems to me, that a culture that changes its moral standards does not as such subscribe to relativism and may not be relativistic, it may be the product of self critique and moral growth. Evidence and argument will determine this, but nothing can be assumed. The more central point, though, is that irrespective of who is raising a moral objection, the question remains: does a moral objection hold true? The question as to whether the Qur'an and Hadith inspire militancy and misogyny is a legitimate moral question. It is also an urgent moral question. As I suggested in the Introduction, to shy away from judgment is to shy away from life. More generally, to shy away from judgment is to be in denial for we make judgments whether we admit this or not, only the less we are open with ourselves about the judgments we make, the less they undergo critical analysis, and this applies equally to radical atheism and to religion adherence.

Qur'an

To begin we shall look at these claims in relation to the Qur'an and consider the first premise of the argument above, that the Qur'an is viewed by almost all Muslims as literally true in every word and as such to be followed to the letter. If this means that there is no room for metaphor, or that careful attention should not be paid to context within the Qur'an to determine whether or not a Qur'anic injunction applies, then it is false to say of all Muslims, both historically and now, that the Qur'an is literally true and to be followed to the letter, for all that they do believe that it is in every word ultimately dictated by Allah. This is evident when we consider the mystical aspect of Islam known as Sufism. This has been both integral to Islam for the vast majority of its history and of great significance in that history. Sufism has propounded a kind of spiritual elitism in which it sees the Qur'an as bearing hidden esoteric truth for those gifted enough to understand. These truths take the believer beyond literal truth and specific legal rulings that have often followed from them.

We might think, though, following Harris, that a sure sign of a fairly universal literalism is the enactment of laws very much in line with Qur'anic diktat and that the enactment of Shari'a law has been the fundamental preoccupation and accomplishment of all Islamic societies. These claims are, however, questionable for several reasons. First, elements of Roman law and also Jewish law persisted within the Islamic world for centuries after the beginning of Islam at a time when they could have been removed by Islamic rulers and jurists.[212] Second, the importance of following law according to the Qur'an has not always been preeminent in the faith.

The eminent Islamic scholar Wilfred Cantwell Smith writes 'as late as the fifth century of Islam (the twelfth century C.E.) it [the following of Shari'a] was still not felt necessary as such to the Muslim's conceptualising of his faith.'[213] Associate Professor of Islamic Studies at Harvard University, Shahab Ahmed adds that across the Middle East between the twelfth and nineteenth centuries law was put under the interrogation of Sufism rather than visa-versa.[214] This supports the view mentioned a moment ago that Sufism has been integral to the body politic of Islam across the centuries rather than being an exceptional or deviant practice within it. Ahmed concludes that to see Islam as the application of a literal understanding of Qur'anic law throughout its history is a profound misunderstanding of Islam. He writes:

> 'The assumption of the legal-supremacist conceptualization of Islam/Islamic *by Western analysts and modern Muslims alike* does the worst sort of Procrustean violence both to the phenomenon at stake and to our ability to understand it: it effectively lops off various limbs of the historical body of Islam so as to box it into a theoretical "Islam" of our own mis-manufacture.'[215]

A couple of the most startling examples of a departure from a literal understanding of the Qur'an is to be found on the front cover of Shahab Ahmed's book 'What Is Islam?'. Here, the face of a Muslim ruler, the Mughal Emperor Jahangir appears, resplendent with wine cup in one hand, and the Qur'an in the other on a coin minted in 1611, thus advertising both the consumption of alcohol and the making of a facial representation, both Qur'anically proscribed.[216] On the second point Ahmed informs us that the more we read Sufi literature we see that we have two divergent trajectories: one that reads the text to prohibit the image, and the other that reads the text to celebrate the image.[217] As regards alcohol, the Qur'an says a variety of things. A key passage, however, reads 'wine and games of chance, and stone-idols, and divining-arrows are an abomination from the works of Satan: shun it, that you might do good works.'[218] The drinking of alcohol is also forbidden by all four main law schools within Sunni Islam. Nonetheless in a key early medical Islamic text *'The Welfare of Bodies and Souls'*, Abu Zayd al-Ballkhi

(849 – 943) writes that wine is 'of all beverages, the most noble in essence.' Ahmed continues 'the positive valorization of wine is, of course, universally evident in the history of the poetical discourses of Muslim societies...where wine served as the pre-eminent and pivotal image for the deepest experience of the meaning of human existence in relation to the Divine.' Neither, insists Ahmed, is this to be dismissed as metaphor since between the twelfth and eighteenth centuries across much of the Middle East 'grape-wine drinking is a persistent and standard feature in the history of societies of Muslims...in which the ideal setting for wine was in a gathering of friends with the accompaniment of poetry and music.'[219] To make plain the range of Muslim societies in which such gatherings were often to be found Ahmed makes clear the names for such drinking assemblies, in Arabic: *majlis al-sharab*, Persian: *majlis-i sharab*, and Turkish: *badeh meclisi* and *cagir meclisi*).[220] So, a literalist interpretation of the Qur'an does not appear always to have been kept to at this point.

More recently, in the nineteenth and twentieth centuries movements arose whose aim was to '*get back*' to the Qur'an and the practices of the earliest followers of Islam known as salaf. These Salafi movements tried to follow the Qur'an in the way that they understood the first three generations of Muslims (*al-salaf al-salihin* meaning pious ancestors) to have done, beginning with the Companions of the Prophet Muhammad. They sought to make optional for all Muslims the interpretations of the Qur'an offered by the various law schools. They also eschewed the metaphysical musings of much Sufi reflection. Today Salafism is diverse, but Salafis hold in common the view that throughout almost all of Islamic history Muslim scholars and jurists have not looked as directly at the Qur'an and Hadith as they should have done in their search for law. Salafis seek to correct these mistakes and some of them, in a variety of ways, seek to be quite literalist, accusing Islamic jurists across the centuries of being anything but this.

The work of the four main Sunni law schools (*madhahib*), the Hanafi, Maliki, Shafi'i, and Hanbali have been at the heart of this problem for the Salafis. Procedures for interpreting the Qur'an developed and were systematised by al Shafi'i (d 822) but ultimately established among all of these law schools in the following way. In order to interpret the Qur'an, if its teachings were unclear, jurists would look next to the Hadith for clarification. In many instances the use of both the Qur'an and Hadith are judged insufficient to establish the right action in a given situation. So here a third principle, that of reasoning from analogy (*qiyas*), is applied. This involves a jurist identifying an underlying cause or reason (*illa*) from an original Qur'anic ruling and applying it by analogy to a parallel case. Finally, the consensus (*ijma*) of scholars, known as the *ulama*, would become the basis of law. Salafis feel that such consensuses have in fact obscured the Qur'an itself by bringing to bear historical and cultural influences to which the law schools have been subject.[221] It should also be clear, that traditionalists, who follow in the traditions of one of the law schools, make up the vast majority of Sunni Muslims worldwide compared with Salafis who are a small minority within that group.

There are further reasons to question how widespread are literalist interpretations of the Qur'an. Many Muslims today learn to recite the Qur'an in Arabic without understanding any Arabic and without reading translations of it in their own languages. Their practice of Islam is based on the teachings of local imams and elders within their communities, their local Shari'a councils and the law school traditions to which they belong. Many such traditionalist Muslims do both less and more than follow a literal understanding of the Qur'an and not understanding the text for themselves, they don't knowingly do either. They do more than follow a literal understanding by adopting practices not mentioned in the Qur'an such as the wearing of the burka for Muslim women, not owning a dog, men growing beards, celebrating the Prophet's birthday... the list goes on. For Salafi critics, traditionalists also do less than follow a literal understanding of the Qur'an since they do not follow the text as such. Instead traditionalists are concerned to follow the consensus of past scholars and the plurality of law schools indicates that there is some considerable variation here.

I have naturally spoken to a number of Muslim Qur'anic scholars about the question of Qur'anic literalism. Dr. Shabbir Akhtar from the Faculty of Theology and Religion at Oxford University was clear that there are many Muslims and Muslim scholars who do not take a literalist approach to the Qur'an and that among literalists there is significant variation as to what literalism means.[222] I pursued this question further with Dr. Shuruq Naguib who lectures in Islamic Studies at Lancaster University. In her general comments Dr. Naguib said something quite remarkable, that in most works of

Qur'anic hermeneutics there is no attempt to pin down a definitive meaning. As such, plurality, to some degree, is at the heart of the text. Speaking about the issue of women inheriting half of what a man would inherit she said that the circumstances that warranted this Qur'anic teaching no longer applied today in very different circumstances, and that the Qur'an is not to be applied literally in this respect.[223]

In addition to this varied account about literalism within Sunni Islam, the other key strand within Islam, Shi'a Islam, also appears to be a movement away from literalism. In much Shi'a understanding of the Qur'an, the text has an inner meaning, inaccessible to the ordinary Muslim. Only the figure of the Imam (a mystical hidden spiritual being who will return at the end of time) can truly interpret the Qur'an and only senior Shi'a clerics like Ayatollahs can communicate with the Imam and therefore properly understand the text.[224]

Finally, I want to add a few points to what has already been said about Sufism, which is to be found in both Sunni and Shi'a Islam. While Sufis regard the Qur'an as the direct speech of God, some Sufis think that the Qur'an lacks the capacity to shed light upon God's essence. As one Sufi master has pointed out, 'why spend time reading a love letter (by which he means the Quran) in the presence of the Beloved who wrote it?'[225] We gain a picture here that the Qur'an and the five pillars of faith are pointers to the truth, but ultimately through spiritual accomplishment are to be superseded. The Qur'an is a means, not an end in itself. It is a first and very crucial step towards Allah, but not the goal. Qur'anic law and ritual *in themselves* will not get Muslims where they want to be. Sufism points in the opposite direction to a literalism focused on regulation and rituals. In Sufism these externals consistently point beyond themselves to a deeper understanding through a series of mystical revelations of God. The path is one of love, not of ritual, law and text.

So, to conclude about the first premise of the argument we are considering, not all forms of Islam either today or in the past have a literal understanding of the Qur'an. Sometimes other forms of interpretation prevail and the law schools have devised methods of interpretation that are at variance with the Salafi return to the text.

Yet while the literalist premise is in part at least false, this does not exonerate the Qur'an as a key cause of militancy and misogyny. If today types of Islam that stick more closely to the text than others appear more misogynist and militant, then literalism or no literalism the Qur'an would appear to be ethically problematic.

This brings us still closer to the issue of the variety of approaches taken to the Qur'an within Islam. Let's look at a present day survey of this variety.

Muslim scholar Tariq Ramadan distinguishes between the following approaches.

First there is a scholastic traditionalism that understands the Qur'an through the various law schools mentioned above. These approaches rely on opinions of scholars that were codified between the eighth and the eleventh centuries. As such Muslim groups found in Britain that originated in Pakistan like the Deobandis and the Barelvis are often conservative in their approach to social issues, not because they are literalists but because they depend in their jurisprudence on interpretations of the Qur'an that date back to a very different time and place. As regards acts of terrorism and suicide bombing, the various law schools more or less universally condemn such acts and are not associated with them.

A second approach is that of Salafi literalism. Salafi literalists are often opposed to scholastic traditionalism because they do not trust the judgments of the law schools. Like the traditionalists, however they have very conservative perspectives on social issues and are also to be found in Britain and the US. For all the conservative and discriminatory attitudes exhibited here towards women, such approaches are generally very much opposed to militancy, especially the killing of civilians, whether Muslim or not.

A third approach is that of Salafi reformism. Like their literalist counterparts, they seek to circumvent the views of the law schools regarding them as suspect in some matters. In searching for the meaning of the Qur'an they look for the overall intention of laws stated there, and they look too to Hadith. There are many Salafi reformists in the West. They were inspired by a wide range of nineteenth and early twentieth century figures, some very conservative like Syed Abul A'la Maududi (1903 – 1979), others less so like Muhammad Abduh (1849 – 1905) and Muhammad Iqbal (1877 – 1938). These groups as they exist today, though, 'seek to protect Muslim identity while recognising Western constitutional structures.'[226] One view, for example, is to distinguish between on the one hand, compulsory acts of worship in the five pillars of Islam: the Shahada, to bear witness that there is one God and Muhammad is his messenger; prayer; charity; fasting and the pilgrimage to Mecca or Hajj, and on the other hand, the social requirements of the Qur'an regarding such matters as; marriage, divorce and the family. With these social requirements, time and place are crucial in deciding how to apply the Qur'an. Some Salafi reformists think of themselves as sticking more closely to the Qur'an than Salafi literalists because they see themselves as being truer than the literalists to the objectives of the Qur'an. Such scholars see themselves as holding fast to the Qur'anic intentions of justice, mercy, compassion and equality, and this marks them out from literalists, who they perceive as adhering quite slavishly to discriminatory rules about divorce, inheritance rights or testimony in a Shari'a court vis-a-vis men and women.

A fourth group of interpreters may be called Political Literalist Salafists. They, as the name suggests, are both literalist and hostile to the West and Western governments. Banned groups like Anjem Choudary's Al-Muhajiroun and also Hizb ut-Tahrir fit this description. Al-Muhajiroun has openly condoned and supported terrorism. Hizb ut-Tahrir seeks to build a non-federal Islamist superstate that spans the globe from Morocco to Indonesia.

A fifth approach is taken by liberal rationalist reformists. They seek a separation of religion and the state. They oppose the seclusion of women and they opposed the lifting of the ban on the hijab in Turkey in 2013. Reason and the importance of the individual and individual rights take precedence over a literal understanding of the Qur'an. In the West such Muslims are assimilationists.

A sixth approach, as we have seen, belongs to a range of Sufi orders or Islamic mystical groups that want to say that Allah is ultimately beyond the Word, beyond ritual and regulation. Such things are simply a means. Such faiths are esoteric rather than exoteric putting the focus on inner truth.

I want to focus from the above taxonomy on the various types of Salafism since they have in their perception returned to the text of the Qur'an that underlies the layers of tradition that have sometimes occluded it. If the Qur'an is very much misogynist and militant we would expect such Salafisms to veer in these directions more than traditionalisms. But this is not particularly the case, and especially not as regards discriminations against women. Muslim feminist scholar, Professor Asma Afsaruddin, remarks that what is interesting is that, like the Protestant Reformation in Europe, the Salafi return to the text has, in effect, encouraged a wide variety of interpretation, because it has called for such close attention to be paid to the text uninhibited by the strictures of jurisprudential tradition. The diversity of Salafisms is fascinating. Aspects of political Salafism often condone some of the worst terrorist atrocities. Almost all other forms of Salafism and traditionalism condemn rather than condone such things accusing political Salafis of turning their back on the Qur'an in their militancy. As regards discrimination against women, traditionalisms have often enforced these in law, based in part on their interpretations of the Qur'an that some Salafis have rejected. Salafism for all its 'return to the text' is interestingly divided here. As we have seen, some forms of reformist Salafism reject practices that discriminate against women. We should be clear too that category five above, of liberal rationalist reformers, eschews traditionalism with its discriminatory perspectives. Such reformers claim that their interpretations of the text are closer to the message of the Qur'an than those of traditionalists. Both traditionalists as well as literalist and political Salafis, though, would reject that claim.

Terminology is, however, at the heart of much dispute and Professor Khaled Abou El Fadl, who calls himself a literalist, all the same regards Qur'anic mandates that discriminate against women as no longer applicable today and looks rather to Qur'anic objectives of compassion, justice and equality as his *literalist* anchor points. Looking at traditionalisms on the other hand, these very much share with political Salafism discriminatory attitudes towards women.[227] So once again there is no clear evidence that it is sticking closely or even literally to the Qur'an as opposed to other factors – such as taking on board the jurisprudence of a law school – that accounts for discriminatory attitudes towards women in Islam today.

As regards militancy, Salafis as we have seen, are divided. The vast majority, alongside traditionalists, liberal rationalists and Sufis condemn militancy and terrorism. In this sense it cannot be a return to the Qur'an that necessarily inspires militancy, if it is this at all, since the vast majority of Salafis don't espouse that view and so it remains to be seen why a small minority do.

We move further from the view that it is the Qur'an itself that is the *key cause* of misogyny and militancy when considering two further issues. First, later juridical developments within the law schools have led some Islamic practice in directions that discriminate against women in ways that the Qur'an does not espouse. The concept of male guardianship over women is a case in point as we shall see later in this chapter. A second factor is the rise and spread of Wahhabism. Abou El Fadl writes 'The story of puritanical Islam should properly start with the Wahhabis…they have influenced every puritanical movement in the Muslim world in the contemporary age. Every single Islamic group that has achieved a degree of international infamy, such as the Taliban and al-Qa'ida, has been heavily influenced by Wahhabi thought.'[228] Wahhabism has tried to pass itself off as Salafism as part of its propaganda campaign. Yet while there have been amalgams of Salafism and Wahhabism in the writing of Sayyid Qutb and Maududi, the idea that Wahhabism takes us back to some pristine unadulterated reading of the Qur'an is false. Muhammad ibn Abd al -Wahhab (1703 - 1792) did not finish his training in Islamic jurisprudence. He tortured those he considered to be hypocritical Muslims despite the arguments of classical scholars at the time that this was contrary to precedents set in both the Qur'an and Hadith.[229] His views were rejected by both his father and his brother as extreme forms of puritanism. Abou El Fadl writes, speaking of the discredited precedents that Abd al-Wahhab used to kill and torture civilians who opposed him, 'extremists like Bin Laden and Omar Abd al-Rahman followed in the footsteps of Abd al-Wahhab by relying on the same exact precedents of cruelty as a means of justifying killing innocent people.' He continues '…[these precedents were cited in] web sites set up by groups that butchered hostages in Iraq.'[230] The alleged precedents are non-Qur'anic, neither do they feature in Prophetic Hadith. The dispute is whether or not they go back to Abu Bakr the first of the four caliphs and classical scholarly opinion is strongly against this view. So here we have a key cause of militancy in a movement that for all it claims to stick absolutely to the Qur'an clearly does otherwise. Sticking closely to the Qur'an it seems to me is not at the heart of moral problems within Islam.

Some readers might be extremely irritated at this point thinking the Qur'an clearly discriminates against women and espouses militancy especially against unbelievers so the idea that there isn't a causal connection here is absurd. Yet, from what we have seen so far things are not so clear. The first premise of the argument that we are addressing in this chapter, that all Muslims have a literal approach to the Qur'an and follow it word for word, turns out to be false both in the past and also today. Among those who claim to be literalists and those who claim to stick most closely to the text of the Qur'an there is significant variation as regards both militancy and misogyny. These tendencies are the product, in some significant part, of other influences as we can see most clearly in the case of Wahhabism. In this instance, despite its protestations to be literalist, Wahhabism goes quite against the Qur'an in the way it has, for example, at times supported torture. Some of its discriminations against women also clearly go well beyond anything that is mandated in the Qur'an. Demands that women wear the burka are an obvious example of this.

So let's turn now to the second and third premises of the argument we are considering about the Qur'an in this chapter, that the Qur'an encourages militancy and misogyny. The problem is that the Qur'an says lots of things. Unlike Sam Harris[231] I've tried to give a range of examples, first about militancy and second about the rights and treatment of women. I simply offer a flavour of the variety of claims that are to be found in the Qur'an. The point here is not to give anything like a systematic account of what the Qur'an says on these matters but instead to indicate elements of consistency and diversity within the text. This will bring to light some of the difficulties that face the reader who seeks to follow it. We shall see that some Muslim scholars regard much of what we are about to read as revelations that were made for specific occasions and are therefore not applicable for all time while the underlying message of God as a constant guide in all circumstances is an eternal truth.

Every chapter (or surah) in the Qur'an except one begins with the words 'In the name of Allah, the merciful, the compassionate.' Some commentators regard what follows in each such surah as therefore already containing Allah's compassion and mercy. As such they argue that the Qur'an is not to be read with any further compassion and mercy. Other commentators see these key announcements, at the head of every surah, about compassion and mercy as instructions to see and read the text seeking out the most compassionate interpretation. So at the outset, as regards both militancy and the treatment of women, the text makes available different perspectives.

What follows, is a glimpse of passages that distinctly advocate militancy, and others that ward against it. In a number of passages we seem to get both messages. It should also be clear how much is dependent on translation as the following pair of translations of Surah 2: 194 make clear:

'Attack anyone who attacks you to the same extent as he attacked you. Heed God, and know that God stands by the heedful.' The second translation reads: 'Mandated is the law of equality, so that who transgresses against you, respond in kind, and fear God, and know that God is with those who exercise restraint.'

Some more militant passages read as follows:

> 'Fight for the sake of Allah, those that fight against you, but do not attack them first. Allah does not love the aggressors. Kill them wherever you find them. Drive them out of the places from which they drove you. Idolatry is worse than carnage. But do not fight them within the precincts of the Holy Mosque unless they attack you there; if they attack you put them to the sword. Thus shall the unbelievers be rewarded; but if they mend their ways, know that Allah is forgiving and merciful. Fight against them until idolatry is no more and Allah's religion reigns supreme. But if they mend their ways, fight none except the evil-doers.' (Surah 2: 190-193)

Often cited in connection with suicide bombing is the statement 'Do not destroy yourselves.' (Surah 4: 29)

Referring to fighting unbelievers with whom one is at war Surah 47: 4 reads 'When you meet the unbelievers in the battlefield strike off their heads and, when you have laid them low, bind your captives firmly. Then grant them their freedom or take ransom from them, until war shall lay down her armour.'

Perhaps the most infamous militant 'proof texts' are the sword verses, (especially Surah 9: 5)

'9:1 A declaration of immunity from God and His apostle to the idolaters with whom you have made agreements: 9:2 For four months you shall go unmolested in the land. But know that you shall not escape God's judgement, and that God will humble the unbelievers. 9:3 A proclamation to the people from God and His apostle on the day of the greater pilgrimage: God and His apostle are under no obligation to the idolaters. If you repent, it shall be well with you; but if you give no heed, know that you shall not be immune from God's judgment. Proclaim a woeful punishment to the unbelievers, 9:4 except to those idolaters who have honoured their treaties with you in every detail and aided none against you. With these keep faith, until their treaties have run their term. God loves the righteous. 9:5 When the sacred months are over slay the idolaters wherever you find them. Arrest them, besiege them, and lie in ambush everywhere for them. If they repent and take to prayer and render the alms levy, allow them to go their way. God is forgiving and merciful. 9:6 If an idolater seeks asylum with you, give him protection so that he may hear the Word of God, and then convey him to safety. For the idolaters are ignorant men. 9:7 God and His apostle repose no trust in idolaters, save those with whom you have made treaties at the Sacred Mosque. So long as they keep faith with you, keep faith with them. God loves the righteous. 9:8 How can you trust them? If they prevail against you they will respect neither agreements nor ties of kindred. They flatter you with their tongues, but their hearts reject you. Most of them are evil doers.'

Yet there is much in the Qur'an that warns against aggression: 'Oh you who believe, stand up as witnesses for God in justice, and do not let your hatred of a people lead you away from justice. This is closest to piety and be mindful of God in all you do for God is aware of all you do.' (Surah 5: 8) As regards retaliation 'And do not let your anger at those who barred you from the Holy Mosque [In Mecca] lead you to commit aggression. Help one another in goodness and piety and do not assist each other in committing sin and aggression, and be mindful of God for God is severe in retribution' (Surah 5: 2) and then again 'Those who seek to please God will be guided by Him to the paths of peace.' (Surah 5: 16). There are also verses such as 'Cultivate forgiveness, enjoin goodness, and turn away from the ignorant.' (Surah 5: 69) and teachings about Christians and Jews 'Believers, Jews, Christians and Sabaeans – whoever believes in Allah and the Last Day and does what is right – shall be rewarded by their Lord; they have nothing to fear or to regret.' (Surah 2: 62)

Significantly in contrast with Surah 9: 5 we find 'If your enemy inclines toward peace, then you should seek peace and trust in God.' (Surah 8: 61) and 'If God would have willed, He would have given the unbelievers power over you [Muslims] and they would have fought you [Muslims] Therefore, if they [the unbelievers] withdraw from you and refuse to fight you, and instead, send you guarantees of peace, know that God has not given you licence to fight them.' (Surah 4: 90)

As regards the forced conversion of people of another faith to Islam, Surah 2: 256 reads 'There shall be no compulsion in religion' and Surah 28: 56 reads in support of this 'You cannot guide those you would like to but God guides those he wills. He has best knowledge of the guided.' The Egyptian Muslim scholar, Jamal al Banna notes that there are more than one hundred verses in the Qur'an that affirm freedom of conscience and religion.[232]

As regards the killing of other Muslims the Qur'an is clear, that penalties are to be imposed in the form of blood money to the victim's family if a Muslim is killed by accident. If a Muslim murders another Muslim, however, he will burn in Hell. (Surah 4: 93)

In Sam Harris's catalogue of militant Qur'anic verses almost all of these refer to how the non-believer will be punished in the afterlife. Many scholars regard this to mean that any punishment for unbelief is *not* to be meted out here but is God's business who is the only one to know who is and is not an unbeliever.[233] I would add, though, that there are Muslim scholars who do not at all shy away from the view that the Qur'an supports Islamic conquest. In my interview with the Oxford-based Muslim scholar Dr. Shabbir Akhtar it was quite clear that he thought the Qur'an supported this view.

As regards discrimination against women a number of significant general claims stand out:

'And He has created for you spouses, that you might repose in them, and he has set between you love and mercy.' (Surah 30: 21), 'Men and women are like members one of another.' (Surah 3: 195), 'They are like each other's garments' (a comfort to each other). (Surah 2: 187), Men and women are to be judged by Allah on absolutely equal terms. (Surah 33: 35), They are also created from the same soul (*nafs wahida*) (Surah 4: 1), which for Asma Afsaruddin and Jamal al-Banna confers basic ontological equality on both men and women.[234] Further notable passages include these: 'Men have the same rights in relation to their wives as are expected in all decency of them; while men stand a step above them.' (Surah 2: 228) and also Surah 9: 71 – 72, a précis of which reads: men and women are allies of each other and equally responsible for keeping the five pillars of Islam and will be equally rewarded after death.

There are also a number of noteworthy passages about specific issues:

Marriage and polygamy: a Muslim man may marry a Jewish, Christian or Muslim woman. By contrast a Muslim woman can only marry a Muslim man. (Surah 4: 22-25) Similarly men may marry up to four wives but Muslim women cannot marry more than one husband, 'Then marry such women as seem good to you, two, three or four at a time. If you fear that you will not act justly, then marry one woman only…that is more likely to keep you from committing an injustice'. (Surah 4: 3) Yet mitigating against polygamy is the caveat 'You are never able to be fair and just between women even if that is your ardent desire.' (Surah 4: 129) As such some scholars view polygamy as in practice unjust and therefore in effect prohibited.

Divorce: No precise grounds for divorce are mentioned in the Qur'an and as such it has developed in Islam that a man does not need to have grounds for divorce but the Qur'an does lay down points about how a divorce should proceed. A man should wait for three months before a divorce can take effect to check whether his wife is pregnant. During this time he must provide for shelter and food as a minimum. At the end of this period they should either be divorced or reconciled with honour. (Surah 65: 1-2) If though the wife is pregnant the divorce cannot take place until the child is two years old. (Surah 2: 228 – 232) 'Reasonable provision should be made for women who are divorced.' (Surah 2: 241) No specific mention is made in the Qur'an about a woman divorcing a man although many see in Surah 4: 128 allowance for a woman divorcing a man on grounds of ill-treatment. Tradition has grown up that this may happen but there have to be grounds, unlike in the case of a man divorcing his wife.

After the death of a husband: 'Widows should wait, keeping themselves apart from men, four months and ten days after a husband's death.' (Surah 2: 234) No such rules are mentioned for men in the Qur'an.

Testimony in a Shari'a court: Surah 2: 282 reads 'and call to witness two of your men; if two men are not available then one man and two women you approve of, so that if one of them is confused, the other would remind her.' Scholars in the law schools have interpreted this to mean that a woman's testimony in a Shari'a court is worth half of a man's testimony.

Inheritance rights: a son should inherit twice that of a daughter, 'Allah directs you as regards your children, to a son equal to that of two daughters.' (Surah 4: 7) It is also clear though that where there are no children, nor parents, to inherit but only siblings, that a brother and sister are to inherit equally. 'If a man or a woman leave neither children nor parents and have a brother or a sister, they shall each inherit one-sixth. If there be more, they shall equally share the third of the estate.' (Surah 4: 12)

Domestic violence: 'Men are the managers of the affairs of women for that God has preferred in bounty, one of them over another, and for that they have expended of their property. Righteous women are therefore obedient, guarding the secret for God's guarding. And those you fear may be rebellious admonish; banish them to their couches, and beat them. If they then obey you, look not for any way against them; God is All-high, All-great.' (Surah 4: 34) Essentially we see here that men are in charge of women in the family. Looking specifically at the phrase 'to beat' towards the end of the verse, this is taken from Arberry's translation of the Qur'an but others (e.g. Dawood and Yusuf Ali) also translate the Arabic *'daraba'* as 'to beat'. This is in contrast with Laleh Bakhtiar's translation as 'to go away'.[235] There is much debate about this passage as we shall discover in the next chapter.

It should also be clear that in the Qur'an, men were very much expected to fight on occasions, most especially in defence of their faith. By contrast, women had no such demands placed upon them.

From the briefest of glimpses at the Qur'an there do seem to be mandates to kill unbelievers and mandates for mercy in relation to unbelievers. 'Believe in Islam or be killed' (as would appear at a glance to be implied by Surah 9: 5) seems a straightforward case of compulsion, yet there is to be no compulsion in religion. (Surah 2: 256) We are left in no doubt that unbelievers will be eternally punished after death but there are quite a lot of mixed messages about how unbelievers are to be treated on earth based on the Qur'an and militancy is in this mix. So while a range of claims are made in the Qur'an, the diversity is such that the reader needs to understand how the various parts fit together, and the contexts of particular verses need to be clearer before much understanding is possible. Discrimination against women clearly exists in the Qur'an in a number of respects while there is also ambiguity and tension between some of the specifics (for example that a husband may according to most interpretations of Surah 4: 34 beat his wife) and some of the more general motifs such as compassion and mercy. Once again, the need to see the Qur'an as a larger whole is essential even on the most cursory of glances about just two issues. As one of the most eminent Western commentators about Islam has written 'the Qur'an is on the surface, very inappropriate as a legal text. If it does make rules, it makes them for the occasions of a developing community, and commonly softens in the next phrase what it has fulminated just before.'[236]

So we begin to see how pressing the issue of Qur'anic interpretation (*ijtihad*) is. The procedures of the various law schools have been one way of distilling what is to be taken from the Qur'an. Within and beyond this a key method used throughout the disciplines of ijtihad is that of abrogation. Especially where there appears to be flat contradiction in the text, the concept of abrogation has been at the heart of much discussion. This concept is very widely used to deal with the kinds of tension we can clearly see above. It illustrates to me once more how to a lesser or greater extent different interpreters and schools find very much what they seek in the text. Let's look at how the concept of abrogation has been variously applied to make this point.

Professor Muhammad Khalid Masud, Director General of the Islamic Research Institute, at the International Islamic University, in Islamabad, Pakistan, explains how the concept of abrogation took three main forms. What follows is my précis of his account. The first form of abrogation is chronological abrogation, whereby what was revealed later in the sequence of revelations to Muhammad nullified previous revelations – and rulings that may have followed from them. A second form of abrogation can refer to changes in circumstances - rulings that conflict are to be understood by identifying the different circumstances for which differing revelations were made. A third type of abrogation refers simply to clarification, where one verse appears to resolve ambiguity that lies elsewhere, and in this way the meaning of an ambiguous verse or passage is aligned with the text where it offers greater clarity.[237] The vast majority of Muslim scholars today do, in one way or another, use some method of abrogation in Qur'anic interpretation. All the same, they differ significantly in the emphasis they place on the various forms of abrogation available.

What is of real interest in all this is the history of abrogation. When did abrogation come to be used and for what purpose and has it been consistently used? The answers to these questions are revealing. Asma Afsaruddin writes:

> 'The hawkish juridical perspective that gained ground from the time of al-Shafi'i (767 – 820) onward relies for its validity on the deployment of the hermeneutic principle of abrogation that emerged over time – a principle that, according to a considerable number of scholars, allows for a number of early Qur'anic verses which are markedly irenic and conciliatory in tone to be superseded by later ones which deal with fighting those who had attacked and persecuted Muslims for their faith alone. It is this theory of abrogation that has allowed for an expansionist conception of the military jihad to emerge in deference to realpolitik.'[238]

Afsaruddin makes clear that a number of modern scholars have gone so far as to disallow this classical type of abrogation, (*naskh*), which they see as having been deployed on many occasions in order to support offensive warfare. Reinforcing this point, that the chronological approach to abrogation has been put to essentially political and ideological ends, Abou El Fadl writes of more recent times 'puritans [Wahhabis would be a clear example] habitually declare any part of the Qur'an that is inconsistent with their worldview to have been abrogated…what they call the jihad verses [for example the sword verses, Surah 9: 5f] have abrogated and nullified all of the Qur'anic teachings on tolerance and forgiveness.'

But perhaps this is being unfair on those traditionalists and recent Wahhabis who regard chronological abrogation as the only way of achieving coherence from the Qur'an. After all there are those who claim that the principle of abrogation dates back to the Qur'an itself and as such does not reflect cultural or political influence. Such scholars cite the following Qur'anic passages:

> 2: 106 'Whatever ayah [verse] We abrogate or cause to be forgotten, We bring one better; or the like thereof.'
> 16: 101 'When we replace an ayah with another – and Allah knows best what He reveals – they say behold you are inventing! Most of them know not.'
> 22: 52 'We never sent a messenger or a prophet before you without Satan intervening in his desires. But Allah abrogates (suppresses) what Satan interposes. Then Allah confirms his ayats. Allah is All-knowing, All-wise.'

This issue is important since if those Muslim scholars who insist that chronological abrogation is Qu'ranically based are right about that, and right that the more emollient verses are abrogated by the more belligerent ones, then the Qur'an is a very distinct advocate of militancy in relation to unbelievers. The sword verses, for example, are thought to come late in the chronology of revelation. Professor of Islamic Studies, Neal Robinson is keen to put the record straight about this question of Qur'anic justification of chronological abrogation. He writes 'It is arguable that the traditional understanding of abrogation is entirely alien to the Qur'an.'[239] For example Surah 2: 106 from its context would appear to suggest merely that the Qur'an abrogates the Jewish and Christian scriptures, the universally accepted view within Islam, not other aspects of the Qur'an. Surah 16: 101 is a problematic text for the purposes of chronological abrogation because it is widely believed to be a Meccan passage earlier than the Medinian passages that include all other alleged cases of abrogation. Being an early text how could it possibly refer to the majority of the Qur'an most especially the Medinian surahs that had not yet been revealed? The reference in Surah 22: 52 to the Arabic *nasakha* (to suppress) is a non-technical use of the word not at all implying that other ayat are to be suppressed.[240] A fourth ayah that has been alleged to support the principle of abrogation reads 'We shall cause thee to recite it, and thou wilt not forget it, except what Allah wills.' (Surah 85: 6) Many scholars have argued that this verse alone is far too slender a basis on which to ground the principle of abrogation, whereby whole sections of the Qur'an are to be ignored as rulings.

But not only does the Qur'an offer a very slender basis, if any, for the practice of abrogation we do not find evidence for the practice of chronological abrogation within a century of Muhammad's death in 632CE. The whole concept of chronological abrogation seems to have grown up in tandem with the political needs of empire building, and any supposed mandate within the Qur'an seems to have been read back into the text during these times.

There has also been considerable variation about where to apply the principle of abrogation. Jurists never agreed about which passages were affected. This has always itself been a matter of interpretation. It has also been a crucial respect in which the needs of time and place can, and did, affect jurists who have been invariably bound up by the political situations around them. For example, Az-Zuhri (d. 742) held that 42 verses/ayat had been abrogated. This grew to an upper limit in the eleventh century when al Farisi claimed 248 verses to have been abrogated. A backlash ensued in the following centuries so that Shah Wali Allah of Delhi (d.1762) considered only 5 ayat to have been abrogated.

Of course the whole concept of chronological abrogation is predicated on the idea that the sequence of revelations is universally agreed upon, and it is not. A significant locus of ideological dispute is which type of abrogation to privilege and when. Thus progressives and modernists, like Mahmud Muhammad Taha (1909–1985), reverse the process of chronological abrogation whereby the earlier Meccan surahs are abrogated by the later Medinian ones. Taha argued that the Meccan surahs focus on universal principles, and these therefore abrogate the Medinian surahs where more specific instructions made for particular circumstances are to be found. What is clear is that just as Wahhabis today and traditionalists for many centuries have pushed their own agendas through the hermeneutic of abrogation, so progressives, like Afsaruddin and Abou El Fadl, emphasise their agendas through alternative concepts of abrogation. In this way progressives reject the sword verses, as of any relevance today, arguing that they applied only to the Medinian context of war. This is exactly the view of the Leeds imam Qari Asim who, in speaking to me about the sword verses, made clear why he thought they could not apply now. Muslims today, he argued, were not under any threat to be compared with the peril they faced when the peace treaty was broken in Medina in the time of Muhammad. I do not wish to suggest that some interpretations of the Qur'an are not more plausible than others. It is reasonable to claim, however, that discussions about abrogation have often been polemic and more to do with the agendas of jurists and scholars over the centuries up until today than to do with a disinterested investigation of the Qur'anic text, its compilation and arrangement.

To sum up at this point: there is some basis in the Qur'an to support discrimination against women and there is also some basis for militancy. All the same, the Qur'an, by its nature and diversity, is open to a wide range of interpretation and a brief examination of some of this indicates that the Qur'an as understood is as much a text with impositions laid upon it as expositions brought out of it. So premises 2 and 3 from the argument we are considering in this chapter - that the Qur'an supports misogyny and militancy - are on a sliding scale of 'half truths'. As regards premise 1 that all Muslims have a literal interpretation of the Qur'an this is false as far as some Muslims are concerned. Equally what cashes out as literalism varies considerably because of ambiguity, context dependency and perspective on the text. Those who appear to follow the Qur'an most closely exhibit no greater tendency towards militancy or misogyny than others especially when we consider elements within Wahhabism where wider cultural and juridical factors have been brought to bear.

Hadith

We shall turn now to the other key foundational texts within Islam, the Hadith and see if these support discrimination against women and militancy.

In considering Hadith, we should make clear at the outset that here we certainly have an admixture of politics, culture and religion. Nevertheless, these texts have been and continue to be viewed today, throughout the Islamic world, as sufficiently religiously foundational that such external forces have become sacralised in the sense that Hadith is honoured and followed with great religious fervour. So are we looking at pure unadulterated Islam in looking at

Hadith? For very many Muslims the answer to this is clearly yes. All the same, as we shall see, this is in one crucial respect quite misleading. Very few ordinary practising Muslims are familiar with Hadith in its very many volumes and are guided into a very selective appreciation of it. We shall also see that there is less than universal agreement among Muslims about how foundational it is.

Let's understand a little more about Hadith before we move on to our key question about how far it supports misogyny and militancy.

Hadith refers to both a single tradition (*hadith*), but also to the entire corpus of Tradition that describes the sayings and actions of the Prophet Muhammad. These *sunnah* (meaning path) are also the source of the word *Sunni* Muslim - meaning those who follow in the well beaten path to Allah. A specific tradition is made up of two parts; the *matn*, or point it expresses, and the *isnad*, or chain of transmitters, listing those from whom the sayings had been heard, going back either as far as the Prophet Muhammad, or else to one of his Companions. There are six main collections of such traditions but the most famous are those of Muhammad Ibn Ishma'il al-Bukhari (d.870) and Abu-I-Husayn-Muslim ibn al Hajjaj (d.875). These are thought within Islam to be compilations of the most reliable hadiths. This, however, is a conservative Muslim account of things. Some non-Muslim Islamic scholars dispute that any hadiths can be reliably attributed to Muhammad himself [241] and within Islam there is significant dispute too about reliability. Abou El Fadl, for example, makes his views clear. While for him the Qur'an 'was preserved exactly as the Prophet Muhammad received it from God…the sunnah or traditions attributed to the Prophet,…are a different question altogether.' He continues 'many of these traditions defy reason, are offensively demeaning towards women and non-Muslims, or are blatantly inconsistent with the ethics and morality set out in the Qur'an.'[242] He firmly rejects the view that al-Bukhari hadith or Muslim hadith are reliable, and points out that they were documented centuries after Muhammad's death reflecting much of the social and political views of the time when they were written. Abou El Fadl follows in a long line of Salafi critics of Hadith such as Shah Wali Allah Dihlawi (d.1762) who was critical of many precedents set in Hadith. He sought to initiate a new phase of independent reasoning about Hadith and also about the Qur'an. Another key Salafi critic of Hadith was Muhammad Abduh (1849 – 1905), who was especially critical of hadiths that were at variance with the Qur'an. Perhaps of greatest significance was Fazlur Rahman (d.1988), who set about a systematic critique of Hadith and took further Muhammad Abduh's approach and rejected all hadiths he saw to be at odds with the Qur'an. A number of significant Muslim scholars such as Nurcolish Madjid (1939 – 2005) in Indonesia and Amina Wadud (b.1952) in the United States have built on Rahman's critique seeking to get back to what they see as 'the egalitarian principles of the Qur'an getting beyond the masculinist exegetical tradition that they understand to have cloaked it.'[243]

A quite different type of tradition is known as *hadith qudsi* or divine sayings. These are said to be part of what Allah revealed to Muhammad and were subsequently passed on, but were not revealed for inclusion in the Qur'an. The content of *hadith qudsi* is mainly about spiritual life and has been particularly valued by Sufis while not all Sunni Muslims accept *hadith qudsi*. A number of Muslim scholars, notably Fazlur Rahman, dismiss the notion of *hadith qudsi* altogether.

Shi'a Muslims call their hadith '*khabar*' – meaning news.[244] They are different in that instead of being authenticated by an isnad, their authenticity is guaranteed by transmission through Ali and the Imams of Shi'ism.[245]

In the centuries following Muhammad's death the doctrine developed that he lived a sinless life and so was the supreme exemplar. The term Sunni Muslim makes this point. This title identifies Sunnis as those following in his path and living through his example. Hadith is their access to this example. In Hadith there are hundreds of tangible illustrations of what can be followed and this has had compelling appeal when it comes to religious perfectionistic striving right down to the wearing of beards and the tying of sandals but also in a quite opposite direction as regards the keeping to a spirituality of right intent or niyyah. As such, Hadith has sometimes been called 'the walking Qur'an.'

Hadith is also essential, as we have seen, for clarifying questions of basic religious practice. For example, the five pillars of Islam are not explained in detail in the Qur'an. To take the example of the second pillar, the daily prayer (*salah*), the sequence of movements during this ritual comes from Hadith not from the Qur'an. As regards the third pillar of Islam, the paying of *zakah*, while this word zakah is found 32 times in the Qur'an, once again we find the practical details about its payment in Hadith, for example, that it is to be paid annually, on gold and silver, on livestock and crops and that it is to be paid by all Muslims who earn above a minimum level known as the nisab.

Hadith was also seen as vital as regards the development of law within an expanding empire. And many Western scholars as well as some Muslim scholars agree that Hadith developed in part in response to this need as much as vice-versa.[246]

The importance of Hadith has gone so far as to mean that at times it has even taken precedence over the Qur'an. The Director General of the Islamic Research Institute at the International Islamic University in Islamabad, Muhammad Khalid Mansud explains that al-Shafi'i (d. 822) and Ibn Hanbal (d. 855), founders of two of the key law schools, thought that since the Hadith explained the Qur'an it incorporated what it said while interpreting it too. As such Hadith was a convenient first point of reference rather than supplementary to the Qur'an. While this view is widely rejected, it has had much impact and underlines the extraordinary importance of Hadith within Islam.[247]

So, looking once again at the first two premises of the argument we are considering about Hadith presented at the beginning of the chapter, that 1. Hadith is regarded universally within Islam as an authoritative guide to the life of Muhammad who is thought to have lived a sinless life and is therefore to be emulated, and 2. as such Hadith texts are foundational and at the heart of Islam and key guides to life and to the Qur'an; Islam turns out once again to speak with more than one voice. For some Muslims the Qur'an seems basically eclipsed by Hadith which is its first interpreter and guide. The vast majority of Muslims take al-Bukhari Hadith and al-Muslim Hadith very seriously. They are foundational as texts. At the other end of the spectrum a tiny proportion of Muslims, known as Qur'anists, reject them entirely. Moderate, progressive Muslims and some Salafis, especially Salafi reformists, look at Hadith through critical eyes rejecting what they find historically unconvincing. Crucially, though, it must be emphasised that Muslims, certainly on a popular level and even on a scholarly level, are not familiar with the vast majority of hadiths. Hadith is used more as an a la carte menu from which different selections are made to suit a great variety of purposes and sensibilities. So we cannot conclude that Muslims are agreed that *all* al-Bukhari hadiths and al-Muslim hadiths are foundational and authoritative. Even while the majority of Muslims will say that they think of Hadith in this way this is more than questionable. The almost inevitable a la carte approach to the text means that the vast majority of Muslims do not act having in mind Hadith as a whole. This point needs emphasis. Muslims will routinely have a copy of the Qur'an. They won't have a copy of al-Bukhari Hadith and won't be familiar with its many volumes. On the contrary they may know a few sayings, or even many passages. However for ordinary Muslims the hadiths they know are what parents and grandparents, imams and elders happen to pass on, and this is, of necessity, more than highly selective.

So let's turn to premises 3 and 4 about Hadith at the beginning of the chapter that claimed that Hadith bolsters the causes of militancy and misogyny. How far are these claims true?

As has been mentioned Hadith is vast, and so while we shall consider the odd generalisation about the texts it is perhaps most instructive to look at how Hadith has been used. Abou El Fadl is keen to point out that as Islam developed in the early centuries some hadith that demean women gained attention while those emphasising equality lost the spotlight. The point is made more forcefully by Hadith scholar G. H. A. Juynboll who remarks that around a hundred years after Muhammad's death we seem to have a breeding ground for hadith that are women-unfriendly.[248] One example relates to the Qur'anic teaching about a woman's testimony compared with a man's. 'The Messenger of Allah "Allah's blessing and peace be upon him" answered: "Do not you see that the two women's witness is considered to be equal only to one man's witness?" [the woman] replied: "Yes." He said: "Then, this is the woman's deficiency of intelligence." '[249] This kind of passage has led Asma Barlas, a key Muslim feminist scholar, to see Hadith as far more problematic than the Qur'an as regards the treatment of women.

Another aspect of Hadith that came into frequent use, and explains how men came to be understood as superior to women, despite the more varied pronouncements of the Qur'an, relates to the figures of Adam and Eve. The story of Eve being created from Adam's rib enters Hadith literature and becomes much lauded among male exegetes as legitimising male superiority in relation to women.

A further example of this kind of development takes place in relation to male guardianship over women. Afsaruddin charts how this has grown to be a relationship in which women are subjugated and that hadiths are used to support this. A key point she makes is that from the vast corpus of questionable hadith, proof-texts that are misogynistic come to be used, that have not been used before, in commentaries on Qur'an and Hadith. Thus one commentator, Ibn Kathir, in the fourteenth century, uses words to describe the relationship between men and women that are unprecedented in the Islamic tradition thus far. 'Thus the man has become the woman's 'head', her 'elder', her 'judge', and 'the one who disciplines her if she should stray.'[250] As a proof-text from Hadith Ibn Kathir cites a single (uncorroborated) report from al-Bukhari in which Muhammad warns that a state will not prosper if led by a woman. Ibn Kathir further insists that a wife should be unconditionally obedient to her husband and cites the purported hadith where Muhammad claims 'If I were to command anyone to prostrate himself before another [person], it would be the wife before her husband on account of the rights he enjoys in relation to her.' Afsaruddin comments 'we had not encountered this hadith previously as a proof-text in the exegetical discussion of Ibn Kathir's predecessors, proving to us once again that male authoritarian attitudes towards women in the later period were progressively projected back to the time of the Prophet in the form of hadiths attributed to him, creating a powerful legitimising source for such changed sensibilities.'[251] What we are also seeing here is that discriminatory and misogynist commentaries and ultimately juridical decisions gain their own momentum sometimes over against much Qur'anic teaching.

There are, though, many more egalitarian aspects of Hadith literature as Professor of Political Science at the University of California, Berkeley, M. Steven Fish makes clear in his detailed sociological study entitled *Are Muslims Distinctive? A Look At The Evidence*. Having examined in some detail a wide variety of al-Bukhari hadiths Fish writes that what seems remarkable, having noted the quotations just mentioned, is that:

> 'in al-Bukhari's depiction of the Prophet's community, rigorous segregation of the sexes in daily life, reflexive female subordination to male authority, and sexual Puritanism are simply absent. After

reading how the hadith was used to justify hyper-patriarchal practices in relations between the genders in the modern [Muslim] world, I have been surprised to encounter Muhammad's wife whipping him in foot races and receiving from him a challenge to a rematch after she had put on some weight; to see Muhammad engaging in all manner of social interaction with women of every station; to see Muhammad following a mentally ill old woman's orders to finish some (probably manual) work for her; and to hear Muhammad tell men that the very measure of their faith was how well they treated their wives.'[252]

It should be added that many of the most trusted narrators of the chains of tradition, the isnads, were women, including for example Muhammad's wife Aisha.

Given these comments, it is all the more alarming that with time, some of the more misogynist manufactures from alleged hadiths came to the fore that had previously not seen the light of day. Hadith literature is highly malleable and, as we have seen, something of an a la carte menu whose constituents can be combined for good or ill. As the centuries passed they were used in many ways more for ill, when it comes to the treatment of women. Again this does not give us reason to generalise even about hadiths not least because hadiths are not seen as a whole within Islam unlike in the case of the Qur'an. The selective use of hadiths has been put to work by rival interpreters in polemic exchanges known as 'hadith hurling'. In this way hadiths were used for the construction of discriminatory law by patriarchal jurists, and hadiths materialised to support this purpose. Yet scholarship is divided about how discriminatory Hadith literature is especially when each hadith is analysed by verifying isnads and checking matn for consistency in relation to the Qur'an. Muslim feminist scholar and Emeritus Professor of Islamic Studies at Virginia Commonwealth University, Amina Wadud calls for more inclusivist interpretations of hadiths,[253] but in the meantime traditionalists and Wahhabists continue, in varying degrees, in the opposite direction.

What about militancy in Hadith? This is certainly present. A short selection from al-Bukhari and al-Muslim hadiths is nothing more than indicative.

'Whoever changes his Islamic religion, kill him.' Sahih al-Bukhari (Vol. 9: Bk. 84: 57)

'Know that paradise is under the shades of swords.' Sahih al-Bukhari (Vol 4: Bk. 55: 73)

'The Messenger of Allah said: 'One who died but did not fight in the way of Allah nor did he express any desire (or determination) for jihad died the death of a hypocrite.' (Muslim Bk. 20: 4696)

'The Messenger of Allah said I have been commanded to fight against people so long as they do not declare that there is no god but Allah.' (Muslim Bk. 1: 30)

We have seen how many scholars will rightly point out that a good deal of hadiths are weak, having just one chain of narration to authenticate them, or have been 'back dated' beyond the starting point of the original isnad. This is true of very many militant hadiths. All the same, whatever their origin, such hadiths have had a deep impact throughout much of Islam especially in times of war. Like much present day media they have been fodder for propaganda machines in such times. The 'arrival' and use of more belligerent hadiths indicate a move towards militancy in time with the rising needs of an Islamic empire. Asma Afsaruddin makes clear that the kinds of militant hadith we find here also had an impact on how the Qur'an was interpreted from the ninth century onwards.[254]

Hadith has been often used as polemic through much of the early history of Islam and this is still true today. For Sunnis it pointed to their identity with the Sunna and as such was a rallying cry validating their claim to the true Islam over against the Shi'a. 'Hadith hurling' continued as misogynist hadiths popped up or were selected. The same is true as regards combative hadiths as the needs of empire arose. Professor of Religious Studies at the University of Cape Town, Sa'diyya Shaikh provides a feminist interpretation of Hadith. She finds affirming passages as regards women in Hadith and describes the Islamic inheritance of the Qur'an and Hadith as a mixture of patriarchy and liberation.

Conclusion

First, the Qur'an lies at the heart of Islam. For many Muslims this is also so as regards al-Bukhari and al-Muslim Hadith. However, some Muslims are not of this view as regards Hadith. What is more, very few Muslims are at all mindful of al-Bukhari and al-Muslim Hadith as a whole. They follow a variously highly selective set of passages within it.

Second, mandates for discrimination against women are to be found within the Qur'an as are warrants for militancy against non-believers. There are also passages that temper, qualify and at times seem to annul these directives. Further, how far possibilities for militancy and misogyny are to be realised raises questions about the context of the revelations and the overall ethical objectives of the Qur'an. An examination of the key process of Qur'anic interpretation through abrogation makes clear that what possibilities become realised says more about the agendas of interpreters than it does about the text itself.

Third, Hadith literature as it has developed, in tandem with empire building, has realised further possibilities for misogyny and militancy beyond what is stated in the Qur'an. Some readers of Hadith don't see it as particularly misogynist and bellicose when read extensively. But Hadith literature has picked up and recycled misogynist and militant values through the body politic of a developing Islam from the ninth century onwards.

Fourth, however the argument we have been considering in this chapter, to say that Islam is *innately* misogynist and belligerent because its foundational texts are, does not hold firm. First, the claim that the Qur'an advocates misogyny and militancy is a half-truth dependent upon interpretation. Hadith, while it has developed misogynist and militant potential, is also a contested text, both now and in the past, and is rarely if ever seen as a whole. Second, Qur'anic literalists and those who stick most closely to the text are not especially more misogynist or bellicose than non-literalists. Sticking closely to the Qur'an is not what correlates with these developments. Some think that a literal interpretation of the Qur'an takes us away from discriminating against women and militancy, often because the context of discriminatory and militant passages makes clear their non-applicability now. Developments beyond the Qur'an and Hadith have been the most discriminatory against women such as some of the consensus rulings of the law schools that at times have been quite contrary to Qur'anic principles. Crucially, the rise of Wahhabism, is the factor most consistently associated with recent misogynist and belligerent developments within the faith and this, in the minds of many, is again a move away from the Qur'an.

In the next two chapters we shall look further at the issues of misogyny and militancy within Islam. Our focus will be much more on Islam today. Where there is misogyny and militancy we shall investigate where this has originated other than from interpretations of the Qur'an and Hadith. We shall see if these places of origin have been primarily religious and specifically Islamic or have they had more broadly political, cultural or institutional origins that are in principle independent of religion.

7

Islam Today: Attitudes Towards Women

Terms of Reference

In this, the second of three chapters that takes Islam as a case study we shall identify evidence that outlines the degree and character of discriminations and prejudice against women to be found within Islam. I shall debate moral evaluations of these inequalities, drawing upon a variety of perspectives, in line with my remarks about the dialogical character of understanding and evaluation mentioned in the Introduction.

In the last chapter we spent some time considering the Qur'an and thought this to be, in a sense, Islam at its most pristine. When we look at Islam today, after many centuries of interpretation, empire, colonialism, neo-colonialism, global Islam and now Islam on the net, we have something far more complex, as we began to see with the evolution of Hadith. Islam today is an on-going product in part of political and cultural influence, and here we are brought back to our discussion in the Introduction about the difficulties of identifying what is specifically religious. So if we are judging religion, and here Islam in particular, I need to be clear at the outset about what it is we are judging.

We noted in the Introduction that religion is often intimately bound up with politics and culture. In fact, whenever religion has a significant influence and effect it is almost certainly bound up in this way. We also noted, for all the difficulties in pinning down the word 'religion' or defining it, that it is used by scholars and by the general public in ways that work. The fact that there is meaningful dialogue about religion underscores the point that, to a fair extent, the word 'religion' and its many translations carry with them a good deal of common understanding. As far as Islam is concerned, however, there is every reason to see it as intimately bound up with the political and the cultural at least on one level. Not only does Islam, like the other world faiths, predate by many centuries modern and Enlightenment distinctions as regards the categories of religion, politics and culture, but many students of Islam have insisted that to place any great emphasis on distinctions between religion, politics and culture is to misunderstand the nature of their integration in the case of Islam because, as a way of life and a polity, Islam moves and continues to move against such distinctions. As such, Shahab Ahmed speaks about the Islamicate as an undifferentiated whole. Following Ahmed I shall use this phrase since this does justice to the way in which these elements are and have been intimately bound together.

However, we are considering the means by which such an Islamicate as it is today is more or less discriminatory against women. Within the dynamic of the Islamicate we can identify - without necessarily separating out - factors, events, and processes that are more or less religious in character. At the same time such is the integration of these factors that it is a mistake not to also see them as a whole. As such I shall make remarks both about the Islamicate and also about the role of religious factors within it.

The integral character of religion, culture and politics, especially in the case of Islam, naturally leads in the direction of its plurality in different times and places because of the diversity of these factors. We have already seen this in the case of Qur'anic interpretation as well as in the use of Hadith literature. Thus the Islamicate in China, Indonesia, Saudi Arabia, Iran, the UK and the US vary considerably today and I shall happily use the term Islams to keep this issue in mind.

Evidence of Discrimination and Misogyny

Looking then at the Islamicate today we can see that, by a wide range of measures, there are some significant inequalities between men and women in Muslim countries compared with in non-Muslim countries. Clear evidence of discrimination and misogyny is also to be found. We shall look at three types of evidence for this before also considering legal and juridical evidence.

Statistical Evidence

First, I shall look at a statistical approach to the question of gender inequality taken by Professor Steven Fish in his book that I mentioned at the end of the last chapter *Are Muslims Distinctive: A Look at the Evidence.*

Indicators of Women's Status

Fish considers three indicators of women's status in public life in Muslim and non-Muslim countries. These are:

First, *sex-income ratio:* in Muslim countries women's income varies between 20 – 70% that of men compared with in non-Muslim countries where this ratio is 30 – 80% that of men.

Second, the *proportion of the national legislature that is made up of women:* just over one tenth of legislatures are constituted of women in Muslim countries compared to just under a fifth so constituted in non-Muslim countries.

Third, the *percentage of women in ministerial positions:* 7.5% more women are in ministerial positions in non-Muslim countries compared with in Muslim countries. Yet when we compare more wealthy Muslim countries and most especially more democratic Muslim countries with non-Muslim countries this difference is, Fish remarks, 'no longer statistically significant.'

Popular Attitudes Towards Gender-Based Inequality

Steven Fish investigates a number of surveys:

The first survey he considers asks whether respondents thought a university education more important for a boy than a girl. Across a range of countries surveyed some Muslim majority and some not, 38.4% of Muslims answered that they thought a university education more important for a boy than a girl compared to 17.7% of all non-Muslim respondents, 16.7% of Christians and 15.2% of no religion.[255]

A second survey again across a range of Muslim and non-Muslim countries, addressed the question: 'If when jobs are scarce should men have more rights to jobs than women?' The proportions of groups answering 'Yes' to this question were as follows: Muslims 68.2%, Non-Muslims 29%, Christians 28.7%, No denomination 25.1%.[256]

A third survey asked respondents whether they thought men made better political leaders than women. Controlling for a range of other variables the probability of a Muslim man in a 95% Muslim country agreeing with the statement is .72 compared with .67 for a Christian man in such a society and .56 for a Muslim woman and .50 for a Christian woman in that situation. This compares with results for a Christian society as follows: Probabilities for agreeing with the statement were .45 for a Muslim man, .39 for a Christian man, .29 for a Muslim woman and .24 for a Christian woman.[257]

Fish remarks that 'being a Muslim increased the likelihood that one would agree with statements that favour a more traditional view of gender-based inequality. Yet gender itself stands out as an important predictor. Support for gender-based inequality seems less a Muslim tendency and more a tendency among Muslim men.'[258]

Structural Inequalities in Well-Being Between Men and Women
Under what he calls structural inequalities in well-being between the genders Fish considers two significant factors:

First, the literacy ratio between men and women in the largest Muslim and Christian countries. This is expressed in percentage form as a female literacy ratio of the male rate of literacy.

The Muslim countries featured appear as follows: Indonesia 92%, Pakistan 55%, Morocco 60%, Malaysia 93%, Afghanistan 29%, Algeria 76%, Bangladesh 76%, Saudi Arabia 87%, Uzbekistan 100%, Malaysia 93%, Turkey 84%, Egypt 72%, Iran 87%, Yemen 47%, Sudan 73%, Tunisia 78%, Syria 84%, Senegal 57%, Niger 35%, and Mali 49%. Average for 20 countries surveyed 71%.

The Christian countries appear as follows: US 100%, Brazil 100%, Russia

100%, Mexico 97%, Philippines 102%, Germany 100%, Dem Rep. Congo 67%., France 100%, UK 100%, Italy 99%, Ukraine 100%, Colombia 100%, South Africa 96%, Spain 100%, Argentina 100%, Poland 100%, Kenya 90%, Canada 100%, Uganda 75% and Peru 88%, average 96%.

On average the percentage of female literacy to male literacy is 21% higher in a country with 0% Muslims than in a country that is all Muslim.[259]

Second, differences in life-expectancy for females and males in Muslim and non-Muslim countries.

Here Fish borrows from statistics gleaned from the World Health Organisation. Granted that female life expectancy naturally exceeds male life expectancy, the World Health Organisation has devised the concept of 'Healthy Life Expectancy'. This is the average number of years someone can expect to live in full health. This provides valuable information on the status and life conditions of females in relation to males. Reflecting on this information Fish writes 'females in a country with 0% Muslims are expected to have a life expectancy advantage that is 2.5 years greater than do females in a country that is 100% Muslim.'[260]

We should of course beware of the very broad brush character of some of what is said in Fish's research. For example, he points out that within some specific non-Muslim countries such as Russia, views about female suitability for political office tend to favour men. Popular attitudes also reflect how respondents see the world around them as much as how they think the world should be, although of course, this in itself indicates inequity. The final two sets of statistics about 'structural inequalities' would appear to reflect facts about the human situation that in effect are discriminatory against women, more so in Muslim countries than elsewhere.

Legal And Juridical Evidence

There is not the space to give any kind of summary as regards the gender discriminatory character of law and custom in largely Islamic countries today. A few points will merely give a flavour of how things stand.

The OECD Development Centre has produced a worldwide Social Institutions and Gender Index (2014) document. In the synthesis report to this, countries are classified into four groups according to the level of gender discrimination in their social institutions. The most discriminatory group of countries are especially discriminatory in their legal frameworks and customary practices across most criteria considered. The category with the highest level of gender discrimination is described as having very high levels of discrimination within legal frameworks and customary practices across most of the criteria considered. It continues:

> 'the family code greatly discriminates against women; almost one third of girls younger than 19 are married, and women face severe discrimination in their parental authority and inheritance rights. Women's rights to own and control land and other resources and to access public space are extremely limited. There are serious infringements on their physical integrity matched by high levels of acceptance and prevalence of domestic violence: 44% of women have been victims of domestic violence, and 59% of women accept that it is justified under certain circumstances.'[261]

The full list of countries to be found in this category are: Bangladesh, Chad, Democratic Rep. Of Congo, Egypt, Gabon, Gambia, Liberia. Mali, Mauritania, Niger, Nigeria, Sierra Leone, Somalia, Sudan, Syrian Arab Rep., Yemen and Zambia, ten of which are Muslim countries. It should be noted that all the countries in this category that are not Muslim are African.

In the second highest category as regards gender discrimination we find Lebanon, Afghanistan, Azerbaijan, Iraq, Jordan and Pakistan. By contrast in the category where gender discrimination is described as very low Bosnia Herzegovina is the only largely Muslim country mentioned. All the other fifteen countries in that category are non-Muslim. It should also be clear that Indonesia - with a vast Muslim population - is in the middle category where the descriptor reads 'women face discrimination in terms of the legal age of marriage' and 'are restricted in terms of their access to public space and political life' and 'on average 39% of women agree that domestic violence is justified under certain circumstances.' It should be emphasised too that a number of key Muslim countries do not feature in the Survey including Saudi Arabia, Libya, Iran and Algeria.

A small selection of laws enacted in Muslim majority countries will make clearer the degree and range of discrimination. In Iran the Family Protection Act legitimises polygamy, marriage at the age of thirteen and temporary marriage.[262] In Syria rape is a felony, although the sentence may be suspended if the perpetrator marries the victim. In Bangladesh as regards the private sphere of family law, the usual discriminations about divorce, inheritance and the custody of children hold. Similarly in Malaysia women do not have equality as regards divorce, custody of children or division of matrimonial property.[263] Also in Kuwait and Qatar a woman's testimony in court is worth half that of a man, although in Qatar this is judged on a case by case basis.

I shall simply add a note about Saudi Arabia specifically since it is not mentioned in the above survey. Besides imposing the burka on women and until very recently not allowing women to drive or vote, failure to comply with the dress code for women routinely involves detainment without access to a lawyer.[264] Less well known is that 'wife beating' is specifically allowed by Saudi law, women are not allowed identity cards but merely feature as adjuncts on their husband's and if not their husband's then their father's or brother's or the most proximate male relative who they may hardly know to whom they must be officially attached. The Qur'anic judgment that in order to have a conviction for adultery there needs to be four male witnesses to the act of penetration, gets transmuted as regards rape into; there needs to be this degree of testimony in order to gain a conviction. So, in effect, rape is, for all intents and purposes, legal in Saudi Arabia. Polygamy is allowed as are temporary marriages and according to some religious authorities fathers may marry off their female toddlers, consummation being delayed until the girl is 9 years old.[265]

We can conclude that discrimination against women is widespread in many Muslim majority countries and most especially in the Middle East where we find some of the worst forms of misogyny today. This, however, is also the case in some non-Muslim African countries. As regards Indonesia discrimination against women is certainly present but not to the same extent as in the Middle East. Discriminatory attitudes towards women are especially marked among Muslim men rather than among Muslims as a whole.

The Many Muslim Voices about Discrimination and Misogyny Today

I made it very clear in the Introduction that this book followed a method of moral evaluation about faiths that was rooted in dialogue with those faiths and a reader might reasonably point out that we have not heard much as regards Muslim points of view about discrimination against women.

A common view I have met in speaking to Islamic Muslim scholars, imams and many ordinary Muslims, is one that rejects ideas of equality between men and women. Men and women are seen rather as *complementary* to each other's existence as Seyyed Hossein Nasr puts it in *Islam in the Modern World*. As a traditionalist he derives his views both from the history of Islam as well as from the Qur'an and Hadith. For example, a text such as 'Women have the same rights in relation to their husbands as are expected in all decency of them; while men stand a step above them' (Surah 2: 228) and 'Men are the ones who support women since God has given some persons advantages over others', (Surah 4: 34) inspire his views as they do those of Cambridge Islamic scholar and cleric Sheik Abdal Hakim Murad[266] and Salafi literalist Haitham Al-Haddad of the Islamic Sharia Council in Leyton, east London. Beyond references to the Qur'an, arguments seem to run something like this: first the individual is not necessarily the primary consideration, society and its needs are of enormous significance too. Therefore questions of individual rights and equality are not inviolable, they need to take their place in the round. To quote Nasr the 'complementarity of men and women was rooted in equity rather than equality and sought to base itself on what served best the interests of society as a sacred body and men and women as immortal beings.'[267] Second, men and women are seen as having different roles, the woman as the primary carer of children, of their education and the home. Men are to provide financially for their families. The argument for this division of labour seems to be that this is natural and part of the different role given by Allah to men and women as *khalifs* or vice-regents. These views are also expressed by some Muslim women. I remember the writer, educationalist and Muslim convert Raqiyyah Waris Maqsood informing a class of 15 year olds that this complementary model rather than one of equality was her understanding of the proper relationship between men and women. It should be made clear that those advocating this 'complementary view' of the relationship between men and women do not at all necessarily support the worst excesses of misogyny we have seen mentioned such as domestic violence against women. I spoke at some length for example to Abdal Hakim Murad because he is one of the most well known senior traditionalist Muslim scholars in the UK. For all that Surah 4: 34 is often translated, as we have seen, to mean 'to beat' your wife, Murad pointed to possible metaphorical meanings. But he was also keen to emphasise that, from his traditionalist point of view, the text is to be seen in the light of Hadith, and Muhammad does not appear, on any occasion, to have beaten any of his wives and therefore, for him, beating one's wife is not allowed in Islam.

However this entire 'complementary approach' to relations between men and women is also challenged within Islam.

Heba Raouf speaks about a 'renewal jihad', a struggle through which the Qur'an is seen as an ally of women's rights. In keeping with this Professor Amina Wadud seeks to return to the Qur'an, away from discriminatory traditional Islam and Wahhabism. Instead of following a line by line approach to the Qur'an she insists it is viewed holistically otherwise one can't see the wood for the trees. Wadud sees equality between men and women at the heart of Qur'anic values in sync with justice and mercy. The view that God is too great to be embodied in law is mainstream Islam and this fits with a key distinction that has been made between *Shar'ia* and *fiqh*.[268] Contrary to much common usage Shari'a refers to law as it is in the mind of God, by definition unknown to humans.[269] The human and therefore *fallible* attempt to enact this in specific times and places to meet the needs of circumstance is fiqh, the laws of time and place. The various law schools in general agree that such laws are fallible and the range of laws enacted through and within those schools indicate the scope of legitimate interpretation or *ijtihad* on a wide range of issues. As one scholar put it, at the heart of fiqh is plurality. This is not just progressivist polemic either. Traditionalist scholar, Murad, made much of this point. In his view Wahhabis stand out in their insistence that their very specific puritanical extremism is alone legitimate. This variety of course stems from the fact that Islam in its early rapid expansion developed in many ways in response to the cultures and situations it encountered. Much classical scholarship accepted that each new generation would take a fresh look at issues. In keeping with this the number and validity of sources has been continually debated by jurists. We have already seen this as regards how many ayat were thought to be abrogated at different points in time in the Qur'an and how the meaning of abrogation has varied and evolved. We have seen how similar discussion has taken place over the centuries about al-Bukhari and al-Muslim Hadith and how dispute has continued about what is meant by the interpretive methods of analogy/qiyas and consensus/ijma among the ulama. At times, for example, in Moorish Spain and in the early Ottoman Empire, a somewhat secular approach to much civil law was practised.

Among the considerable diversity that has been Muslim practice across the centuries some, seeking to bolster women's rights, have looked back to a group of Muslim scholars known as the Mutazilites. The Mutazilites argued that the use of reason was key to understanding the Qur'an and the practice of Islam that followed from it. Laws were not to be irrational, and not to be out of keeping with God's qualities of justice and mercy. The Ashirites, who took a much more faith based, even fideist view, won out, generally speaking, but not entirely. In recent times a key Egyptian Salafi figure, Muhammad Abduh – who we met in the last chapter – was extremely critical of the ulama at the prestigious Islamic Al Ahzar University in Cairo. In response to their views he declared himself a neo-Mutazilite announcing every manmade source of law – the sunna, ijma, qiyas, and the like, to be subject to rational discourse. Even the Qur'an, he maintained, must be reopened to debate but from all sectors of society. Abduh proposed a proletariatisation of Islam redefining key terms such as consensus/ijma to mean popular sovereignty, and in keeping with this he pushed for universal suffrage.

The reader may think Abduh's ideas a radical departure from traditional Islam and in some ways they were, though Abduh, being a Salafi, claimed his ideas were nearer to the Qur'an than traditionalism. Abduh's thinking was for sure less of a departure from the historical Islamicate than hardline Wahhabism that introduced stoning for adultery, more or less unheard of at the time in eighteenth century Arabia. Abou El Fadl makes clear that the vast majority of Muslims today are not puritan in the Wahhabi sense, and do not support the kind of *hudud* punishments routine within Saudi Wahhabi practice. In Murad's estimation, Wahhabis worldwide constitute roughly 2% of Muslims.

My point here is that Islam has been, throughout its history, considerably varied and fiercely contested. Today those seeking equal rights for women are part of that contest, one based in part on the plurality of interpretation and practice that has been and continues to be Islam. Making this case for greater gender equality within Islam, a highly selective précis of points, made by some recent scholars and activists, runs as follows. Several wives of the prophet would appear to have been jurists in the fledgling Islamicate. There is therefore every reason to ensure that women are well represented in the judiciary and in other positions of authority and influence in Islamic countries today. Egyptian hardline clerics, who recently opposed the election of thirty female members of the judiciary, were unsuccessful in their efforts.[270] Until the sixteenth century thousands of women jurists and scholars taught male jurists in the mosques of Damascus and Cairo.[271] Muslim women were of key importance in early Islam. For example Fatimah, daughter of the prophet, was said to be a perfect saint, and Zaynab bint Ali gave one of the most important Islamic discourses to the victorious Yazid at the battle of Karbala, where for Shi'a's their Imam Husayn was martyred. This is notice too to modern puritans that certainly some Muslim women were well educated, presumably with the approval of Muhammad. It should not be forgotten that Muhammad was himself employed by his first wife Khadija. Reflecting on this, many activists see the centuries of male exegesis as being 'due an overhaul' since gender is a human bias, and the Qur'an as we have seen regards men and women as spiritual equals.

In relation to the specific issues of divorce, inheritance, child custody and court testimony activists today are speaking out and achieving some success. The Sisters of Islam organisation, possibly the foremost organisation challenging traditional male interpretations of the Qur'an, was founded to examine and critique Islamic legal practice in Malaysia where it remains clearly discriminatory against women. It has challenged decisions in relation to inheritance, divorce and child custody. Some liberal religious clergy have entered into dialogue with Sisters of Islam. The founder, Zainab Anwar believes that the agenda is gaining ground not simply in Malaysia but elsewhere in the Muslim world too. Anwar also set up 'Musawah' (meaning 'equality)' that in February 2009 brought together 250 Muslim scholars and feminist activists from nearly fifty countries to engage in 'knowledge building' about gender justice in relation to Islam. There are also several US based Muslim organisations such as Muslims For Progressive Values that have a global reach. MPV campaigns against human rights abuses carried out in the name of Islam in Muslim majority countries. It especially focuses on women's rights and LGBTQI rights.

Many Muslim majority countries have signed up to the Convention on the Elimination of all forms of Discrimination against Women (CEDAW) which reads that signatories must 'adopt appropriate legislative and other measures, including sanctions where appropriate, prohibiting all discrimination against women.'[272] Those Muslim majority countries that have ratified the treaty either by signature or accession include: Algeria, Bangladesh, Bosnia, Chad, Egypt, Indonesia, Iraq, Kuwait, Malaysia, Morocco, Pakistan, Palestine, Qatar, Oman, Syria, Tunisia and UAE. Clearly duplicity is not the preserve of the West and many of these countries don't keep to what they have signed as we have seen, but what emerges is that a battle is on-going. It is worth mentioning in terms of Western human rights finger wagging that the US has not signed CEDAW.

In the UK today there are a range of progressive organisations such as The Inclusive Mosques Initiative, British Muslims for Secular Democracy, Inspire and the Quilliam Foundation, all of which seek to promote equal rights for women. I would also mention the work of imams such as Qari Asim, whose MBE is a recognition of his speaking out within the Muslim community against forced marriage and domestic violence within families and for his work in building positive relations between the Muslim community and the wider society.

In addition to activism about discrimination further progressive interpretations keep emerging about key issues.

As regards equality in divorce, the renowned Muslim feminist sociologist, the late Dr. Fatema Mernissi points out that Muhammad seems to have been repudiated by three of his wives. It would seem that, in Muhammad's time, women could absolutely repudiate their husbands without the requirement that they give any further reason than men needed to give. Dr. Shuruq Naguib, who I mentioned in the previous chapter, also informed me that there is also *some* evidence that jurists have allowed husbands and wives to choose between options as regards divorce. This adds to the Islamic precedents for parity between men and women in this respect.

Mernissi also points out, regarding polygamy, that it is hardly mentioned in the Qur'an, but where it is, this is with the proviso that all wives are treated equally. Yet, as we saw in the last chapter, the Qur'an also states 'you cannot be perfectly equitable to all your wives even if you so desire' (Surah 4: 129), which would seem to imply that polygamy is inadmissible. For all the legislation that we have seen allowing polygamy at present across the Middle East, it is all the same in decline across the region today and banned in Tunisia and Turkey.

As regards inheritance, Abou El Fadl remarks that before the time of Islam it would seem that women had no inheritance rights because people only inherited what they fought for in battles and women did not fight. Yet in Medina some Muslim women chose to fight, and they therefore claimed their right to inherit. A subsequent revelation, suggesting that women inherit half of what a man inherits, seems then to reflect changing circumstances in relation to what had gone before; the implication being that circumstance, not some imagined eternal law irrespective of circumstance, is where critical reflection on practice and law should begin. The very different circumstances of the varied Muslim communities across the planet today require much rethinking especially in the light of the fairly consistently held distinction that we have identified across Islam between Shari'a and fiqh. In my conversation with Dr. Shuruq Naguib I was informed that, both among British Muslims and elsewhere, property is often given equally to sons and daughters today, and that Muslim jurists have found ways in which women can inherit equally by such provisions being written into wills.

Abou El Fadl also comments about Surah 4: 34, that we considered in Chapter 6, to do with domestic violence. The beginning of this ayah reads 'Men are the *managers/guardians* of the affairs of women'. The Arabic for managers/guardians is *'qawwamun'* and can also be translated as supporters/masters/servants. However this 'progressive' translation seems to me odd. Even if Bakhtiar's translation of 'daraba' later in the verse as 'to send away' rather than the usual translation of 'to beat one's wife' has credence, nonetheless 'daraba' comes as the third and final step in a series of sanctions that the husband can mete out against his rebellious wife. If misogyny has a heart within the Qur'an it is here. In her unflinching opposition to this, Professor Amina Wadud writes about 'daraba', 'I have come to say "no" outright to the literal implementation of this passage.' [273] She continues, 'this verse, and the literal interpretation of hudud (penal code) both imply an ethical standard of human actions that are archaic and barbaric at this time in history.'[274] The reader should be clear that this is a Muslim scholar rejecting some of the Qur'an! Wadud is in-line with the Mutazilites - subjecting the Qur'an to rational scrutiny - long may the innovation of which she is accused continue.[275]

As regards testimony in a Shari'a court, where a woman's witness statement has been generally thought to constitute half the evidential value of a man's witness statement, it has been pointed out that the context of the relevant ayat in the Qur'an (Surah 2: 282), upon which this is based, refers specifically to a loan transaction. Yet even that very specific discrimination has in effect been abrogated today, according to scholars such as Afsaruddin, since unlike in Qur'anic times, women are now equally experienced in financial matters implying their equal status as witnesses. More generally, as regards hadith testimony, in the process of tracing isnads back to their sources, a woman's testimony is regarded as equal to that of a man.[276] This, as we saw in Chapter 6, is reflected in the fact that very many al-Bukhari hadith are traced back to the prophet's wife Ai'sha.

Locating Responsibility for Discrimination and Misogyny

We have seen then how allegations of discrimination and misogyny within the Islamicate, most especially in the Middle East, seem to be accurate, in part at least. We have also observed, both historically and today, how much Islam is contested, in the meaning of its sources and the nature of its practice, and how there are many within Islam now who seek an egalitarian Islam as regards men and women while there are also very many who bitterly oppose this.

Of key importance is the point that some specific injections of discriminatory and misogynist rhetoric and law have their origins in tribal culture, tradition and politics beyond the degree to which they have already been imbibed within bedrock sources such as Hadith. There are those, at the most politically correct end of the spectrum, who, for their own genuine moral reasons, would seek to absolve Islam of much discriminatory practice on these grounds. Some Muslims, either out of denial, ignorance or understandable self-protection against the barrage of media onslaught, seek to do the same. As such, all the statistics and evidence at the beginning of this chapter, from the least discriminatory to the most misogynist, miss the mark in judging Islam if it is local culture, rather than global faith, that is responsible. For this kind of view to be at all tenable some attempt has to be made to distinguish between religion on the one hand, and culture tradition and politics on the other. We saw, at the outset of this chapter, that this is perhaps possible, even in the case of Islam and the Islamicate that so often eschews such distinctions. Still, in the extreme form of the argument, as I have presented it here, in which Islam is left more or less unscathed by critique as regards its attitude and practice towards women, this, it seems to me, is quite implausible. If Islam were essentially egalitarian as regards men and women, this might be clearer in the Qur'an and in Hadith and in the majority of traditionalist Sunni commentary and scholarship that very often takes the opposite 'complementary' perspective about the relationship between men and women. The idea that Islam has fought or expounded an egalitarian battle against the forces of local misogyny across the Middle East and Indonesia and in the West, when it has come West, is simply false. Those fighting for equal rights within Islam don't believe a word of it when the argument is put in such a strong form. They have lived through and fought against the opposite reality.

What about modified forms of this argument that say that some of the most misogynist aspects of the Islamicate are of local cultural origin rather than being Islamic in nature? The rise of Wahhabism, in eighteenth century Arabia, is perhaps a prime candidate for such an alleged acculturation of religion. Abou El Fadl tells us that Al Wahhab, brought in much Bedouin culture and practice from the Najd region of eastern Arabia into the faith. I don't want to delay the reader with this issue. Suffice to say that this view has been strongly disputed by scholars equally eminent in the field and crucially even if Abou El Fadl is right to regard Wahhabism as a significant product of Bedouin culture nonetheless it is Islam all the same.[277] Wahhabism, whatever Bedouin influence may or may not have given rise and sustenance to it, still draws heavily upon similar views found in the writings of very influential Muslim scholars such as Ibn Taymiyya (d1328). Notably, Al Wahhab was building upon the discriminations against women we have seen in the Qur'an and Hadith and taking them much further. If, on grounds of going beyond these sources, we are to judge Al Wahhab's development of Islam as beyond Islam, by the same token, we must exorcise all egalitarian types of Islam as deviant in the opposite direction. Wahhabism, of course, has also come to have political weight today and, backed by Saudi finance, it has some influence worldwide. As such Wahhabism is a cause as much as an effect as it also enacts stoning for adultery and, as we have seen, requires that four male witnesses are needed to the act of penetration to secure a conviction for rape. Very many Muslim moderates judge it, correctly, as a key engine of misogyny in the modern world.

Deobandhi Islam is a further example of an alleged hybrid of Islam and local northern Indian cultural practice that is routinely discriminatory against women. Nonetheless, for all the hybridity at play, with its political origins in the Indian mutiny in Delhi in 1857, and its birth in rural Deoband near there, Deobandhi Islam is also Islam through and through. Part of the motivation for founding a seminary in rural Deoband was to preserve Islam in its perceived purity that was taken to include discriminatory practices and attitudes towards women. This is not of course what progressives would call the purity of Islam, but then, as we have seen, even the Qu'ran cannot be agreed upon in this respect. What is clear is that seminal Muslim scholars like Syed Abu A'la Maududi have given an Islamic basis to Deobandhi practice. Maududi's Qur'anic commentaries are to be found in some of the 1695 or 40% of UK mosques that are Deobandhi today.[278]

Some, arguing that responsibility for misogyny lies more with local culture than with Islam, suggest that this is seen most clearly when we consider some specific issues rather than when we consider particular sects and movements within Islam. Female Genital Mutilation is perhaps the most often cited issue in this respect, so let's look briefly at whether or not this is the case as regards FGM.

FGM is not mentioned in the Qur'an which generally proscribes mutilating the body. It is condemned by very many Muslim leaders and scholars today as non-Islamic. For example, Dean of Faculty of Shari'a at Al-Ahzar University in Cairo, Ahmed Talib (2005), described FGM as a crime that had no relationship to Islam. Al-Ahzar's Grand Mufti, Ali Gomaa (2006), also denounced the practice and Ayatollah al-Sistani of Iraq (2014), issued a fatwa declaring FGM a non-religious tradition and denied parents permission or justification for subjecting their daughters to the practice. FGM is also found not just in Muslim countries, but more widely across Africa and Asia. For example, in Kenya and Ethiopia, more Christian than Muslim women are affected.[279] For these reasons, FGM is widely regarded as a matter of culture and tradition rather than religion. The issue is, all the same, not quite that simple. Some weak hadiths mention FGM, but no consensus emerges from these. There is also division among the law schools, whose views range from regarding FGM as forbidden, permitted, or left up to parental discretion, through to regarding FGM as obligatory.[280] Bringing matters up to date it is worth quoting scholars John L. Esposito and Natana J. Delong-Bas:

> 'In [Muslim majority] Malaysia FGM has become a widespread practice among the middle class, which considers it a religious obligation. Although the government has outlawed the practice, the National Fatwa Council declared it obligatory in 2009... Similarly, in Indonesia, [by far the most populous Muslim country in the world], where 85 percent to 100 percent of girls are believed to have undergone FGM, or are at high risk of it, it is believed to be an Islamic requirement. In 2013, the Indonesian Ulama Council issued a statement, that female circumcision is recommended, but not mandatory.'

We might ask, for example, if Islam is quite opposed to FGM, why, in a Muslim majority country such as Egypt, have 91% of married Muslim women between the ages of 15 and 49 been subject to it, and why, when it was outlawed in Egypt in 2008 was this condemned by Islamist clerics in Egypt despite the pronouncements against FGM from the senior clerics at Al-Ahzar that we have seen.[281] [282] In many cases the Islamicate has appropriated FGM as Islamic. As such it is to be included as one of its moral failings. We should be equally clear that very many mainstream Islamic organisations and movements, such as Sisters-In-Islam, have campaigned and are campaigning valiantly against FGM; this is also Islam.

Discriminations, prejudice and the abuse of women are to be found the world over, however, the first section of this chapter made clear that these attitudes and behaviours are particularly prevalent in some Muslim majority societies as well as some non-Muslim parts of Africa. It makes no sense to simply attribute this to certain non-Islamic cultural and political influence, that exonerates Islam as a purely passive phenomenon and separates out religion, culture and politics to a degree that the vast majority of Muslims and non-Muslim Islamic scholars would reject.

So, attempts to sideline issues of discrimination and misogyny as matters of culture set apart from the nature of Islam do not succeed. We have also seen that there are very many moderate Muslims who do seek an egalitarian Islam as regards men and women and they have their successes too. All the same, both in the Middle East as well as elsewhere, including in the UK the potential for an egalitarian Islam has often yet to be realised. When I interviewed Temina Kazi, founder of British Muslims for Secular Democracy in early 2016, I asked her what progress organisations like BMSD, alongside other progressive and egalitarian minded Islamic ventures, such as the Inclusive Mosques Initiative and Inspire, had made in achieving gender equality in British Islam. She explained that it was very much a game of 'catch up.' A great many Muslims in the UK have essentially secularised she explained. Many drink alcohol and don't keep Ramadan. Problems also arise where an older generation of Muslim men fail to inspire while also refusing to relinquish power within their communities. This can all too easily give rise to a listlessness among younger generations who, caught in the twilight between cultures, often struggle with their own questions about their own identity. Into that vacuum some self-appointed hardline preachers, not simply the notorious ones like Anjem Choudary, but also non-militant conservatives like Dr. Haitham al-Haddad and activist, preacher and writer Hamza Tzortsis, have been making very clear their view that men and women are not at all equals. In Haddad's Shari'a council in Leyton men and women are not equal in divorce. Tzortsis has done what he can to segregate men and women at Islamic Society meetings on university campuses, a first step in the direction of discrimination.

Dialogue about the Veil

Before concluding this chapter about the treatment of women within Islam something should be said about the veil and its meaning. Again, this issue illustrates the battles being fought within Islam. It points once more to how

Western perceptions can so easily miss the mark, and makes clear how when considering issues to do with people, the specific people we are considering should have their perspectives centre stage.

The vexed question of the veil, in all its forms, is both topical and important. The veil has been so many things; an instrument of repression and subjugation at the hands of the Taliban and ISIS, the reason for exclusion from British education in the case of Shakira Begum in Luton in 2004, a source of fear that is prohibited in several European countries and an object of ridicule from the pen of senior politicians within what has become a mainstream discourse within British public life. The issue of the meaning of the veil is inextricably intertwined with assessments of the appropriateness of its prohibition, or the acceptance of it as a requirement, and everything in between.

The veil appears in various guises notable among which are: first, the hijab; a scarf covering the hair, second, the chador; a cloak covering the head and body, but leaving the face uncovered, third, the burka; covering the entire head and body including the eyes - the wearer sees through a cloth mesh eye veil sewn into the burka and fourth, the niqab; a veil that leaves the eyes clear and is worn with a headscarf.[283]

Once again the concept of judging the veil, like judging religion, is highly suspect. We cannot stand outside the histories that we, as individuals and cultures imbibe, to find an objective place from which to judge. At the opposite extreme, simply walking away, suggesting that nothing can be said, as part of a relativist capitulation is equally mistaken. That approach disengages from the world. It abrogates a responsibility to seek to understand each other, a crucial ingredient of the good life. A middle path of dialogue will investigate something about the meanings of the veil, and about the circumstances that have given rise to those meanings.

I have spoken to a small number of Muslim women who wear hijab. One such conversation was with a colleague, a student teacher who appeared after the school holiday wearing hijab whereas before she hadn't done so. I wanted to know why she had presumably decided to wear hijab. She said she wanted to assert her identity as a Muslim woman. She claimed she was under no pressure to wear the veil, and I believed her. She showed no nervousness or reluctance to speak to me about the issue and, if she was coerced, I was left asking why she wasn't coerced sooner? This is consonant with the accounts of many Muslim women in the UK as to why they wear some form of veil as Muslim women.[284] It also fits with recent research by Anabel Inge, by her own account a non-Muslim feminist, who having spent years researching the lives of Salafi Muslim women living in London, found not one case where a women was compelled to wear the veil.[285] I remember a graduate seminar, at King's College London, where a number of Muslim women spoke in an impassioned way about their ownership of the veil. It carried their meaning, and they refused the impositions of meaning upon their dress from others, whether Iranian mullahs, Saudi imams, Western feminists or secularists. I think we should take seriously what people say about the meaning of what they wear. We might want to psychoanalyse their accounts, we might be right to do so, but we should by the same token psychoanalyse our own motivations and intentions for doing this. We might also look at the history of the meaning of the veil for there are those who say that this is inescapable and that, for this reason, the King's graduate students could not simply own the meaning of what they were doing, what they were doing had baggage, vast historical baggage. I don't want to pre-empt this question. Instead I want to look at a history of the meaning of the veil in order to take further the question as to whether its meaning can be somehow independent of its history. Let's look at a thumbnail sketch of the history and significance of the veil. That may help us to understand more about the meanings that are available to draw upon today.

A number of leading Muslim scholars have argued that the Qur'an at no point insists that Muslim women cover their heads or faces even in public.[286] The injunction that both men and women dress modestly is no more specific than that. Sheikh Zaki Badawi (d. 2006), once Principal of the Muslim College in London, went further insisting that a proper reading of Hadith gives no instruction either although other sources indicate that a woman should not show more than her hands and feet. From what we can tell, the only women who Muhammad insisted were veiled were his own wives. Influential Muslim scholar, Yusuf al-Qaradawi, dubbed by Wahhabis as the wicked Mufti, argues that in Islam what is not distinctively forbidden is permitted which would imply that veiling of any kind is not required in Islam. Much commentary argues that Muhammad improved the rights of women compared with in pre-Islamic Arabia, ending the practice of female infanticide and allowing for women's inheritance and for dowries although significantly Dr. Fatema Mernissi contests the extent to which this is so. Professor of Religion and International Affairs at Georgetown University John Esposito suggests that four or so generations after the death of Muhammad veiling began as a practice.[287] It seems too to have been promoted by seminal Muslim theologian and jurist Al Ghazzali (c.1056–1111), and later by Ibn Taymiyya (d1328) to whom some repressive Salafist and Wahhabi regimes today look back for inspiration. The word *hijab* seems to have originated from a Persian root '*jhb*'. Wearing hijab seems to have developed as a status symbol for aristocratic women, separating them from the lower classes within society. It seems too to have arisen in the fourteenth century when Persia was invaded by the Mongol empire in order to distinguish Muslim from non-Muslim women.

In the twentieth century, with the rise of mass education and more and more women being in the public sphere, especially from the 1950s onwards, a conservative reaction has gathered pace with accompanying puritanical sensibilities and violent insecurities. It is well known that gender apartheid prevails in Saudi Arabia with separate lifts and floors in shopping centres for men and women. Infringements of women's dress code in Iran or Saudi Arabia have also incurred zealous wrath. Following the Iranian revolution in 1979, the hijab was enforced, and people protesting against this were attacked. Unveiled women have been blamed by one Shi'a cleric as 'sources of all that is bad in society' and accused of inviting men to rape them.[288] The *Program for Social Safety* gives the Iranian Special Guidance Police the authority to apprehend and detain any woman not appropriately dressed. Repeat offenders may be fined and sentenced to flogging. One sickening case occurred in March 2002 in Saudi Arabia when 800 girls were trapped in a school that had caught fire. They were beaten back by police because they were not wearing the mandatory headscarves for a public place. Fifteen girls died and fifty were injured.[289]

How this history affects the meaning of wearing the headscarf, hijab or burka in the UK and elsewhere in the West now, is contentious. In Pakistan, Iran and Saudi Arabia it would seem to be clearly an instrument of oppression and persecution. If children wearing hijab is more important than their lives then the hijab, in that instance, is the most severe form of persecution and violent oppression. This conclusion is reached not via some superimposed Western perspective of human rights. That accusation, made against criticisms of Islam, actually assumes a relativism that conflicts with concepts of absolute truth that many Muslim commentators seek to uphold. Many Muslims are at the forefront of criticisms of Wahhabi Islam in Saudi Arabia, and especially critical of its treatment of women. It is Muslim women's rights organisations that have brought the incident of the Saudi girls' school massacre to light as an atrocity. But something else is important. Such Muslim women reformers, in many cases wear the veil themselves while they also identify it as a form of oppression wherever it is coerced. For those who wish to argue that Muslim women today can never escape the repressive resonances of the veil, they need to explain how meanings ever get started, how symbols change their significance through time and with events. The veil may have baggage but there is more than irony in saying to a Muslim woman 'your veil stands for oppression' or that it stands for anything else. To say you cannot give it your own meaning is oppressive in its own right. As such the veil has all the meanings that women who wear it say it has when they wear it out of choice. It is a form of Muslim identity, despite the fact that it is not required in many forms of Islam. It is a protest, a means of privacy and anonymity, a provocation, a proclamation, a choice, an act of courage in the face of Western suspicion and abuse; it is a badge of honour and source of pride.

All the same, if a primary perspective is that of the women who wear the veil, the perspective of those who are observers is also significant, especially when they agree - and there is agreement, not just about Pakistan and Saudi Arabia, but also about cases in the UK - that the veil and the burka are sometimes coerced. In some Somali and Pakistani communities in Britain some very young girls wear the veil. Despite the important research of Dr. Anabel Inge within specifically Salafi London based Muslim communities, more widely there do seem to be some limited cases in the UK where the wearing of the veil is mandatory for girls and women. I join the consensus opposition to such enforcement, and to the influence of Wahhabi, and some Salafi groups in some Muslim communities, where they have advanced this. Further, if as some studies have indicated, wearing the burka can lead to low self esteem and depression within girls and women, then that is further reason for opposition as are issues of vitamin D deficiency.

I would agree with the Canadian political philosopher, Professor Will Kymlicka that community rights are most important when under threat from the wider society, and of vanishing importance when they restrict their own members. No culture should absolutely impose itself on its constituent cultures and by the same token: no such constituent culture should impose itself on its members. In contrast with these options, active dialogue is crucial between the wider society and its various constituencies since all cultures bring their children up in certain ways while such ways, in all societies, are best open to wider critique. It would be crazy to ban the burka in the UK while complaining about its enforcement in elements of British Islam. Both are acts of coercion, and if such a government prohibition was a response to such a constraint it would also be an act of hypocrisy. Banning the burka might have the effect that women, now forced to wear it, would then be further restricted by being generally kept at home.

The British journalist and commentator Yasmin Alibhai-Brown identifies the burka as a potential means of hiding domestic violence.[290] I mention that because, as we have seen, Australian psychiatrist Ida Lichter notes that incidents of domestic violence against women in Pakistan, Iran, Indonesia and, I would add, Saudi Arabia, are alarmingly high. Clothing that hides such violence and that can be imposed by the perpetrators needs to be vehemently opposed. [291] [292] As fellow human beings we should take an interest in the plight of women in Pakistan, Iran, Indonesia and Saudi Arabia, and support Muslim women's rights groups there. In Britain it seems important to me for non-Muslims and society more generally to work with elements within the Muslim communities to make the veil, in all cases and in all its forms, a matter of choice. This recognises the primacy of what Muslim women wearing the veil say, and may feel unable to say. It starts with their concerns about oppression and those of observers, and this has significant implications. It means not importing imams from Pakistan who cannot speak English and who may well bring further frankly misogynistic baggage into UK Muslim communities. It means that the wider society needs to engage more with Muslim communities in the UK beyond the conversations with 'gatekeepers' of such communities. These are the sentiments of the late Zaki Badawi who was appalled by the ignorance of many imams from Pakistan as regards both Islam and British society.²⁹³ Badawi looked forward to a time when such baggage was a thing of the past and Muslim women could have choice about their dress and be the drivers in interpreting phrases like 'modesty', which, we should remember, applies as much to men as to women in the Qur'an.

On-Going Struggle and Dialogue

What should be very clear is that a battle is on-going within Islam about women's rights and about Muslim perceptions of women, most especially Muslim men's perception of women and Muslim women. Discrimination against women and misogyny are not givens within Islam. Of course, those organisations and individuals that seek gender equality inside the faith, as well as decidedly egalitarian sects like the Shi'a Ismailis, will be dismissed as being non-Islamic both by some within Islam and by others beyond it. This is part of the endless posturing and bickering within religious power politics whereby opponents are castigated and defined as being beyond the pale. There is no Pope within Islam, no over-arching authority that can arbitrate a definition. What then of the future of Islam with respect to women's rights?

There is some sign of change even in some of the most discriminatory regimes within the Islamicate. It may come as a surprise to know that today there are more women than men studying at university both in Saudi Arabia and also in Iran. In Saudi Arabia considerable status is conferred on a family whose sons and daughters graduate from university which explains something of this story. The new King Abdullah University of Science and Technology is the first co-educational university in Saudi Arabia. There are also reports that the impact of the religious police in Saudi Arabia, the *mutaween*, is at present in decline amid a general feeling, among much of the population, that they are something of a nuisance. One example of change is that the Saudi authorities didn't want women to go to the London 2012 Olympics. Women's rights groups, largely in Saudi Arabia, put pressure on the Olympic committee who told the Saudi government that if Saudi women could not compete then the same prohibition would apply to Saudi men. The ruling worked, and both Saudi men and women competed. All of this, however, sits alongside the fact that in Saudi Arabia, for example, attempts to eliminate child marriage have achieved only limited success, and that Wahhabi clerics have remained divided on this issue. This came to light in a particularly disturbing case in 2009 when an eight year old girl was married to someone to whom the father owed a debt. The mother's appeal was overruled on the pretext that the girl could divorce when 18! Even all-women fitness centres were banned in the 1990s although some have now started to reappear. Only 15% of women work outside the home, although the dependency upon ex-pat workers, consequent in part on this fact, is a pressure for further change.

It is equally important to be clear that while Wahhabism is very much a minority ideology within the Islamicate, as we have seen from the comments of Abdal Hakim Murad, nonetheless it is influential today due to its zealously evangelical character backed by the petrodollar. Much Saudi funding does not necessarily go to Wahhabi 'educational' centres but it does fund conservative versions of Islam. The Saudis, for example, have supplied funds for the setting up of Islamic Studies centres and university chairs at Harvard and also at Cambridge, in the UK. Between 1982 and 2005, during the reign of King Fahd of Saudi Arabia, 200 seminaries, 210 Islamic centres, 1500 mosques and 2000 schools were established outside Saudi Arabia by Saudi and Wahhabi funding.[294]

Other influences, though, are also apparent. In Egypt the senior cleric al-Qaradawi has recently pronounced a fatwa to the effect that women should be allowed to be heads of state. In agreement with the Grand Mufti of Egypt, Sheik Gomaa, he has also pushed for women to have an absolute choice about their spouse.[295] Still, in Egypt under Hosni Mubarek until the Egyptian revolution in 2011, while there were many women in positions of power in business, only 7.6% of such women were members of political parties. Egyptian scholar, Professor Heba Raouf Ezzat, however, also advocates more local political involvement of women - grassroots empowerment. This, she argues, is as effective as women being in positions of political power where they can more easily be manipulated by the state.

In Indonesia the conservative ideologies of Wahhabism, the Muslim Brotherhood and Maududi have had a significant impact especially after some student volunteers returned from assisting the mujahedeen in Afghanistan, in the 1980s. All the same, conservative forces have also met much resistance from Islamic NGOs like Rahima, associated with the largest Muslim organisation in Indonesia, the Nahdlatul Ulama. Rahima opposes patriarchal interpretations of Shari'a, and seeks to have influence through education, especially in poor rural areas, for example, in Java.

In a country like the UK, it needs to be made clear to conservative clerics, like Haitham Haddad, that their discriminatory and patriarchal versions of Islam are optional *in Islamic terms*, that religion needs to be always in dialogue with the state and that Islam, in any form, cannot operate without regard to state rules. The state in its turn has every reason to disallow 'under the radar' practices that discriminate against women. Persuasion, rather than coercion, is always to be preferred, and the waters would be much less muddy in a situation where the Church of England was disestablished and in which no special privilege was accorded to any religious body whatsoever. As equal citizens in the UK, Muslims, alongside everyone else, should contribute to British values, and should not be 'othered' by some procrustean notion of what those values are, independent of, and prior to, the contribution that British Muslims make. Any other approach is, in effect, to make British Muslims 'secondary' citizens. Instead, British Muslims, as equal citizens, have their equality logically tied to the equality of women, and as citizens they have to accept not simply a democracy that mandates gender equality, but a much needed deliberative democracy, that eschews a ghettoisation of lifestyle and values, in favour of intercultural exchange.

The hostile, totalising approach taken towards Islam and preached by evangelical atheists, like Sam Harris, builds further divisions between Muslims and the West. It alienates Muslims who belong in the US, in Britain and in the rest of Europe, and its stereotypes are the building blocks of prejudice founded on the mistaken belief that Islam is simple and monolithic. This is, as we have seen, false. The resources to overcome the discrimination and misogyny to be found within Islam, that is most effective, does, and will, need to come from within Islam, especially in Muslim majority countries. And this is a part of the contest that is integral to Islam today. This contest can, and should, be supported by non-Muslims, both to diminish tribalisms across boundaries, but also in the belief that an egalitarian Islam is possible having a valid basis in Islamic sources, and in modern and ancient exegesis.

8

Islam Today: The Making And Countering Of Militancy

We saw in Chapter 6 about the Qur'an and the Hadith that there is militant potential in these texts but that in themselves they fail to explain the rise in Islamic militancy in recent decades. This last chapter in our case study of Islam aims to give us our bearings about issues of militancy within Islam. In particular, I shall seek to identify how far religious factors cumulatively and more generally have been a driving force behind militancy, and how far largely non-religious factors are decisive in understanding these developments. We shall also consider the claim that Islam has and continues to be an important counter to belligerence.

I shall begin by first setting out a wide range of factors and perspectives that have played a role in the rise of Islamic militancy in recent times. Some of these are non-religious in character while others in part implicate religion, specifically Islam in the way that they have played out. This sets the scene and gives a context against which we can, secondly, examine how far theological concepts such as jihad and the categories of the House of Islam/Dar al Islam and the House of War/Dar al Harb are the main drivers towards militancy. In turn we shall then be better informed to, thirdly, understand and evaluate attitudes within Islam towards militancy, specifically terrorism and suicide bombing.

Accounts of the Rise of Islamic Militancy in Recent Times

The following contributory accounts of the rise of militancy within Islam need to be seen cumulatively and in correspondence with each other. The first four factors are largely non-religious descriptions of its ascent.

i. Colonialisms And Neo-Colonialisms:

Historically we should mention two developments: first, aspects of colonial rule that have played their part in augmenting Islamist resistance and second, neo-colonialist interventions as the West has continued to influence and dominate much of the Middle East. Let's turn to the first of these factors.

Following the annexation of Algeria by France in 1834, Britain seized Aden on the Arabian peninsula in 1839 and went on to occupy Egypt in 1882. Historian and writer, William Dalrymple recounts how the British empire similarly plundered and wrought havoc in Afghanistan in the nineteenth century.[296] In India at that time key Islamic Salafi thinkers like Jamal ad Din Al Afghani witnessed British imperialism at its worst. Like Gandhi who when asked what he thought of Western civilisation retorted that 'it would be a good idea', Al Afghani was unimpressed with the British. He began to look back to Muhammad's community in Medina and saw, as he imagined it, an ethnically non-hierarchical polity, the opposite of the British Raj. Al Afghani saw Islam as the only socio-political identity that might be able to resist the British, and resist too the propaganda of imperialist writers like James Mill who advised British officers about to set sail of the 'perfidious character' of the Indians and how India had made 'but a few of the earliest steps in the progress of civilisation.'[297] What comes across again and again is that British, French and US propagation of the virtues of rationality and the Enlightenment, went hand in hand with imperialist brutality rather than civilisation. In response to the 1857 uprising in Delhi, British forces ravaged most major Indian cities. British soldiers in Allahabad killed everyone in their path and razed Lucknow and

Delhi to the ground. 'It took two years of plunder and carnage for full colonial control to be restored.'[298] In 1904 France secretly split Morocco with Spain. Following the collapse of the Ottoman Empire after World War I, the League of Nations agreed Britain's right to keep its armies in the region and to rule Transjordan and Iraq, while France received the rights to Lebanon and Syria. Britain and France had privately agreed this rough division of territory contrary to prior agreements with the Arabs who had been promised land that stretched from Persia to the Mediterranean in return for their services in fighting the Ottoman Turks. By 1943 the US under Roosevelt had concluded that not only was the Middle East vital to US defence, but that the region's oil reserves should come under US control indefinitely.[299] Against this background we begin to see why key Islamic ideologues like Maududi equated Western secularism with exploitation. He objected to the British use of Muslims as civil servants for the British during the Raj. In India Maududi helped set up the ultimately militant Jamaat i Islami. Meanwhile in Egypt, in the 1940s, the founder of the Muslim Brotherhood, Hasan al Banna (1906 - 1949) sought to harness Islam against colonialism organising it into a series of paramilitary cells influenced in part by fascist and communist organisations from the 1930s.

The second factor we are considering here is neo-colonialist intervention. Surveying the post-colonial era in the Middle East, France failed to live up to its cherished values of democracy when in Algeria in 1992 a secularist coup, supported by France, ousted the democratically elected Islamic National Salvation Front resulting in civil war. The post-colonial era has of course been the heyday of US Middle Eastern intervention. The journalist and writer, Abdel Bari Atwan in his book *The Islamic State: The Digital Caliphate* points out that the US has intervened in the affairs of fourteen predominantly Muslims countries since 1980. These are Iran, Libya, Lebanon, Kuwait, Iraq, Somalia, Bosnia, Saudi Arabia, Afghanistan, Sudan, Kosovo, Yemen, Pakistan and Syria.[300] In addition, however, to offering reason for resistance to the West, the US in the 1980s and 1990s also supplied training, expertise and arms to Islamist groups giving them support in Afghanistan, Iraq, Libya and Syria before then turning against them. As is well known the CIA funded and armed the mujahedeen in Afghanistan against the Soviets between 1982 and 1992. Reza Aslan writes 'they were trained in terror tactics [in Pakistan] and indoctrinated with a militant combination of [Islamist] religio-political ideology and Wahhabism's radical Puritanism, all under the supervision of the then CIA chief William Casey.'³⁰¹

The Soviet Union played no small part in feeding the development of jihadism. I spoke to Professor Pervez Hoodbhoy about the Soviet invasion of Afghanistan in 1979. Professor Hoodbhoy, a significant public figure in Pakistan, said that, in his view, the Soviet invasion of Afghanistan was a turning point in paving the way towards the global jihadism we have today. It acted as a magnet for those who sought to fight for Islam who then became career jihadists, moving from one theatre of war to another as a succession of conflicts ignited across the Middle East in the last decades of the twentieth century and up to the present day.

In 1990-91, during the First Gulf War, the US inspired further anti-Western sentiment following its bombing campaigns in Iraq and its strict regime of sanctions upon the country. Saddam Hussein judged that his best response was to now encourage Islamic militancy - that he had so far repressed - so long as it was focused against the West.

Following the atrocities of 9/11, US President George W. Bush's 'global war on terror' was seen and felt by many Muslims, especially in the Middle East as a war against Islam. Bush's response to 9/11 took shape on three fronts as he invaded Afghanistan in October 2001 in pursuit of the Taliban and Al-Qaeda, supported Israel's suppression of the Second Palestinian Intifada (2000 – 2005) and invaded Iraq in March 2003. The aftermath of this Second Gulf War though did not feel very much like liberation for many Iraqis despite the image touting frenzy around the toppling of the statue of Saddam Hussein within the Western propaganda war. As US personnel led by Paul Bremer (Chief administrator of the Coalition Provisional Authority) privatised the state-owned oil fields, doling out the booty to friends and acquaintances, the US army uprooted orchards, bulldozed homes and destroyed the infrastructure upon which many Iraqi civilians depended. This strengthened the resolve of Islamist belligerents and gave more weight to an anti-Americanism and an anti-Westernism that they remarkably failed to comprehend and less remarkably failed to contain. In fact, as news about detainment without trial and the humiliation and torture at Abu Graib came to public attention, all that was needed was for Nouri Al Maliki to take over as Iraqi president in 2008 and dismiss all Sunni Muslim personnel - some of whom were highly skilled and well trained military operatives - and the ingredients for a powerful Islamist militant movement were assembled. Now unemployed, ISIL was delighted to pay these people well to work for an alternative dark side. Torture was also an effective recruiting sergeant in Abu Graib, radicalising characters like Abu Bakr Al Baghdadi who in 2010 became emir of ISIL.

Against this background of colonialism and neo-colonialism a more insidious colonisation has been resented in much of the Muslim world leading to a strong desire to assert an independent Islamic identity in a variety of ways. The media from all forms of advertising and commerce to film, pornography and what is seen as Western propaganda is perceived as a special threat to the Muslim mind and soul, beckoning the young away from the ties of tradition and family, cultural history and religious identity. Supplementing the physical assault of Western powers media colonialism is a profound irritant, raising the ire of belligerents and non-belligerents alike as they fail to come to terms with the asymmetries and, as they see it, the injustices of globalised media.

ii. Israel

Integral to the narrative of colonialism and neo-colonialism is the issue of Israel and the war that led to its founding in 1948. We noted in Chapter 3 how this is known among Palestinians and many Muslims as the catastrophe, the Nakbah. This war and the forced removal of Palestinians from their homes created the refugee populations that still surround Israel today. Estimates of the number of people who became refugees at this time vary; a rough figure is about 711,000.[302] Many Muslims worldwide identify themselves with Palestinians - most of whom are Muslims – since they see them as part of the global Muslim community or *umma*. The continued backing of Israel, especially by the US, is therefore experienced as an on-going injustice by the worldwide Muslim community as a whole. As such, this support is a perpetual source of bitterness and anger that reinforces a communal bereavement and victimhood within the *umma*. US support in particular has been consistent despite the fact that Israel has contravened and continues to flout international law in its building of settlements in the West Bank, and regardless of Israel's disproportionate use of force within the region. For example, in the second Lebanon war in July – August 2006 Israeli retaliation against Lebanon for a handful of Israeli soldiers killed would seem to have been excessive. According to Human Rights Watch 'the conflict resulted in at least 1109 Lebanese deaths, the vast majority of whom were civilians.'[303] It also led to the displacement of 1 million people within southern Lebanon. Human Rights Watch was also highly critical of Hezbollah's indiscriminate rocket attacks on Israel but noted that in this conflict as a whole these resulted in 55 Israeli deaths. Again in 2008, in response to Hamas rocket attacks that killed 13 Israelis, Israeli assaults on Gaza resulted in 1417 Palestinian civilian fatalities including 313 children. It also led to the displacement of tens of thousands of Palestinians in the Gaza Strip.[304] Avi Shlaim, himself an Israeli and Professor of International Relations at Oxford University, wrote at this time 'Israel has an utterly unscrupulous set of leaders…it is a rogue state…its aim is not peaceful co-existence but military domination'[305], a view with which Jewish groups such as *Jews For Justice For Palestinians* would very much agree. Palestinian resentment that develops into militancy has in turn fuelled further belligerence from a series of hardline Israeli governments. Islamism has, among its many causes, grown out of these circumstances of political violence. It should be made clear, however, that Palestinian resistance to Israel has often not been particularly Islamic in character. As we identified in Chapter 3, the Palestinian Liberation Organisation was rooted in nationalism and socialism rather than in Islam.[306] The emergence of Hamas, on the other hand, has clear links with the Islamism of Egypt's Sayyid Qutb and his belligerent follower Muhammad Abd Al Salam Faraj (1954 – 1982).

iii. War As A Catalyst Of Militancy

The case of Israel fits with the view that acts of Islamist terrorism tend to occur in what are already theatres of war or conflict. We shall later consider how far Islamic ideologies lead to militancy. But for now - considering non-religious factors - it is important to ask the equally pertinent question how far does war and conflict lead to the rise in these ideologies.[307]

Professor Michael Howard, founder of the War Studies Department at King's College London, was convinced that war was a key engine of change in history at every level. What has also arisen in recent times is the concept of intellectual history as distinct from the history of ideas. Whereas the history of ideas has seen the thought of a given time and place as essentially a response to the thought that preceded it, intellectual history by contrast sees ideas as fundamentally rooted in events. The amplification of events through medias, the internet and social media adds strength to this view and means that we need to look at the narrative of recent Middle Eastern wars as much as a cause of militancy as an effect.

In his extremely informative text *Salafi-Jihadism*, Dr. Shiraz Maher, Director of the International Centre for the Study of Radicalisation and Political Violence (ICSR) at King's College, London, makes clear that the development of three key concepts within militant Islamism have grown in a distinctly belligerent direction 'as a response to war and crisis.'[308] Maher takes the example of the concept *al-wala'wa-l-bara* that means most basically 'loyalty and disavowal' for the sake of Allah. Such vagueness in meaning, though, has offered great latitude for interpretation as we saw to be the case more broadly with the Qur'an and Hadith in Chapters 6 and 7. According to the political needs of time and place the *al-wala'wa-l-bara* doctrine has been forged in a variety of directions. Before its militant usage it referred largely to Muslim distinctiveness for example in dress, in greeting others and in performing festivals. Muhammad ibn Abd al-Wahhab (1703 - 1792), however, in his aggressive opposition to the Ottomans marshalled the phrase so as to polarise Islam. He set out his specifically puritanical version of the faith to defy and combat all other available forms of Islam, most especially Ottoman Sufism. Anyone who did not align with his thinking was to be disavowed. To love the good involved hating what is not Islam by his definition. Radicalising the doctrine of *al wala'wa-l-bara* further, Abu Muhammad al-Magdisi wrote *Milat Ibrahim* in 1984. Written in part while fighting the Soviets in Afghanistan al-Magdisi gave the doctrine of *al-wala'wa-l-bara* a further twist. It comes to mean more than simply disavowing or even hating evil. It is not enough to hate what is not Muslim because it would be more hateful to demonstrate this through militancy since the teaching evolved to say the more you hate the evil the more you will love the good. The logic is therefore that taking up arms is a demonstration of your love for Allah.

Anything less means that your love for Allah is insufficient.

A further case where a doctrine has taken on a distinctly belligerent character has been in the development of the notion of *takfir* during the Algerian civil war that, as we have seen, began in the 1990s and cost 200,000 lives. Scott Atran points out how, in this war, one way to justify killing civilians who claimed to be fellow Muslims was by engineering the doctrine of *takfir* to do the job. Roughly *takfir* means to excommunicate, to judge someone a non-Muslim, which then - in league with militant radicalised concepts of 'jihad' - means that they may be killed. We see again the growth of militancy within theological doctrines to meet the needs of belligerents within specific theatres of war.[309] The doctrine of *takfir* had certainly been used for aggressive purposes in the past, by Al Wahhab, and also by the Kharijites within the first generation of Muslims. However, rather than being a source of protection for the Muslim community from intra-Muslim strife - as it often operated in more peaceable times - in times of conflict *takfir* becomes used for the opposite purpose of generating division and belligerence.

Perhaps the key example that Maher gives of the shaping of theological doctrine in a hostile direction to meet the needs of war, is the case of *tatarrus* or human shields. Needless to say, the Qur'an says nothing about *tatarrus*. All the same, when unable to fight an enemy in open warfare, Salafi-Jihadist groups such as Al- Qaeda, have seen the killing of civilians as part of their war of terror and integral to their propaganda. How they then justify what they do - given a history in which civilians are not to be killed and certainly not intentionally - leads to the kind of theological recalibration we have been witnessing. Maher concludes about the killing of *tatarrus*/human shields 'the exigencies of war have proved to be a driver of theological change.'[310] A further indication that war gives rise to militant theological development, as much as if not more than the other way around, is that those operational in the field seem to hold the most belligerent versions of such doctrines as *takfir* and *al-wala'wa-l-bara*. Less hostile understandings of such teachings prevail among those not engaged in the front line.[311]

Two additional points should be made here both of which we have alluded to but they need more emphasis.

First, repression and specifically the torture of people has led to militancy and to the radicalisation of key figures within Islam. Abou El Fadl points out a number of figures who, having been tortured, became radicalised, Sayyid Qutb in Egypt, about whom more will be said in a moment, is perhaps the most famous example of this. The incarceration of many other members of the Muslim Brotherhood by President Gamal Abdel Nasser taught the Muslim Brotherhood that forms of quietist Sufism would have no effect in reinvigorating Islam in Egypt in the face of Nasser's repression, so they became militant. Abou El Fadl also mentions further influential figures who through torture became radicalised including Salih Saraya (ultimately executed in 1975), and Shukri Mustafa (executed in 1978) who was very much inspired by Qutb. The repressions of the Syrian regime in 1982 had a similar effect on the Muslim Brotherhood there as was also the case in Saudi Arabia. The despotic secular nationalisms of Iraq and Libya have had the same kind of consequences over the last thirty years.[312] Besides the well attested point that torture all too often desensitises its victims to violence[313] puritanism in one form or another is a refuge for people suffering extreme hardship including torture. If the demands that you make upon yourself outstrip the pain inflicted by another, then that pain can be contained and possibly even transformed as part of one's own narrative of honour and heroism. If there is a cause beyond oneself one is not being tortured alone but for the sake of something worthwhile, a companion in your own mind that never leaves you. Of course when released from torture where can the fortitude and grit within the human spirit find traction in the outside world more than on the battlefield, facing death? Torture is a rite of passage that ensures the victim is battle ready and battle worthy; it perfects in many ways the spirit of the soldier and the martyr.

Secondly, successive wars have given rise to the 'career militant' who has earned a living from being hired to fight in a succession of arenas. Word gets round among the disenfranchised, the unemployed and those inspired by an opposition to injustice that there is a cause awaiting their allegiance and loyalty, their life and death. In a far off land their ultimate destiny awaits and they will also get paid in self respect and honour as well as money. Militant Islamism is the ideology at large in this narrative in the way that communism and anarchism have been in past centuries but belligerent Islamism and career militancy would not have been so able to gain a foothold were it not for wars in Afghanistan, the Balkans, Algeria, Chechnya, Iraq and Syria that are largely the product of foreign invasion, intra-ethnic conflict or totalitarian dictators seeking to maintain their grip on power rather than Islamism in its own right. A highly selective sketch of such a militant's curriculum vitae begins perhaps in Afghanistan in the 1980s following the Soviet invasion in 1979. Bosnia in the Balkan wars of the early 1990s, offered further opportunities for engagement while there was always fighting to be done in Algeria at this time as we have seen. Following the Russian invasion of Chechnya, the first Chechnyan war between 1994 and 1996 recruited significant numbers of militants too and they found a further opportunity to fight in the second Chechnyan war in 1999. Meanwhile Al-Qaeda sought recruits for its various operations in Kenya, Tanzania and Yemen. US strikes on Afghanistan in 2001 offered yet more opportunities for combat for much of that decade and Saddam Hussein's attempt to recruit jihadists against the US and its allies led to further opportunities in 2003 that were made all the greater by the rise of ISIS and the civil war in Syria. The fall and death of Muammar Gaddafi in Libya in October 2011 offered prospects too for the formation of a satellite of IS well armed with pickings from Gaddafi's arsenal. When Al Baghdadi declared the establishment of the ISIS Caliphate from Mosul mosque in July 2014 yet more recruits joined. An estimate of the numbers recruited to ISIS in 2014 stood at about 30,000. The point is that these various wars with their accompanying career militants have inspired aggressive jihadism at least as much as the other way around.

iv. Youth Psychology

One thing that politicians and the media seem utterly perplexed about is the attraction of jihadism for some aspects of Muslim youth. There seems to me an image problem here. Politicians and the media need to put across an utter lack of comprehension about such things or at least they need to fain this, since to understand and explain radicalisation can all too easily be spun by media opponents as justifying or condoning it – which of course would be a public relations disaster. Yet explaining radicalisation and condoning it are of course quite distinct.[314]

By examining the paths leading towards radicalisation that we have so far outlined we can make a lot of sense of why some Muslims have become militant. It is of particular interest that most Muslims who have become radicalised across a variety of cultures tend to be young.[315] So what is it about some elements of Muslim youth that leads them towards militancy that is to do with the youthful mind? Elements of Muslim youth, it would seem, both in the UK and elsewhere in the West, have often been brought up betwixt two cultures; a Muslim culture in which they sometimes have little or no say, and an outside, wider culture that can easily feel alienating and agoraphobic. A deference to older generations dis-empowers them in their local community at times while strictures, for example, about alcohol and fasting keep them at a distance from much Western youth into which they may struggle to entirely integrate. Caught between identities, and pushed towards conforming in either direction, which at points is impossible, the option of rebelling against both cultures can seem appealing.

The German philosopher Frederick Nietzsche remarked with both prescience and derision that 'the last of men live only for a pitiable comfort', that in modern times there has been a loss of heroism, of things for which to live and die as we retreat into a variety of self chosen narcissisms buying our freedom at the cost of identities and commitments that reach beyond ourselves. The youth generations from the 1960s onwards have in a number of ways encapsulated this type of life. A rebelliousness has come to the fore that has tended to eschew traditional community commitments in favour of individual choice alongside various modes of hedonism and self definition. A rebellion of today - in order to make its mark - needs again to turn against what has gone before and militant Islamism fits the bill quite well. It condemns and rails against the West while it also sneers at an obstructive paternalistic Islam that will keep a younger generation in its place to wait its turn. In this way it is also continuous with a Western 'doing your own thing', and here the jihadist while rejecting the West also doesn't feel 'left out.' Yet this youthful rebellion also involves claiming the moral high ground in every direction through its lens of puritanical self-righteousness - drawing upon the idea of moral payback from fragments of the colonialist and neo-colonialist narrative we have seen. It involves admonishing parents for being too docile and not angry enough about the oppression of Muslims. Such elements of Muslim youth then find others like them - a community - that thinks the same, and the gravitational pull towards an evolving identity starts to gather pace. Add in the vocation to save your faith and bolt on an ISIS ideology that beckons you to be there at the end of time on the winning side of the final battles and a natural youthful hunger for adventure coalesces with compensations in terms of self-esteem and identity that only the convert knows. The average age of women travelling to Syria to join ISIS from the UK and France in recent years is 19 – 20. Reasons that such women have given for leaving to join ISIS include dealing with often restrictive home lives in conservative families and avoiding arranged marriages they don't like. Disinclined to believe Western media reports about ISIS, they imagine the grass can only be greener there.

In support of these points counter-terrorist adviser Dr. Marc Sageman makes clear that 78% of terrorist attacks in the West are 'home grown.'[316] Sageman adds that the tendency has been for some youth to 'seek out radical preachers rather than vice versa.' Scott Atran's research supports the point too that youth peer pressure is invariably pivotal. Many, while not all of course, who become radicalised, are also recent 'converts', not those who have been brought up within Islam. Much has been written about the psychology of religious conversion. Two central claims within such writings are first, that the new convert is vulnerable and second that conversion and a re-orientation of values is of a piece with adolescent psychological development.[317] In other words to re-orientate ones values sometimes radically is within the normal spectrum of what adolescents do.

The remaining factors that account for the rise of militancy refer more specifically to Islam.

v. Islamic Reformations

We need to look back to the nineteenth century at least in order to bring into focus the titanic changes that have occurred within the worlds of Islam - including the rise of militancy - within recent times. Changes that began then have sometimes been referred to as an Islamic reformation. Western colonisation led to the demise of the Islamic law schools; lawyers trained in Western law took over and when countries such as Egypt gained their independence, centres for the study of Shar'ia such as Al Ahzar University in Cairo became state owned and the role of jurists became restricted to leading prayers and at most serving

THE MAKING AND COUNTERING OF MILITANCY   201

as judges in personal law courts away from considerations about jurisprudence. Many Shar'ia schools closed down and by the 1960s there were few new jurists and those that there were, were poorly trained to the point of no longer being legal experts.[318] This process, replicated across much of the Muslim world, left a vacuum in religious authority that has been filled by a range of mainly Salafi self-appointed experts that parallels, at least superficially, the plethora of protestantisms and fundamentalisms that have come to fruition in Europe and America since the sixteenth century. Significantly this religious power vacuum developed shortly following the colonial era and was also seen by religious conservatives to be the consequence of yet another form of oppression, the post-colonial state with its attendant ideologies of nationalism and secularism, hostile to Islam. In these circumstances the selection of militancy from the Qur'an and Hadith by a minority of Salafis has appealed; it has been less constrained in an age where the interpretation of the primary texts is more than ever up for grabs.

vi. Hypermedia, the Internet and Social Media

Various types of media have been a means of advertising and idealising the life of the militant as well as promoting the cause. Dr. Fraser Egerton in his *Jihad in the West: the Rise of Militant Salafism* has made the case that the rise of militant Islam in the West following the wars in Afghanistan and Iraq is greatly inspired by what he calls hypermedia. Explaining this further, Egerton writes specifically about the dissemination of images of torture, footage of the killing of civilians in coalition bombings and drone strikes and pictures of the abuse of inmates in Guantanamo and Abu Graib detention centres. Images of such atrocities against Muslims are readily available and easily used as polemic to incite hatred and violence. They unite a minority of Muslims in a fraternity of victimhood and collective anger and reach out through their visual impact beyond the limits of any specific language. Such images were, for example, orchestrated as part of programmes of indoctrination by, for example, Abu Hamza at Finsbury Park Mosque. Egerton points out that of the 186 files recovered from the Madrid bombers in 2004, only 19 related to logistics and secrecy. All the rest were about propaganda, inspiring others to get involved, showing Chechnyan Muslims being driven over by tanks and thereby reinforcing the message of Muslims as a victimised global community. Hypermedia makes available a collective consciousness, in this case of victimhood and anger. Sociologist and Michael Ramsey Professor of Modern Theology at the University of Kent, Gordon Lynch, has looked into this kind of phenomena further and researched the question, 'what makes some violent images pass from people's short term to long term memories', and found that identification with the victims of violence is a key factor.

Whereas the puritanical Taliban were repulsed by technology; they smashed TV's and regarded the advance of global media as the 'Westoxification' of Islam and the world, Al-Qaeda, by contrast, began its own online news service *The Voice of the Caliphate* in 2005.[319] Anwar al-Awlaki, dubbed the 'bin Laden of the internet', created his own blog, facebook page and YouTube channel to promote *Inspire,* his radicalising online magazine while working with AQAP (Al-Qaeda in the Arabian Peninsula)[320] encouraging lone wolf attacks. ISIS have also developed jihadist networks in English and Chinese. Scott Atran notes how the internet 'now allows anyone who wishes to become a terrorist to become one, anywhere, anytime.'[321] It is also true that ISIS was, at its height, the richest terrorist organisation in history both as a result of oil, but also due to its trade in bitcoins!

Hypermedia as a factor is more an account of how Islamist militancy has been proliferated than spawned. It is part of the explanation of the global character of Islamism. It adds to the socio-psychological account of the amplification and traction that militant Islamism can and does have in places, but in itself it leaves unexplained the rise of Islamism before this factor took hold in the new millennium and it would seem not to be the main account of its continued generation. For these things we need to look to some of the other factors mentioned and not dismiss out of hand the view that militant Islamism is best explained and understood as part of the wider mainstream Islamic body politic - which is why this factor does not particularly point away from Islam in the way that some of the previous factors would appear to do.

What has been outlined so far in this chapter is not an attempt to exonerate Islam from charges of playing a key role in the process of radicalisation. Rather the factors that we have so far identified to be at work within developing Islamic militancy should make us alert to some of the complexities at issue, aware of cross-currents of explanation and more concerned to examine these than draw cursory conclusions. Against this background we shall now examine claims that despite the wide range of factors so far identified, key long held Islamic teaching is still at the heart of any reasonable explanation of militancy.

Are Key Islamic Teachings At The Heart Of Explanations Of Radicalisation?

We have seen how in various ways teachings such as *al-wala'wa-l-bara*, *takfir* and *tatarrus* have mutated in a matter of decades to have a radical and then militant set of implications. There are those who argue, however, that some Islamic teachings have always been belligerent and that these are therefore the drivers of militancy. As such the rest of the explanatory paraphernalia that I have so far set out merely orbits these primary militant principles. Let's look at some of these alleged innate militancies to see how far such claims are true. We shall look again at the Qur'an and Hadith here. But we are looking now at the trajectories of specific concepts and principles that may or may not have their origins there and not at the general tenor of those texts as we were in the Chapter 6.

Jihad

The first such principle is that of jihad. From its origins in the Qur'an and Hadith this concept is the subject of much dispute. Jihad is the verbal noun related to the verb 'jahada' meaning to endeavour, to strive, to struggle towards a commendable aim. It is distinct from the word 'qital' to fight. Much is made of the distinction between the greater jihad and the lesser jihad based on the questionable hadith attributed to Muhammad on returning from a military campaign 'we have now returned from the lesser jihad to the greater jihad.' Many seeking to downplay the aggressive character of jihad as a concept emphasise that the 'greater jihad' is the real focus of jihad and this is an inner striving for closeness to Allah, an aligning of intention along the straight path to him. This pious and in some quarters mystical path has not been, and is not now, marginal within Islam.[322] The life of prayer and fasting and, for example, of hospitality to the stranger is a struggle to love God within the everyday life of very many ordinary Muslims. We should note too that the idea of a greater jihad is not Qur'anic, while Asma Afsaruddin remarks that it is very well grounded in the Qur'anic concept of 'sabr' or patient forbearance. However I would agree with Rudolf Peters who writes that in about two thirds of cases where the word jihad and its cognates are used in the Qur'an it denotes warfare.[323]

Muhammad too seems to be involved in twenty seven or so raids and his Muslim followers, at that time, a further fifty. Jihad is to be distinguished from 'razzia' - pre-Islamic raids that tribes made against each other. By contrast with these, jihad had a religious motivation, to defend Islam but also to spread it and convert the unbeliever. As such some have identified jihad with holy war[324] and this has often been how 'jihad' has been translated. Many Muslim scholars reject the connotations implicit here too. Abou El Fadl, for example, makes the point that Islam has never had the concept of holy war in the sense of divinely ordained militancy validated by a central institutional authority like the papacy. It just hasn't had anything parallel with such an institution. While this is a sound point, not least about the pitfalls of the now dated discipline of 'comparative religion', Islam does have in the form of jihad, a mandate to fight that is religious. Jihad must be led by a religious leader who is acknowledged by the Muslim community - albeit with various restrictions attached - such as not killing Muslims or non-combatants, not destroying vegetation and livestock and, according to some authorities, not fighting at night. Abou El Fadl points out too that the further Qur'anic qualifications about fighting almost always include the need for restraint, to forgive and to seek peace. Whatever we make of such qualifications though, we should be clear that jihad as the waging of war, both defensively and offensively against resistant non-believers, is a central while not undisputed meaning of jihad in the original sources.[325]

As such, for all the variety of interpretation to which the Qur'an is open, a militant interpretation, as well as more irenic ones, has accompanied Islam throughout most of its history and, with the spread of empire, offensive jihad was seen as an Islamic mandate based on texts such as Surah 9: 5. Martyrdom in battle, as a fast-track to paradise, acted as an additional Islamic imperative and the lightning speed with which the Islamic empire developed was, for many, miraculous confirmation of providential support.

As the four law schools developed and we move into the age of classical Islam, jurists also suggested to emperors to lead one conquest a year, at least to keep the idea of jihad alive - it could always be useful. This is a good example, in addition to what we have seen already, of religiously originated and inspired militancy.

Continuing to emphasise this kind of militancy as normative, Dr. David Cook, Associate Professor of the History of Islam at Rice University in Texas, in his book *Understanding Jihad*, claims that with the rise of non-militant Salafism in the nineteenth century we have for the first time a reformist Muslim scholar, in Sayyid Ahmad Khan, who emphasises the idea of a purely defensive jihad. This, says Cook, is quite new. This perspective, though, is too emphatic. Abou El Fadl reports that, following the twelfth century, when very influential jurists such as Ibn Kathir extolled the virtues of offensive jihads, that the majority of Muslim jurists had opposed such jihads against unbelievers. In terms of the track records of Muslim emperors there are extremes - of both tolerance and militancy. Most famously the Moghul emperor Akbar celebrated peaceful co-existence between Islam, Christianity, Hinduism and other faiths besides. Not long after his rule, however, the emperor Aurangzeb won himself a reputation for being, what today we might call, an Islamist militant of the first order.

It is worth being clear about what an offensive jihad amounted to in practice for non-Muslims, compared with what being conquered by many non-Muslim empires meant for a civilian population. Non-Muslim civilians who were conquered by Muslim empires were, by and large, left in peace, and offered a fair degree of protection against others, so long as they did not offer violent resistance, and so long as they paid the required *jizyah* poll tax. Looking back across the centuries the Islamic scholar Hamilton Gibb writes about Islam:

> "It possesses a magnificent tradition of inter-racial understanding and cooperation. No other society has such a record of success uniting in an equality of status, of opportunity, and of endeavours, so many and so various races of mankind."[326]

More recently, Bernard Lewis - not known for his sympathy towards Islam - has written,

'Until the seventeenth century, there can be no doubt that, all in all, the treatment by Muslim governments and populations of those who believed otherwise was more tolerant and respectful than was normal in Europe...there is nothing in Islamic history to compare with the massacres and expulsions, the inquisitions and persecutions that Christians habitually inflicted on non-Christians, and still more on each other. In the lands of Islam, persecution was the exception; in Christendom sadly, it was often the norm.'[327]

Of course there were persecutions of non-Muslims who had been conquered by Muslim empires, but Muslim empires seem to have behaved actually better than their non-Muslim counterparts. Marshall Hodgson in his epic work on Islam *The Venture of Islam*, makes clear that those conquered were sometimes persecuted by their Muslim overlords but that 'rarely can any substantial amount of conversion to Islam in a broad area be ascribed to direct persecution.'[328]

What I want to consider is whether this history of the concept of jihad is the key motivator and explanation of the rise of militancy within Islam in recent years or are the other factors we have observed of greater significance?

To bring this question into perspective, it is worth realising that without concepts of jihad at all, we can still see why there would have been a violent reaction to the Soviet invasion of Afghanistan and Chechnya, and why the Balkans would still have imploded through its ethnic divisions following the demise of the Yugoslavian President Marshal Tito. Without the concept of jihad we can also see why the US invasion of Iraq, followed by the US take-over of its oilfields, might have triggered a militant response, and why the Syrian people would have revolted against the brutality of their President Bashar al-Assad. None of these theatres of war were spawned by Islam, or even by Islamism, but Islam and Islamism have reacted to them. Each of these scenarios supports the view that existing militancy and violence has given rise to the use of militant concepts of jihad in these scenarios, rather than the other way around.

Scott Atran conducted research among Palestinians about their attitudes towards the killing of non-Muslims. 91% of those surveyed believed that Islam did support the killing and the suicide bombing of Israelis in some circumstances. Yet, of that 91% only 4% believed that it was the duty of

Muslims to fight and kill non-Muslims in any general sense. According to Atran the more bellicose interpretations of the Qur'an were not driving their views. Neither did they focus on concepts of jihad. From Atran's interviews, what caused his respondents to say that they thought it was a Muslim's duty to kill Israelis, including by suicide bombing, were basic (non-religious) desires for retaliation within a theatre of asymmetric conflict. So in one of the most violent and fraught parts of the Muslim world the Muslim population today are not it would seem motivated, to any great extent, by offensive concept of jihad against non-Muslims.

Still the idea of jihad has been involved and has evolved throughout the Islamic world during the course of recent crises and military engagements.

At the militant end of the spectrum an offensive jihad is justified and linked very much to the spread of Islam. Sayyid Qutb (d.1966) regarded the spread of Islam as necessary so as to give everyone the choice to follow Islam. His follower Muhammad abd-al-Salam Faraj went further, claiming that jihad would for sure lead to the conversion of all to Islam thus pressing it as an imperative, alongside the re-establishment of the Caliphate. Faraj finds reason to kill Muslims - according to his extended concept of jihad - moving against centuries' old juridical prohibitions about this. For him, those who oppress Muslims are themselves only nominal Muslims, and may therefore be killed. Faraj thought that the time for the greater jihad was over - it was obsolete. This combative milieu within the Muslim Brotherhood and within the writings of Qutb and Faraj went hand in hand with their incarceration. Qutb was horrifically tortured, for example, by the Nasser regime. The film maker Adam Curtis tells us the story of how he was stripped naked, covered in animal fat in a cell and set upon by dogs. Following his subsequent heart attack he recovered to write *Milestones* and *In the Shade of the Qur'an*. His writings grew in militancy, but he also became a hero, and *Milestones* sold millions of copies worldwide. What Qutb could not come to terms with was how a purportedly Islamic government could turn on fellow Muslims like himself with such brutality. The only way he could think this through was by reasoning that Nasser and his government were not Muslim after all. They thought they were, but they had deceived themselves and others. Qutb, influenced significantly by Maududi in Pakistan, saw Nasser as having regressed to a time of ignorance (*jahilliyah*), parallel to the time before Muhammad from which Muhammad, as the great exemplar, had sought and achieved liberation. As such, it was a Muslim's duty to overthrow Nasser's secularist regime, for whose attempted assassination Qutb was executed in 1966. What begins to emerge in these postcolonial times of the 1960s is a puritanical way of imagining and dividing humanity; there are real Muslims, non-Muslims and an especially problematic category of those apparent Muslims who are actually hypocrites and deceivers. To excommunicate/takfir this third group becomes an imperative for such evolving jihadists.[329] Here we see the doctrine of takfir and jihad brought together and bonded in part through the brutality of Nasser's regime and twinned with the militancy that lies within the history of jihad itself. The idea of jihad, however, does not evolve of its own accord in this instance. In keeping with the idea of intellectual history it gains traction through events and in this case through the writings and the dissemination of people who have been brutalised and turned militant.

Qutb and Faraj did not directly inspire a global jihad for all that their militant concepts of jihad looked ultimately towards global liberation. A number of scholars make clear that the transition to the concept of a global jihad only really gained traction in Afghanistan following the Soviet invasion in 1979.

Consistent with what we have seen so far, that war and violence radicalise theology more than the other way around, the Afghan war initiated by the Soviets took the concept of jihad to another level. It gave it renewed global pretentions now that it was pitted against a global military force. David Cook writes that Afghanistan at this time was the incubator of global radicalism. An aggressive Islamism evolved in response to the Soviet invasion, binding together people beyond the limits of kinship and tribe in the face of a common enemy. There were of course key figures that helped develop the notion of a global jihad such as the Palestinian Abdallah Azzam, for whom as Cook puts it 'warfare was salvific'.[330] Still it is within theatres of war that Azzam developed and most successfully propagated these views. The concept of jihad, like the concepts of takfir and tatarrus that we have already observed, became more belligerent, and more popular, and kept that character, following conflict. Ideologies of jihad continued to evolve alongside the career jihadists as they moved from one theatre of war to the next, deriving from, and giving significance to, their lives and deaths.

More mainstream views of jihad within the last fifty years are, however, quite diverse. There are those who emphasise the defensive character of jihad such as the extremely influential conservative scholar Sayyid Abu'l-A'la Mawdudi. More radical figures such as Hammad Al-Ghunaymi and Muslim al-Qadiri see an aggressive jihad as mandated in much classical Islamic scholarship and see no reason to reformulate matters now.[331] Salafis are also divided, circumventing codified law and looking simply at the Qur'an and Hadith. Some regard these original sources to be supportive of a more militant jihad and others do not. For example, Scott Atran takes the view that the most effective opponent of violent jihad is Salafism itself with its potential to see the Qur'an anew - and perhaps through irenic eyes. Asma Afsaruddin argues too that today, in a time of international treaties between nation-states, the default position is one of peace not war, and classical Islamic jurisprudence on jihad is out of date. She reflects the view of many Muslim leaders and scholars, including Muhammad Fethullah Gulen, that in general the time for a violent jihad has passed.

The practice of the greater jihad is also very much alive today while it gains little publicity in a sensationalist oriented media age. It isn't just among Muslim mystics and Sufis that it predominates either. It is, as I suggested earlier, written into the intentions and spirit of the daily practice of Islam by ordinary Muslims. This deserves emphasis because this is an Islam that isn't so visible to the outside world.

The concepts of jihad that have evolved into our times have as often as not been militant and in this sense Islam, its juridical history and the belligerent potential of the earliest sources play their part in that development. All the same, the wide range of non-religious factors that we have identified are decisive. They seem to explain the narrative as to when and how the worst aspects of concepts of jihad have come to the fore. In recent decades, war - invariably not caused by Islam - but involving Muslims, in Muslim majority countries, has been a catalyst for bellicose ideology more than the other way around. This is not to exonerate concepts of jihad. The persistently, if not consistently, militant complexion of this concept, for all the other aspects of it, means that it lies at the ready, in times of threat and tension, to support and offer religious justification for belligerence notwithstanding that, whether it is Afghanistan, Iraq, Bosnia, Chechnya or Palestine, such militancy invariably operates on a political level. The vast majority of Muslims in all these situations have been victims far more than perpetrators, and have drawn upon notions of the greater jihad as a source of inner strength and peace within their own psychological and communal struggles. This is the untold story about jihad; how it has for many ordinary Muslims offered a spiritual option in the face of violence, a place in the soul of solace where, as the Qur'an says, God is closer to you than your jugular vein.

Dar Al Islam And Dar Al Harb

A second principle that has a militant pedigree within Islam is the distinction between Dar al Islam and Dar al Harb, meaning respectively; the 'house' or abode of Islam, and the 'house' or abode of war. These terms do not date back to the Qur'an, while Dar al Islam has been equated by some with the Qur'anic phrase Dar al Salam, or abode of Peace, which is a reference to paradise as found in Surah 10: 25 and 6: 127. These phrases have evolved considerably over time. According to Asma Afsaruddin they evolved to meet the needs of political empire building for many centuries. The realms of Dar al Islam and Dar al Harb reflected respectively those territories so far conquered by Islam and those that remained to be conquered. An intermediate realm developed 'the realm of Truce' (Dar al Sulh/al-Ahd), that non-Muslim nations could sign up to, thereby agreeing to amicable relations with a neighbouring Muslim realm. This was, though, clearly seen as a convenience of empire building before the next phase of expansion. The founder of the Hanafi law school, Abu Hanifa (c.699 – 767CE) developed a series of conditions that needed to be met if territory was to be admitted as part of Dar al Islam, and the Abbasid jurist, al-Shafi'i (767 – 820CE) went on to divide the world into these two mutually hostile realms. Afsaruddin paints al-Shafi'i's view as reflective very much of his time, and as such the Islam he presents is militaristic being engaged with the expansion of empire. We should be careful, though, not to exonerate Islam here by suggesting that militancy has its origins in a purely political source. Yes, politics very much forged Islam in the ninth century, but to the point that politics and Islam were fairly indistinguishable within the Islamicate. As we have seen, Al-Shafi'i was a founder of one of the four main law schools within Islam. As such, he remains a key *religious* figure within Islamic history and his *theological* distinction between Dar al Islam and Dar al Harb has cast a long shadow across many centuries - especially now - as it raises a very ugly head within ISIS and more broadly within jihadist practice and propaganda.

Some scholars have remarked that it has been a sectarian and minority view in the history of Islam to speak purely about the abode of peace and the abode of war; that you have allegiance to an Islamic state but enmity towards anything else. Contrary to this view, however, after al-Shafi'i's pronouncements, those opposing these concepts were not on the winning side and the mantra of Dar al Islam vs. Dar al Harb, continued to be a clarion call within expansionist Islam for many centuries.

Speaking about today, the influential Syrian scholar Wahbah al Zuhayli regards the application of Dar al Islam and Dar al Harb as extremely limited. He writes 'Islamic countries have joined the United Nations covenant that stipulates the relationship between nations is peace not war.'[332] The Islamic scholar Tariq Ramadan writes that according to tradition, where Muslims can practice their faith freely, that is, worship freely and perform the five pillars of Islam, then this is not the abode of war but rather the abode of safety (Dar al-Amn). This sentiment was echoed by an Imam I spoke to at East London mosque who commented that even if there is any validity to the concept of Dar al Harb it certainly does not describe the UK or the US now. He continued, Dar al Harb cannot apply to the UK since Muslims can live here in peace having more freedom to practice their faith than they do in Saudi Arabia. The Leeds based imam, Qari Asim, told me that the distinction between Dar al Harb and Dar al Islam was now blurred beyond recognition. He commented that in an internet age the concept of territory, of place, is fast disappearing and with it, the application of these terms. Ramadan also makes the point that even where Islam is not accepted and not allowed to be practised, a variety of definitions of Dar al Harb show that the existence of an abode of war does not necessarily mean that a state of war exists between the opposing abodes.[333]

Ramadan summarises the situation as follows; jurists in Islam today do not agree about what counts as Dar al Islam. Some say it refers primarily to government; some to the populous as a whole. There are broadly three approaches to the concepts of Dar al Islam and Dar al Harb today: the first approach is to accept some understanding of these concepts as still valid; a second approach is to think instead of non-Muslim countries as the abodes of treaty and the abodes of safety (an approach within the Shafi'i Law School) and the third approach is to reject the concepts of Dar al Islam and Dar al Harb as not at all applicable now.

Nevertheless, parallel with such mainstream Islamic comment, in the worlds of Salafi-jihadism and Wahhabism, the Dar al Islam/Dar al Harb distinction has been taken up with avengeance. As we saw with the development of concepts of jihad, the Dar al Islam/Dar al Harb distinction has been used not simply to justify hostilities, against both combatants and civilians, but also against fellow Muslims. The trick is, once again, as we have seen, in bellicose 'takfiri' fashion to simply decide that a regime and its laws are non-Islamic; this then implies that the populous is non-Islamic. They then become legitimate targets of war and conquest as part of the mission to purify the faith. It is hardly surprising that most victims of Islamist terrorism and attack have been self-confessed fellow Muslims.

The focus on Dar al Islam and Dar al Harb as defining the Islamic world and the West as essentially in conflict, or awaiting conflict, has a long history within Islam but this does not mean that it holds centre stage now. Today this binary division comes from the ideologies and activities of belligerent forms of Salafism and Wahhabism, which are inflammatory in their polarisation of the world. Militant Salafiism seeks to convert mainstream Muslims and others to its cause. It also has some strong financial backing. All the same, the majority of Muslim scholars and ordinary Muslims do not think in these terms. Professor of sociology at Fatih University in Istanbul, Tahir Abbas, writes that today the application of the concept of Dar al Harb to the West as a whole, indeed the application of these concepts at all, is the work of a minority of puritanical Muslim jurists. Nonetheless, the polemics of Salafi belligerents, and radical secularists like Sam Harris, push to the fore this terminology as the consensus view - and this is false. All the same, the history of Islam has laid down lethal ideological tools in the form of these concepts that have been readily picked up by those who are so inclined. While this is the co-option of religion by politics, both now and in the past, it is also true that the Dar al Islam/Dar al Harb binary is a religious category and a theological motivator which, especially in tandem with the takfiri theology of excommunication, has bred militancy. As with other aspects of theology, the most hostile developments of the concept of Dar al Islam and Dar al Harb have taken place in theatres of war where in effect theology and violence have forged a poisonous symbiosis.

Terrorism and Suicide Bombing

Before I consider what relationship if any exists between forms of Islam and the various phenomena of terrorism and suicide bombing directly, a few points about these behaviours should be made.

There are cases for saying in extremis that terrorism and suicide bombing, even where civilians are involved, may be justified it seems to me. I am for example an admirer of those who sought to assassinate Hitler even though a number of such plots would almost certainly have involved the death of civilians. There can be good terrorists. Further examples might include the French resistance during WWII or perhaps those who travelled to Spain in the 1930s to oppose Franco's fascism. Many are happy to grant these kinds of argument. The cases are safely in the past and the stuff of ethics seminars and discussions about forms of utilitarianism, but what about the present or the much more recent past? We have of course been conditioned into not raising the question about whether or not terrorism could ever be right. A teacher discussing this question today in the UK might well find themselves the wrong side of the government's PREVENT policy. Yet the degree to which, and the circumstances in which, terrorism might ever be right is a very pressing ethical question for our time just as it has become taboo.[334] Like many key ethical questions for any given time it is avoided where it most needs to be faced.[335]

Some of the Middle Eastern dictators within the largely Muslim world may or may not compare with the likes of Hitler or Franco, Mussolini or Stalin, within their own arenas, but some of them have been brutally murderous, vindictive and repressive when their regimes were not under direct threat. That many Muslims in the Middle East are rarely, but still sometimes, in favour of terrorism or suicide bombing, having in many cases lived through brutal repression, does not seem to me on all occasions to be a morally outrageous response. I am clearly at odds here with the evangelical Westerner and atheist Sam Harris. By contrast with human bombs, Harris suggests in extremis that nuclear bombs might be dropped on Iran[336] and worryingly Harris' views reflect those of a wider American populous. In one poll about these matters 59% of the US citizens interviewed thought that a nuclear strike killing 100,000 Iranian civilians would be justified if Iran attacked a US aircraft carrier killing 2000 military personnel.[337] Let's put it mildly; support for suicide bombing, for all its utter horrors, pales into insignificance against support for dropping nuclear bombs. A desire to defend yourself when under attack or when you sense an imminent threat is wired into the human evolutionary heritage and not as such anything to do with Islam, except that like all other faiths and human enterprises Islam has evolved to be congruent with these needs.

Looking briefly at civilian victims of coalition attacks in the Middle East, the Iraq war of 2003, left 116,000 civilians dead and many more injured according to one report. A further report reveals that the overall 'War on Terror' begun by US President George W Bush in 2002, killed over 1.3 million civilians as a result of the actions of coalition forces. These figures, however, only refer to deaths in Afghanistan, Pakistan and Iraq. Further US led operations in Libya, Somalia and Yemen add to this toll.[338] Atrocities, including the murder and rape of unarmed civilians, would also seem to have taken place on several occasions in Iraq during the second Iraq war, including in Haditha, Hamandiya, Sadr City, Samarra, Ishaqi and of course we shouldn't forget Fallujah.[339]

Not surprisingly there is also good reason to think there is a direct connection between drone strikes and the rise of anti-US and anti-Western hostility. In July 2016 the Guardian[340] reported that:

> 'Survivors of the strikes and relatives of the dead consider drone strikes to be proof that the US is waging an indiscriminate war on their largely Muslim countries…the threat of the strikes has created an ever-present fear in their countries amongst civilians while having a negligible impact on the terrorist groups they are meant to

contain or destroy. Survivors also resent the lack of official apology, acknowledgement and compensation from the US for mistaken strikes, and bitterly note that Obama was quick to take responsibility for an errant 2015 strike that killed two Westerners.'

Just as the Western media reinforces a list of terrorist attacks in the West, so other medias make the most of Western atrocities against civilians in the Middle East.

I do not align with some in the Middle East who support terrorist attacks against Western soldiers even in cases where their civilian relatives and friends have been killed as 'collateral damage' in the 'war on terror'. But we should as always ask ourselves the question, how would we feel if we were them. If those who would zealously 'nuke' Iranian civilians, as mentioned a moment ago, suffered the plight that many civilians have suffered at the hands of Western troops, it is hard to see that they wouldn't equally support terrorism. For all of this, however, attacks that specifically target civilians in order to cause terror, move into a realm of immorality that is, I believe, altogether different. As such, in the research we shall examine shortly, where attacks on civilians are thought to be *often* justified rather than sometimes or rarely, I think that there is every reason to ask some tough moral questions. It is, of course, another thing to connect such views specifically with Islam, and still a further issue to suggest that Islam, in any of its many varieties, is responsible for such views.

How Islamic Are Terrorism And Suicide Bombing?

I shall look at terrorism in general, but also more specifically at the phenomenon of suicide bombing as an example of terrorism. This is because when it is aimed at non-combatants and large scale civilian populations, suicide bombing is surely extremely morally reprehensible. In such circumstances it targets those least able to protect themselves. It is also relatively easy to set up, and virtually impossible to detect in advance, making people especially vulnerable and also fearful. The intention is clearly to create whole cultures of fear.

Professor Steven Fish is keen to investigate any correlation that might exist between Islam and Islamism on the one hand and this kind of wide-scale terrorism and suicide bombing on the other. He analyses Dr. Monty Marshall's account of 'High Casualty Terrorist Bombings'. This is a list of terrorist bombings across the globe that killed 15 or more people between September 1994 and September 2008.[341] Fish finds that: first, Islamist terrorist attacks were responsible for 125 of 204, or 61% of high casualty terrorist bombings that took place between later 1994 and 2008. These attacks caused 69.6% of all deaths from terrorist attacks on this scale during that period. Fish writes 'terrorism is not a uniquely Muslim disease, but its perpetrators in recent times are disproportionately Islamists.' Secondly, 73% of the terrorist attacks during the period studied are concentrated in Afghanistan, Algeria, India, Israel, Pakistan, Russia and Sri Lanka. Terrorist attacks are relatively very rare in the West. Thirdly, most terrorist attacks are embedded in wider conflicts.

These statistics then, to some extent, correlate Islam with terrorist attacks, while, as we have seen, there are many good reasons to think that, given the variety of assaults on the Middle East and the range of other factors indicated, Muslims and non-Muslims alike would have responded violently had they found themselves in similar circumstances. Are there further reasons then to associate or disassociate Islam with terrorism and suicide bombing in a way that is morally reprehensible?

To begin to answer this question, the Qur'an and Hadith both forbid suicide (Surah 2: 195 and 4: 29) and give no reason for thinking that there should be an exception to this rule. We have also seen that the killing of civilians (non-combatants) is largely discouraged, if not condemned in the Qur'an, and especially if those civilians are Muslim. Consistent with the Qur'anic prohibition on suicide, Muslim countries have also had low suicide rates in comparison with non-Muslim countries. Even among those facing torture or certain death, Muslim suicides are relatively rare.

Continuing to look at some individuals and groups that have become radicalised gives us further insight into how a commitment to terrorism and, in places, suicide bombing has arisen. Fraser Egerton, in his study of these issues, concludes 'the journey to becoming a militant Salafist in the West is rarely the result of prolonged self reflection, theological investigation [within Islam] and political analysis. Many of those who have gone on to militancy demonstrate a very poor grasp of the Qur'an and hadiths.'[342] In his book *Perfect Soldiers*, Terry McDermott[343] describes the faith of the members of the Hamburg cell, responsible for 9/11, as 'unthought'. Ruud Peters, an expert witness at their trial, and an academic expert on concepts of jihad, duly corrected just about everything the Hofstad group had to say about jihad on that occasion. When one Hofstad group member tried to form another cell he needed to use the internet to read the Qur'an aloud. He didn't know it, even enough to recite some of it in Arabic, which is the most basic beginning of a Muslim education, as every Muslim child who goes to a madrasah will tell you. Reinforcing this point, a tape found in a van belonging to the Madrid bombers, was a tape of Qur'anic recitations for religious novices. Scott Atran informs us that:

'None of the nineteen 9/11 hijackers or thirty-odd Madrid train bomb conspirators attended a madrassah and the one 7/7 London underground suicide bomber who did attend a madrassah in Pakistan did so very briefly. In Pakistan and Indonesia, the two countries with the greatest number of madrassahs as well as jihadi groups, less than one percent of madrassahs can be associated with jihadis.'[344]

An in-depth knowledge of Islam does not seem to be the inspiration for terrorism. Egerton's studies reveal instead, as we saw earlier, that the use of violent images, of the torture and killing of fellow Muslims, acts time and again as a catalyst and rallying cry of belligerence.

Those who do seem to have an in-depth knowledge of Islam seem not to be particularly involved in militancy, instead Muslim jurists across the world universally condemned the terrorist groups responsible for 9/11 and 7/7. The Islamic scholar Abdal Hakim Murad dismisses suicide bombing and Al Queda as non-Islamic, and writes that, in the vast majority of Islamic judgments in Shari'a law, any killing has to be agreed by the state. Dr. Zaki Badawi, the chief imam at Regents Park mosque in London at the time of 9/11, wrote that it was 'a violation of Islamic laws and ethics.' He described terrorism as 'a declaration of war on God and on His Messenger' and wrote about terrorism and suicide bombing:

'it is a negation of every rule of the Shari'a which decrees that innocent life is sacred, property is inviolate and that the peace of mind of the public must be safeguarded. Those who preach the message of hate serve no religious cause and those who incite the ill-informed, maladjusted and alienated to commit criminal acts do so not as servants of a noble faith or a legitimate cause but as operators for base ambitions disguised as pious and religious.'[345]

In 2010, senior Pakistani Muslim scholar Dr. Tahir ul-Qadr, gave a 600 page judgment or fatwa that was a point-by-point theological rebuttal of every argument used by al-Qaeda inspired recruiters. In 2013, Sheikh Abdul Aziz bin Abdullah Al Sheikh, Grand Mufti of Saudi Arabia, also condemned all terrorism and suicide bombing as non-Islamic. Saudi Arabia's senior clerical leadership also issued a fatwa in 2013 declaring terrorism to be a heinous crime under Shari'a law. Other Wahhabi clerics have very much followed suit; their allegiance in Saudi Arabia is to the Saudi state and in opposition to the likes of Osama bin Laden who ultimately sought to overthrow it.[346] Yet, while condemnation of 9/11 has been more or less universal among Islamic jurists, things are different when it comes to Israel, the place where modern Islamist suicide bombing was born as Hamas responded to the killing of 29 Muslim worshippers at Friday prayers in Hebron on 25th February 1994. One of the most influential Muslim scholars alive today, Yusuf al-Qaradawi, who donated blood to the victims of 9/11, and has condemned suicide bombing as non-Islamic has also made an exception to this rule in the case of Israel. He has argued that because Israelis, both men and women, are conscripted, and since Israeli civilians have settled in the West Bank, violating the Fourth Geneva Convention and contrary to UN Security Council Resolution 446, suicide bombing is one of the few forms of resistance available to Palestinians in the absence of an armed force that can in any way match the Israeli military.

Research that has looked into potential links between adherence to Islam and support for terrorism and suicide bombing indicates that factors other than being a Muslim correlate much more with such support. A Pew Research survey from 2005 that looked precisely at the issue of support for terrorism and suicide bombing in 'the Muslim world' examined the views among Muslims in Indonesia, Pakistan, Jordan, Morocco, Turkey and Lebanon. It found, for example, in Indonesia (Muslim population 204 million, by far the largest on the planet), Turkey (Muslim population 74 million) and Morocco (Muslim population 32 million) that there were strong majorities that thought that terrorism and suicide bombing could *never* be justified. Only in Jordan (Muslim population 6 million) did a majority of those Muslims interviewed report that they thought that terrorism and suicide bombings could *sometimes* be justified. Lebanon was somewhere in the middle. Here 39% said that terrorism and suicide bombing could *sometimes/often* be justified. Regional variation then, rather than adherence to Islam, seems to correlate more consistently with attitudes supportive of terrorism and suicide bombing. This research also indicated that views about terrorism and suicide bombing changed considerably, even over a short period of time. For example, unsurprisingly, support for terrorism tended to decline, in the wake of terror attacks which is a further indication of how being a Muslim fails to correlate when set alongside some other factors as regards support for terrorism. The only demographic variable that did correlate more with support for terrorism and suicide bombing was being male. The only link with Islam that did emerge was that when Islam was perceived to be very much under threat this correlated with a support for terrorism.[347] There is a great deal of evidence to consistently connect imagining being under attack or feeling that you are under attack and of course actually being under attack with a militant response.[348] The connections with Islam, as we have seen in these instances, are much more tenuous.

So is Islam generally exonerated as regards the rise of terrorism and suicide bombing? We might think this from what we have seen of the Qur'an. Also those who would appear to have become most radicalised have quite often been least educated about Islam and the Qur'an. By contrast, those most educated across a very wide range of Islamic traditions appear to roundly condemn acts of terrorism, on almost all occasions. Research too, among Muslim populations in a number of countries, doesn't indicate that what support there is for terrorism and suicide bombing is connected with Islam as such. From what we can tell large proportions of the Muslim population across the planet condemn terrorism and suicide bombings against civilians altogether. The factors that seem to correlate most with being sometimes supportive of terrorism and suicide bombing is being or feeling that you are under attack and even with being male!

Yet there is more to this narrative about the development of terrorism that does make connections with some specific aspects of Islam, and this involves considering further those who have become radicalised within the faith. The key links with Islam here appear to be forms of Wahhabism.[349] Abu al Wahhab (1703 - 1792) developed, what Muslim scholars of that time saw to be, an excessively puritanical and militant Islam that significantly deviated in these respects from even the most conservative perspectives of the four established law school traditions. Al-Wahhab began the Islamist *takfiri* practice of regarding those Muslims who did not comply with his puritanical and bellicose ideology as hypocrites, who could duly be tortured or killed. He claimed that he was simply re-establishing the practices of the first Rightly Guided Caliph Abu Bakr. But most scholarship, both then and now, is engaged in disputes about such traditions as we observed in Chapter 6 to do with discussions about the authenticity of, and the variety of, hadiths. Al-Wahhab regarded Shi'as and Sufis to be non-Muslims. He preached that Muslims could never live in peace with non-Muslims. Harnessing such belligerence Al-Wahhab's forces committed massacres across Arabia during the eighteenth century. His grandson, Sulaiman ibn Abdullah, wrote against befriending the infidel, which included all *Muslims* in Syria, Iran, Iraq, and Egypt. Wahhabism failed to gain power for any great length of time during the nineteenth century despite several military campaigns. In the twentieth century, however, its alliance with the Saudi dynasty helped to give that regime legitimacy in the eyes of many within Saudi Arabia. In turn, Wahhabism achieved strong financial support following the discovery of oil, and most especially after the spike in oil prices in the mid-1970s. Wahhabism then came to have the monetary resources to spread itself far beyond Arabia. The so-called Sinjar Records, (documents captured in Iraq by Coalition forces in 2007) indicated that 45% of foreign jihadists came from Saudi Arabia, where Wahhabism is the only Islamic option to speak of.[350] Abdel Bari Atwan goes further when he states that the 'Saudi education system produces youth who are already radicalised'...'every school child is required to study *Kitab al-Tawhid* by Al-Wahhab, considered by many to be the key written source of militant Islam, in which [militant] jihad is normalised, becoming part of the vocabulary of everyday life.'[351] In an online opinion poll conducted in July 2014, 92% of Saudi citizens interviewed believed that IS conforms to the values of Islam and Islamic law[352] and 80% of the Saudi secret police, the *Mabahith* would seem to sympathise with the views of Osama bin Laden.[353] Atwan reveals a little more about the situation in Saudi Arabia when he makes the point that despite $250 billion taken in oil revenues in Saudi in 2013, a quarter of Saudis live below the poverty line and state education focuses so much on Wahhabism that many within the younger generations do not have the skills to be employed in the job market. Atwan's reflection on the situation is that with Saudi youth unemployment standing at about 30% they 'are not really qualified for anything…except perhaps recruitment for jihad'.[354] We shouldn't forget that 15 of the 19 attackers in 9/11 were Saudi. What is of particular interest is that many from a Saudi background, who do become radicalised, are radicalised to the point of becoming terrorists outside Saudi Arabia, in theatres of war and conflict like Afghanistan and Iraq. It is situations of conflict that, when brought in contact with belligerent Wahhabism, transforms such theology into militancy without limits.

Equally disturbing is the very well financed export of Wahhabism, partly in response to the Iranian export of radicalised Shi'ism following the 1979 revolution. King Fahd (reigned in Saudi Arabia 1982 – 2005) spent $87 billion funding Wahhabism in the form of 210 Islamic centres, 1500 mosques, 202 colleges and 2000 madrasahs in Pakistan, Nigeria, Bosnia, Chechnya, Canada, USA and Britain and this funding is on-going today.[355]

The Wahhabi-Saudi alliance has, from its inception, been one of religio-political convenience, but following Al Wahhab himself, Wahhabism is an extremely conservative theology that uses the more radical concepts of jihad, Dar al Islam/Dar al Harb and takfir. For sure, many of its clerics, as we have seen, have roundly condemned, 9/11, ISIS and Al-Qaeda, and I am sure their condemnations are genuine. Nonetheless, such is the nature of puritanical theology that there are always those who seek to perfect it, to be purer than the pure, such is its trajectory. Osama bin Laden began by respecting the Saudi government and seeking their blessing to fight jihad elsewhere. Only when they proved not to live up to the purity they had inspired in him, did bin Laden turn against them, regarding them also as takfir and a legitimate jihadi target.

This narrative about Wahhabism again points to a significant religious and theological strand within the explanation of radicalised Islam. Abou El Fadl is keen to point out how deviant al-Wahhab's thinking was in relation to Islam more broadly at the time when he lived, but religions are what they become, not some notional ideal. The alliance of the House of Saud and Wahhabism continues to be religiously and politically convenient. But it is hard to avoid the conclusion that Wahhabism today is an engine of belligerence, and this seems to be a very widespread opinion within Islam too. In 2016, 200 clerics from the most prestigious Islamic institution on the planet, Al Ahzar university in Cairo, referred to Wahhabism as a dangerous deformation of Sunni Islam. As the Middle East journalist and writer, Robert Fisk, put it, it was as near as Sunnis have got to excommunicating the Saudis and Wahhabis.[356] Some Muslim groups are more reticent, and, of course, Wahhabism is itself on a spectrum, often condemning terrorist attacks when they occur. We should also be clear that Western regimes, including the US and UK, often conveniently ignore the Wahhabi basis of some terrorism as they pursue their economic and commercial agendas in relation to the Saudi-Wahhabi alliance.

Wahhabism is not the only extremely dubious and belligerent influence that has sought to push Islam in the direction of Islamism either. The figures of Qutb and Faraj play no small part in that story. Both Qutb and Faraj were what we might call primordial utopians. They looked back to an imagined utopia when Muhammad ruled Medina and they understood this paradigm polis to be a signpost towards the truth for all time. Utopianisms, however, whether theological or political are so often ideological liabilities. Bolted together with the idea of divine decree, that God has a plan in which it is the duty of loyal Muslims to play their part, and that this decree is to reinvent the new Medina, that will achieve Dar al Islam, a permanent state of peace - what price and sacrifice is not worth paying for this result - the return of a heaven on earth? Unlike the ideologies of Gandhi or Martin Luther King Jr., in this kind of Islamist utopianism, it is very much believed that violent means can lead to peaceful ends. This perspective is further emphasised when such utopianisms are forged with hostile notions of takfir, and set free from the constraints that the vast majority of modern Islamic scholars mention in relation to jihad. So, for the militant, if suicide bombing is the means available at present to step closer to the Caliphate, then God willing, it must be justified.

To suggest that belligerent theology plays no part in the rise of militancy is hard to maintain, although other factors that we have considered are also crucially important. For example, we have seen in the case of the concepts of jihad, Dar al Harb/Dar al Islam and takfir that theologies are so often a product of events as much as the other way around.

Finally, to get a still closer look at connections between Islam and militancy, I shall consider how far militant theology actually leads individuals to personally engage in terrorism and hostility rather than merely assenting to such things. This is an important moral distinction. The person who is a fascist in his heart is not to be equated with the tub thumping evangelical fascist zealot, who is also not to be equated with the engineers of the final solution in Nazi Germany in 1943. That spectrum of immorality constitutes a series of giant leaps however easily they are made.

We have good reason to think that it is more than bellicose Islamism that is needed to turn someone into becoming a militant. Wahhabi theology, for example, is unfortunately widespread today while still very much a minority form of theology within Islam as a whole. Yet the vast majority of Wahhabis, whether ordinary practitioners or scholars and clerics, are not at all violent for all the implied militancy within that theology. It is in theatres of war, invariably not initiated by Islamism, that terrorism and suicide bombing has arisen within the militarily asymmetric contexts of Iraq, Afghanistan and Syria. In these contexts the militant theologies of jihad, Dar al Islam/Dar al Harb, takfir and what I have called primordial utopianism turn into violence. Of themselves they tend not to spontaneously combust.

An exception to what I have said here about militant theology not 'spontaneously combusting' are the cases of the very small number of home-grown terrorists in the West. They are I believe the product of the most belligerent religious ideologies we have seen, the youth psychology that we have identified and the influence of hyper-media that, in combination, has led to the commission of atrocities at home, and the flight to join ISIS abroad. Fraser Egerton's study, that I mentioned earlier in this chapter, is significant in this respect because those enclaves of the internet that ISIS has spawned are designed to put the viewer in the theatre of war, to generate the emotions of hatred and loathing of non-Muslims and most especially of the West and so to ignite the militant theologies already in place.

Looking specifically at the issue of suicide bombing, Scott Atran paints the briefest of thumbnail sketches of its recent history which gives us more insight into these questions. He writes, 'Modern suicide terrorism became a political force with the atheist anarchist movement that began at the end of the nineteenth century.'[357] In recent decades up until 2001 the most numerous group involved in suicide bombing were in fact the Tamil Tigers, not any form of Islamic or Islamist group at all. They were a nationalist liberation group, avowedly secular, whose supporters were nominally Hindu. Repressed by the Sri Lankan government and fighting in asymmetric conditions, terrorism and suicide bombing was their militant resort. As regards the Middle East until 2001, most suicide bombings occurred in Lebanon and about half of those again were unrelated to Islam, being instead associated with the Syrian Nationalist Party, the Lebanese Communist Party and the Lebanese Ba'ath Party.[358] Consistent with this picture Muhammad Khayr Haykal's three volume text on jihad written in 1993 doesn't even mention suicide bombing or 'martyrdom operations'!

This thumbnail sketch of recent suicide bombings indicates that, while in much of the popular press Islam is associated with suicide bombing today, historically it has been more associated with other ideologies and movements. Arising within the Muslim body politic at a particular point in time, it is not Islam that is at the heart of why it emerges but rather other factor(s) that it shares with the other situations in which it has arisen. We are pointed here towards a conclusion drawn more widely by Steven Fish about terrorism that is consistent with what we have seen so far, that the most consistent variable associated with terrorism are *circumstances rather than perpetrators*. Whether it is Basque separatists or the IRA, nineteenth century anarchists or the Italian Red Brigade, the Tamil Tigers or Al-Qaeda, a belief that one is oppressed by a violent and far more powerful enemy leads more consistently than anything else to the kind of asymmetric tactics that we call terrorism. This is also supported by the report I mentioned earlier from Scott Atran about how Muslim militants in Palestine think about jihad. Their motivation appears to be more about revenge than theology. Terrorism is a strategy in such asymmetric circumstances. Militant theologies of course play their part, but they are, as we have seen, more often than not significantly engineered by non-religious factors such as war and violence. Wahhabism, though, seems to have a militant pedigree that has pushed some, significantly influenced by it, in the direction of theatres of war. Muslim scholars such as Afsaruddin, Abou El Fadl and Amina Wadud are to be praised for their critique of it. The most effective counters to Islamist militancy today come from within Islam. Scott Atran makes clear that 'the only organisations I have found that have actively enticed significant numbers of voluntary defections from the ranks of would-be martyrs and jihadis – in Indonesia, Saudi Arabia, Pakistan, Egypt and elsewhere – are Muslim religious organisations.'[359]

9

Problems Of Evil And Suffering: From Theory To Practice

The ethical appraisal of religion through dialogue that lies at the heart of this book has by now charted a quite varied course. With respect to Islam, it has attempted a more in-depth analysis than elsewhere. We have sought to identify specific religious inputs with respect to practice and belief and have observed interactions between religious commitment, behaviour and lifestyle with the wider world as well as between religions. Looking specifically at belief, we have seen how it has been forged within Islam, as elsewhere through very varied circumstances. We have seen how much belief is effect just as much as cause but we have seen its effects too in Chapter 4 as regards mission, prayer and meditation; and in Chapter 5 as regards the religious upbringing and schooling of children.

In this chapter, we are going to look at the ethical profile of religious belief in a different way and I shall look specifically at belief in a God as the cornerstone belief of the Abrahamic religions of Judaism, Christianity and Islam. We shall consider the ethical profile of believing in a benevolent God *in*

PROBLEMS OF EVIL AND SUFFERING   227

itself, without reference to how it affects people's lives or is culturally generated or perpetuated in the ways that we have observed so far. To be clear about what I mean, some atheists claim that to believe in a benevolent God, to be a theist, is to believe something that is ethically problematic in itself, irrespective of how the belief was generated or of the effects it may have. Given the dialogical character of this book, such a point of view is worth including and assessing. If there is any truth in such a claim, our dialogue about religion would be lacking if we didn't give it some attention.

Let's consider what is at stake here a little more.

Some atheists for example think merely that theism lacks evidence and argument to support it, but they don't particularly want to make an issue of this. They have no objection to someone else believing in God and certainly no moral objection to it at all. Other atheists, such as the new atheists, however, go further, claiming that there is positive evidence to reject theism, and they very much want to persuade others that they are right. Some in this second group say that this positive evidence is to do with ethics. God, they say, is to be rejected on moral grounds for being a mastermind of a universe of untold suffering and pain. Evil and suffering, they say, offer positive reasons for claiming that God does not exist or is not all good. Richard Dawkins, for example, speaks about 'the appalling role-model of Yahweh'. If this version of atheism is convincing, and the central belief in the Abrahamic faiths turns out through examination to be a belief in someone who is immoral in some respects, then that is certainly relevant to our aim of morally evaluating religion. The strongest versions of such an argument go still further, and contend that to believe faithfully in God, to be a theist, is to collude and ally with God's monstrous designs, that belief in God and most especially any attempt to defend God in relation to problems of evil and suffering is itself immoral. We find such a view forcefully expressed by the physicist and atheist Professor Peter Atkins, in dialogue with Richard Dawkins and with the philosopher and Christian apologist Professor Richard Swinburne. Dawkins recalls a particular exchange of views:

'Swinburne at one point attempted to justify the Holocaust on the grounds that it gave the Jews a wonderful opportunity to be courageous and noble. Peter Atkins splendidly growled, "May you rot in hell.".'[360] Such an issue is a flashpoint, where passionate atheistic moral repulsion clashes with religious conviction, and sparks fly.

Both these claims then, first about the goodness of God and second about the ethics of believing in and defending belief in such a God in the face of evil, are clearly relevant to a moral appraisal of the Abrahamic faiths. In the first section of this chapter, we shall examine in some depth these philosophical arguments that offer a moral challenge to belief in God. In the second section we shall seek to set these challenges for all their strengths in a wider moral context which is how this chapter once again keeps with the theme of dialogue that runs through this book.

The philosophical theory - problems of evil and suffering

What follows is a classic philosophy of religion debate with which some may be very familiar, and I invite readers to consider for themselves whether the following atheist contentions – i) that God is a moral outrage when reflecting on the nature and degree of evil and suffering; and ii) that belief in such a God is immoral because it refuses to face up to this truth and in effect sides with God against humanity and sentient life – are reasonable claims in the light of the arguments that follow.

I shall look specifically at belief in an all-good God, who is thought to be omnipotent and omniscient – a view generally shared by the Abrahamic faiths. As such, the problem of evil and suffering I wish to consider is whether it is coherent to believe that such a God exists while also agreeing that there is evil and suffering in the world. If there is convincing reason to think, in the light of problems of evil and suffering, that belief in God is not, or is probably not, coherent, then the ethical problems we have raised about belief in God may seem insurmountable. Let's look further then at this question of the coherence of belief in God in relation to the existence of evil and suffering.

Very broadly, this kind of problem of evil and suffering takes two forms.

The first is known as the logical problem of evil because it alleges there is a contradiction in believing the following claims:

That God is perfectly good
That God is unlimitedly powerful
That evil exists

This argument suggests that this kind of God must want to abolish evil, because the Abrahamic faiths each assume that evil is by definition absolutely opposed to goodness, and that God is perfectly good. Second, God must be able to completely abolish evil because God is omnipotent. Yet, while both willing and able to remove evil, evil still exists. Therefore either, God is not perfectly good because despite being able he will not remove evil, or he is not unlimitedly powerful since he cannot remove evil despite wishing to do so, or he is neither perfectly good nor unlimitedly powerful because he neither wants nor can remove evil.

This kind of logical difficulty seems to multiply when, as is generally understood by theists, God is also taken to be omniscient, and the creator and sustainer of the universe. Being omniscient, God then knows all evil that is happening at present and has ever happened. Omniscience can also involve knowing all evil that will happen in the future. With this knowledge, God has always allowed evil to take place despite being utterly opposed to it and despite wanting and being able to remove it. Also, being the creator of the universe, God, it would seem, is responsible for the origin of evil too, because nothing exists without God's permission for, and active willing of, that thing.[361] Where would any being get the idea of evil from? Being the creator of everything, only God can have put evil there as a possibility, despite being opposed to evil and able to do otherwise. Furthermore, being the sustainer of the universe, God is not a mere passive observer of the universe or of evil. Evil is as such something God actually supports and keeps in existence – despite wanting and being able to remove it.

A second formulation of the problem of evil is often called 'the evidential problem of evil', because its focus is on the weight of evidence for its conclusion, as distinct from the assertion that there is a logical contradiction involved in believing a cluster of claims to which many religious believers adhere.

It has been summarised by the philosopher Stephen Evans as follows:
'If God exists, he does not allow any utterly pointless evil
Probably, there is pointless evil.
Probably, God does not exist.'[362]

The first premise in this argument would seem to hold true for the perfectly good, omnipotent, omniscient God of the Abrahamic traditions.

Having these qualities, God would, being fully aware of all evil, be both able and willing to remove it. Evil that had no purpose for God would surely then be removed. If not, then we are left asking of a perfectly good, omnipotent God what it means to be perfectly good, while not entirely wanting to remove pointless instances of evil; and/or, what it means to be omnipotent, and yet not be able to do this. The strength of this argument as a challenge to belief in God, compared with the argument from the logical problem of evil, is that the burden of proof is lower here and the conclusion therefore more easily reached. It only has to seem likely that some instance of evil is pointless for belief in God to be less than reasonable.

Both the logical and the evidential problems of evil involve a consideration of moral evil and natural evil. Moral evil is evil that is the result of the misuse of free-will by free agents, so as to cause harm or suffering either to themselves or others and other sentient beings. Natural evil is harm and suffering caused by the forces of nature, such as the effects of earthquakes, floods, disease and severe disability upon sentient beings.

Initial responses to the logical problem of evil

A number of initial responses to the logical problem of evil seem to be problematic. One response on the part of apologists for God has been to reject or qualify the assumptions of the problem; to say either that God is not all good or not all-powerful or neither. Belief in God's goodness is so basic within the Abrahamic religions that few have rejected this and remained members of these faiths in their own understanding or that of others. However, there have been attempts to qualify what is meant by God's omnipotence, and some have sought to defend a notion of God that rejects omnipotence altogether. Others have sought to modify the claim that evil exists so as to address the logical problem of evil. I shall look briefly at two examples of this second approach and return to discussions of omnipotence shortly.

A first response from a minority of believers is to say that in some respect evil is an illusion. We find this in the writings of Mary Baker Eddy the founder of the marginal Christian sect, Christian Science. Christian Science rejects the reality of any seeming suffering and evil as an error of the mortal mind. As such, in relation to both the logical problem of evil and the evidential problem of evil, the issue would seem to dissolve, because suffering and evil are no longer realities in need of explanation. The key objection to this kind of view of evil as an illusion is to consider what the difference is between illusion and reality. Evil and suffering seem such convincing illusions that the problem of evil simply shifts to the level of asking why there are such convincing and painful illusions about evil and suffering.

A more mainstream attempt to tinker with the claim that evil and suffering do exist was made by St. Augustine of Hippo (354-430 AD), who described evil as a privation or lack of the good. Evil is seen then as an absence of goodness, an unrealised potential where there could be goodness. For Augustine, it has no existence as such. He explained it in this way:

> 'What, after all, is anything we call evil, except the privation of good? In animal bodies, for instance, sickness and wounds are nothing but the privation of health.'[363]

Evil therefore neither comes from God nor from goodness, and it cannot challenge God. Not being a thing in existence, it is uncreated and God therefore holds no responsibility for it. From God's point of view, evil and suffering are what Augustine described as 'non-being', however real they are to us. In addition to this, as inheritors of Adam and Eve's misdemeanours in the Garden of Eden, all humanity throughout time deserves the suffering it receives for now and for eternity.

I mention this extraordinarily archaic understanding of evil since it is alive and well in the writings of some Catholic thinkers today who seek to communicate with a wide audience. For example, Terry Eagleton in *On Evil*,[364] fails to mention the metaphysical leaps apparent in Augustine's theology but suggests that, in symbolic form at least, this kind of thinking can help us understand something of the nature of evil and suffering. Why, though, anyone should ever buy into this way of thinking apart from the prejudice of following in a tradition, I fail to see or to understand. The whole metaphysics of non-being makes no sense to me. Additionally, the notion of inheriting sin from an original human couple, as well as being justly blamed and punished for such an inheritance, brings into view further vistas of dubious moral reasoning and improbability. As long as evil and suffering are justified from God's point of view all seems to be well for Augustine, irrespective of how humans feel about this. Even if the metaphysics were at all worth considering, such an impersonal God seems hardly worthy of worship.

The free-will defence

The free-will defence is at the heart of most attempts to defend God against accusations of malevolence and/or impotence because of the presence of moral evil in particular. It is a response to both the logical and the evidential problems of evil. The argument suggests that freedom is of great worth for human beings, and of especially great worth for them in God's eyes. According to the free-will defence, our worth is inextricably tied to our freedom. Only by being able to do other than as we do, can we be moral or immoral. Only in this way can we grow in character and spirituality and come to love God or anyone else in a way that truly reflects who we are. Commitment to God can only be at all meaningful and of worth if it is freely given. Therefore, God creates humanity free, both individually and as a species. Of course, for most Christians today who are not fundamentalists or conservative evangelicals, this is a rather convoluted process: God has allowed evolution to give rise to a free species. In other words, to use Daniel Dennett's phrase, freedom evolves but it would seem that God has put in place a mechanistic system to bring this about.

The crucial step in the argument then follows. Since God, out of love, has chosen to create free beings, and because the alternative of programmed beings would not have allowed for the development of morality and goodness in them, it follows that God is justified in creating free beings that by definition are beyond his control. They are therefore free to do both good and evil. Moral evil then cannot be prevented even by the God who created them without also violating their freedom.

Responses to the free-will defence

In response to the free-will defence, the British philosopher John Mackie suggests that an omnipotent God should be able to create beings so that they always freely do the right.[365] He argues that if human beings can freely do what is right on one occasion, why can't they freely do what is right on every occasion? The logic of Mackie's argument seems to me however to hang on an equivocation. Mackie confuses two meanings of 'freely doing the right'. In principle, free beings are not barred from doing the right, otherwise they wouldn't be free. At the same time, being free, it is highly probable that, across an entire life, free beings will not always do the right. A defender of the free-will defence can reasonably say that humans might be able to do the right on every occasion if that is what they freely chose, but they can't do the right on every occasion in the sense of being guaranteed to do that.

The view that if God is omnipotent, then he can make people freely choose the good just like he could make square circles usually provokes the response that this is to misunderstand the concept of omnipotence. Omnipotence is said at most to be an ability to do the logically possible not the logically impossible. There is, in fact, nothing more than the logically possible. Square circles are not an option, not because God lacks omnipotence but because there is not and could not be such a concept as a square circle. Similarly, God could not logically guarantee that people on every occasion freely chose to do the right.

A more significant critique of the free-will defence runs like this. Freedom seems on all occasions to be preferable to control for the free-will defence and therefore no control at any point is admissible no matter what the cost in terms of suffering. Nevertheless, it seems fairly clear that freedom is not an all-or-nothing thing. We find ourselves to be more or less free, in a variety of respects. If this is part of our circumstances, then why couldn't God have intervened to very occasionally limit some human freedom to prevent enormous suffering? To say that the preservation of human freedom is absolutely crucial is to ignore the fact that human freedom is not at all preserved in so many cases at present, and more especially in the past. Take the case of slavery. The free-will defence would have to maintain that preserving the freedom to make someone a slave is more important than the freedom of the slave. For those who would respond by saying that even slaves can on occasion make some moral decisions and build character, ignores the fact that in some instances this seems hardly to have been the case, for example when we consider the thousands of child slaves who died incarcerated on the slave ships from Africa to the New World and elsewhere. Our newspapers tell us of such hideous cases of child abuse, where a toddler who has been terribly tortured and mistreated eventually dies from their injuries. The free-will defence would appear to maintain that the free-will of the perpetrators of such abuse was more important than the freedom of the toddler to have a chance at life. The question for the free-will defence becomes: why has God chosen the specific degree of freedom for humans, so very unevenly distributed, so that some people seem to have a great deal of freedom, while others have very little, if any? What is so precious about this precisely irregular state of affairs that no extra restriction on freedom in any instance, however small and however beneficial the consequence, would make that restriction worth it? By the same token, what is so precious about this state of affairs that no further freedom could ever be granted to anyone across history, in any instance? The free-will defence tells us that freedom is a precious commodity that God seeks to preserve. But that is hard to see. It would seem instead that what any God has preserved is a very irregular pattern of freedom and limitation. The free-will defence does not seem to address what about this inequality and irregularity is so worth preserving.

Another form of this problem about the worth of freedom within the free-will defence looks like this. If freedom is so crucial to preserve that it justifies an abundance of moral evil, then why doesn't God intervene when freedom is threatened by things that are not themselves the result of human choice? We shall revisit the question of natural evil soon but for the time being it has a key bearing on the free-will defence. For example, some are born with significant propensities for addiction. Addictive personality types are well documented. We are no doubt hugely conditioned by culture and parenting, which it now seems in themselves can, through epi-genetics, have a further impact on our genetic make-up. And yet the free-will defence appears unperturbed by these questions about how free we are after all. The free-will defence would have us believe that freedom is so important to God's plan for creation that he will never intervene to inhibit it, while also not intervening when impersonal forces like addiction do precisely that. I remember working as a volunteer with some quite severely disabled young men. One autistic gentleman seemed to me the least free of all. His hands were partially tied together because if they weren't he would hit his forehead with his fists very hard. What was to be gained from his severe lack of freedom? Not some 'compensating' freedom on the part of someone else, as the free-will defence alleges in the case of slavery. So according to the free-will defence, human freedom is such a moral imperative that the Holocaust, the Soviet gulags and the Chinese 'Great Leap Forward' are sacrifices worth making for its preservation. Yet, freedom is also so unimportant that individuals and whole groups of people are allowed to lose it all the time – or never have it in the first place – and this not for the sake of others exerting their freedom, but for no apparent reason.

I would add as regards human evolution that freedom is as yet the most fleeting episode within an extraordinarily long process. If you take a twenty-four-hour period as representing the evolution of life as a whole, freedom has been on the scene for only a second or so. This fledgling emergence of freedom further indicates how it is very erratically distributed. As human consciousness and other similar forms of consciousness emerged, and with them the glimmers of self-consciousness, language and freedom, much indicates that there was randomness to this process. We are now clearly discussing the issue of mutations and their cumulative effects over many generations, leading over the long term to some naturally-selected advantages and, in the vast majority of cases, disadvantages. God, then, has presumably allowed the mechanism of natural selection to take its course and the engine of random mutation to play its part. However, this hands-off approach on the part of God, that as it were delegates evolution to mechanistic and random forces, would seem to be a very blunt instrument to achieve the requisite amount of freedom in all cases of human consciousness that the free-will defence requires in order to work.

This brings the debate about the free-will defence to another level. The believer may well claim here that the point of all suffering is not a case of saying that there is a point to every instance of suffering. Rather, that the evolutionary system which was the best to install for the purpose of bringing about free beings who can both choose good and love God, has written into it these vast inequalities as regards freedom. Some theologians have suggested that natural selection was the best system available to bring about God's purposes. The theologian Peter Vardy, for example, writes about evolution that it 'is the best and most effective way of creating a world of great beauty, richness, diversity and adaptability which has within it the possibility of love and the higher virtues.'[366]

This of course begs the question: how could anyone, with any confidence, know all the possibilities available to God, and with equal confidence know with God-like precision which was the best? The question remains: how reasonable it is to believe that an omnipotent, all-loving God would choose evolution as the best conceivable mechanism for the creation of free beings who would respond to him with love? It is hard to imagine how it is the best in every respect, with all its attendant evil, and suffering and unequal distribution of freedom. When I was in school teaching and I taught the free-will defence, I introduced an exercise in which pupils had to try and design a universe from their imagination in which evil and suffering were minimised, while at every turn human freedom was promoted and this without it being at all obvious there was a God. Most classes came up with a wide range of what seemed plausible options. By contrast, Christian theology over the last 2,000 years has not been particularly fruitful in this respect, when asked to consider ideas counter to its doctrines. There is no small irony in the fact that an institutionalised lack of freedom in the Church across the centuries has promoted the free-will defence.

Where do we stand now, therefore, in relation to the logical and evidential problems of evil, having looked a little at moral evil, and especially at the free-will defence? As regards the logical problem of evil, one might expect a perfectly good, omnipotent God to have done a better job. This conclusion, though, does not address the character of the logical problem of evil, which suggests by deduction a certain conclusion that either God is not omnipotent, or not perfectly good, or that evil does not exist. Just maybe, there is some conceivable explanation in terms of a system that God has instituted which was the best an omnipotent God could have done. However unlikely this might be, it is not a logical contradiction. It may even be possible to conceive of how God did this. I will therefore move on to focus in the rest of this first section of the chapter on the evidential problem of evil which I think, unlike the logical problem of evil, presents an insurmountable problem for belief in the kind of God that very many within the Abrahamic faiths believe in.

The key point about the free-will defence in relation to the evidential problem of evil is that every single act or aspect of moral evil has to have a point. If freedom can be sacrificed in the eyes of God on one or many occasions as in the case of addicts or people who are severely disabled, why couldn't it also, on any other occasion across the entire history of humanity, have been sacrificed so as to slightly or significantly reduce suffering? Alternatively, if our present system is the best an omnipotent, omniscient, perfectly good God could have devised, this scenario has to be more probable than one where God lacked any of these qualities; or where God doesn't quite have them entirely; or where God doesn't exist; or where there are many rival gods; or indeed that we are part of a computer game that a galaxy of deities play as a pastime. The entire collection of alternative cosmic scenarios in which pointless suffering is involved would have to be collectively less likely than there being a system instituted by a perfectly good, omnipotent God, that gives all suffering a point. All the evidential problem of evil has to establish is that *on the balance of probability* there is pointless, unjustified suffering. It seems to me that at this point we have made significant steps in that direction.

Natural evil and the 'for a greater good' defence of God

A systematic theological defence of God in relation to problems of evil and suffering is known as a 'theodicy'. We have already seen something of Augustine's theodicy. In relation to natural evil, Augustine maintained that earthquakes, typhoons, cancers and insanity are all the product of the fall of Adam and Eve, a product of their free choice. I shall not give any further consideration to this kind of theodicy because in our focus on the evidential problem of evil we are looking at the question *'Is there probably pointless evil?'*, and any theodicy that begins by assuming that human evolution is false begins with a weighty improbability. This is before we compound improbability upon improbability with the successive layers of dogma I mentioned a moment ago, regarding the inheritance of original sin – that nature itself is fallen as well as notions of fairness about inheriting original sin. Such a theodicy is hardly going to approach anything more than a high degree of improbability, and so could not be used to effectively counter the claim that 'probably there is pointless evil'.

Let us get clear the scale of the problem of pointless evil when looking at natural evil. Much theodicy has suggested that natural evil is best explained by saying in some guise or other that 'it is for the greater good' that natural evil exists. Here, then, natural evil is justified as a means to a greater good. Before we go further to look at instances of this kind of theodicy there are objections to this sort of theodicy in principle.

The philosopher John Mackie points out a basic difficulty about any form of theodicy that suggests that evil, whether moral or natural, is 'for a greater good' in the way that we have been considering. Any 'for a greater good defence' subjects God to causal laws that in effect should surely be understood instead to be subject to him.[367] A God who can only bring about the greatest good by the means of natural evil does appear on the face of it to be somewhat impotent. It would seem logically possible that an omni-benevolent and omnipotent God could have created a world in which, without natural evil, the greatest good was possible, but if there is a God this clearly hasn't happened.

John Stuart Mill, in discussing the problems of natural evil, made clear that while good may sometimes come from evil, evil may just as equally come from good, but that, by the law of averages, evil comes from evil and good comes from good.[368] The point seems to be about efficiency. While some natural evil may play its part in bringing about a greater good (whatever that greater good may be), it will more surely have other, far worse, effects most of the time.

Finally, we might ask whatever that greater good might be, for the sake of which natural evil is deemed necessary, why can't moral evil perform that role sufficiently well, so as to make this role of natural evil redundant? This argument is best explored while considering the specific instances of what the 'greater good' might be.

So let's look specifically at some instances of the 'for a greater good' argument with respect to natural evil.

Perhaps the most popular case of such a greater good is that of character formation. For example, through the experience of natural evil it is suggested we will be capable of exhibiting and practising courage in the face of threat, determination in relation to difficulty and adversity, compassion and empathy beside the sufferings of others, and altruism and sacrifice where they might be called for. It is easy to see how these kinds of virtue can be generated in the process of dealing with the pain and suffering that comes from natural evil. Yet we are also left considering whether or not moral evil isn't *probably* sufficient to generate these virtues of itself. In returning to the question 'Is there probably pointless evil?' we might rephrase this question as follows: 'Would an omnipotent, infinitely imaginative God find every instance of natural evil

PROBLEMS OF EVIL AND SUFFERING   239

in our present world absolutely necessary for character building or might his ingenuity extend a little further, however slightly, beyond this point? On the balance of probability which is most likely?'

A second argument suggesting that natural evil is necessary for a greater good was advanced by the Christian philosopher John Hick in his classic text *Evil and the God of Love*.[369] I shall look in some detail at Hick's ideas, since they constitute one of the most well-known and widely discussed modern theodicies. Hick contends that we could only make plans to do anything if we lived in a predictable environment. We could only have meaningful moral characters if our plans and actions stood a chance of taking effect. Therefore, we need fixed laws of nature – of gravity and so forth – with the consequence that floods and other natural catastrophes follow. Natural evil is therefore a necessary concomitant of a regular, relatively predictable world, which is the only context in which moral decisions and therefore moral character can be made.

The arguments here, though, don't seem to take us very far. Indeed, a somewhat consistent and predictable environment seems to be what is needed to make human planning and character building possible, but all of this might be far better achieved without cancer, earthquakes or volcanic eruptions. Presumably an omnipotent creator had at his disposal every conceivable type of universe that humans could imagine, and far more besides that we cannot imagine. It is not difficult for humans to imagine a consistent and fairly predictable universe with less natural evil than this one. On the basis of this particular argument, a very great deal of natural evil would seem to be probably pointless.

John Hick has championed a further version of the argument that natural evil, in addition to moral evil, is needed to bring about a greater good than could be achieved otherwise. Hick claims that only through a great deal of suffering and an altogether ambiguous world where it is unclear whether or not there is a God will we be sufficiently free to decide to believe in God or not. This degree of intellectual freedom, he suggests, is a necessary pre-condition for moral choice. If we knew there was a God, we would know that there was a source of supreme goodness and this would impair our free choice about whether or not to do the good. Therefore, to safeguard our moral freedom it needs to look as if there could be a God or there might not be and this requires vast amounts of suffering including natural evil and what may appear pointless evil in order to create this environment for free choice. A clear assessment of this argument can be made with reference to animal suffering.

Animal suffering stands out to me within the range of issues that surround the 'for a greater good defence' as very problematic. John Hick and others suggest that there may be a purpose found for human suffering in an afterlife. For the vast majority of Christians, Jews and Muslims, however, there is not a belief that animals live on after death, so no post-mortem resolution for them. What then could be the reason or purpose for which animal suffering is justified? Hick suggests in a pivotal argument within his theodicy that animal suffering is essential as part of the landscape or backdrop against which humans make their moral and spiritual decisions and destiny. His point is that without us genuinely left wondering whether or not there is a God, we would not be sufficiently free to decide either way. Similarly, if we are to be morally free, we need to be in a situation where it is ambiguous as to whether there is a God. The presence of animal suffering and natural evil puts us at the right knowledge distance to enable us to freely decide both about our religious beliefs and our ethical choices. This is of course an extension of the free-will defence and a troubling one, as if it did not have enough problems already.

Human beings have been around for only a fraction of the time that other animals have existed, so we might reasonably ask what was the point of animal suffering before humans evolved? Most animal suffering is of course not observed by humans either, so apart from a general awareness of such suffering, what is the purpose of each specific instance? Philosophers such as Hick have sought to downplay the significance of animal suffering reporting that vertebrates which clearly feel pain, do not remember it as we do. They do not have the psychological fears of death and pain that we have. But this controversial claim completely misses the point of the evidential problem of evil. Again, to remind the reader, our target question is 'Is there *probably* pointless suffering...of any sort in any time or place?' Would one less antelope being torn apart while still half alive before humans ever came on the scene or a million fewer caterpillars eaten alive by the larvae of digger wasps be sufficient to make anyone stop and think, 'Ah there must be a God after all,' – and so rob someone of that precious freedom, for the sake of which natural evil has been a constant accompaniment to all life? To join this up with a previous point, this precious freedom is in fact erratically distributed not least due to natural evil itself.

God could, it seems, have created us in a Garden of Eden and allowed things to have gone wrong in the way that fundamentalism suggests, but he chose not to do this as far as most Christians, Jews and even some Muslims are concerned today. Instead, God instituted evolution as the *best possible* means of bringing about free creatures that might eventually, after the end of a very long process, come to worship God. We have already observed that for an omnipotent being, this appears breathtakingly inefficient.

Looking more specifically at natural evil as suffered by human beings, is there probably pointless evil there? Hick suggests that we cannot decide about this now. Only in an afterlife, where we continue to grow towards God through free choice, will all people – including the worst of people – ultimately come to see the point of all suffering and evil. Hick rejects any notion of eternal hell where people unceasingly suffer, as well as the simple annihilation of those who have rejected God, as both add to problems of evil and suffering, rather than resolve them. He suggests that in either case, there would seem to be suffering that is unresolved and unredeemed. His liberal Christian alternative proposes an eternity for all. The early stages of this process will still be painful. If everyone lives on after death, that includes the worst of people. While such people will continue for a limited time to perpetrate evil they will ultimately freely come to do good. Over eternity, God will be able to persuade them of this without violating their freedom. In the end, all will be able to see all suffering and evil in retrospect as a learning process that has enriched their eternal life in knowledge, understanding and love of each other and God. In this way, Hick suggests that we can begin to see how all of our suffering, of human suffering, including natural evil, may work towards a greater good and be worth the price paid.

Two responses to Hick's views deserve mention:

First, his theodicy is nothing if not imaginative, but by the same token it pays little attention to what may be probable. So, contrary to Hick's view, it could equally be that there is no afterlife, or that any such afterlife is not a type of personal survival, or that not everyone survives, or that some go to an eternal hell. Each of these scenarios is rejected by Hick precisely because he thinks they would involve the existence of pointless evil. Then there are more specific ingredients that just as easily might not be the case: why should we expect the worst of people in an afterlife to ultimately always do the good?

In order to justify and redeem human suffering, whether in the form of moral or natural evil, Hick installs the various post-mortem characteristics that we have seen and omits others. Yet contrary to his intention, for every feature he suggests about the afterlife, another vista of improbabilities is revealed. Far from countering the claim that probably there is pointless evil, Hick's view of the afterlife makes this seem more than likely. This is because in terms of probability, with every feature that Hick installs, it could just as easily be otherwise several times over and it therefore probably is.

Second, some evil and suffering is of such a nature that there could never be a question of compensation or purpose, of restitution or rehabilitation. This sort of point gets to the heart of the issue of this chapter.[370] This kind of view is expressed by people who have experienced great suffering, beyond what many of us have gone through and to dismiss it with some theoretical construct in the shape of a theodicy seems to me both callous and metaphysically and socially inept.

Let's sum up the chapter at this point before we move on. The logical problem of evil that maintains there is a contradiction between belief in an all good and omnipotent God and the existence of evil – however convinced we may be by the logical tension between these claims – does not actually reveal a logical contradiction between them. On the other hand, the evidential problem of evil, that merely claims that probably there is pointless evil, and that an all-good omnipotent God would not allow this, raises real difficulties for those who want to claim that their belief in the kind of God at issue is reasonable. We have seen at a number of points that probably there is pointless evil and suffering, and in this sense, there would seem to be good reason to call into question either the goodness, the omnipotence or the existence of this kind of God.

As we saw at the beginning of this chapter, a further aspect of this critique of belief in God due to problems of evil and suffering moves beyond questioning the morality of God to questioning the morality of *believing* in God.

To reiterate this argument, and to build upon our reasoning so far in this chapter: God could probably have created a better world, with some reduction in suffering to say the very least, based on the arguments we have seen concerning the evidential problem of evil. His choice not to do this, given his omnipotence and omniscience, makes such a God probably morally culpable – if he exists at all. To believe in such a God is to ally with him. It is to submit to God's judgment about what suffering is permissible, despite having reason to think that God is probably morally culpable, and thus it is to side with God over against the sentient life that has paid the price for such judgments from time immemorial.

One response to this view, from some religious believers, is to champion irrationality or at least to champion believing the improbable as a true hallmark of faith. There are, though, serious ethical problems with this approach to faith as I indicated at the outset of this chapter.[371] To choose to believe what one realises is improbable would seem to amount to turning away from what seems to be true and this is in itself a moral and a theological issue for the Abrahamic faiths that regard God as the supreme truth, and the creator and sustainer of truth.

There is, though, a much more significant point to be made in defence of believers at this point. Across the planet, the vast majority of believers in an Abrahamic God have little or no time for theology or philosophy, they are busy doing other things in life – including of course dealing with, and helping others to deal with, problems of suffering. The idea that they are colluding with a God they have reason to suspect is not all good after all is, it seems to me, grossly unfair. They may have thought about and countered all the arguments posited by the evidential problem of evil mentioned above. They may have thought about many other arguments besides. Far more likely, their faith operates on a much more practical level, and it may or may not be morally creditable for that in ways that we have seen throughout this book.

Moving beyond theory

We have been looking at problems of evil of a rational or, as it were, technical sort. Can God escape the accusations laid against him about the problems of evil and suffering on a technicality, or be found guilty on the same basis?

If only the whole thing were a game, we might reasonably ask this question; but it is not. Going through the arguments I have rehearsed so far can begin to look, in relation to human suffering, rather like a computer simulator does to real life. All the better, some would say, for being detached and so, potentially, more objective. Yet, such a notion of objective ethical evaluation is extremely flawed, as we saw in the Introduction. It actually doesn't take seriously enough, or appreciate sufficiently, the nature of the dialogue this book is about. We cannot begin to debate the significance or justification of suffering without insight about the experience of profound suffering. As such, the perspective of those who suffer most is pivotal. This has far-reaching implications for the arguments so far advanced in this chapter, because it diversifies our conclusions.

Some people who have suffered immensely have found that a perspective involving a God is crucially important in coping with suffering. Others feel that theory and theodicy have no place, that theodicy is an evil in itself insofar as it reduces suffering to an object of contemplation and as such misunderstands the problem at issue. Still others feel convinced that in their personal experience theodicy fails, for the kinds of reason we have seen.[372]

Does this then completely subjectivise the whole discussion about the validity of theodicy? It doesn't look that way. The problems of moral evil are to do with being with others and the best responses to both moral and natural evil are similarly discovered. When people suffer they so often come together in response. This is the best way to overcome division and to avoid moral isolation and moral ghettoization: by reaching out above all, if we can, to people who think morally differently to ourselves.

We can now see the discussion in the first part of this chapter in a wider moral context. It seemed there, on a theoretical level, that probably there is pointless evil and that, on that basis, probably a perfectly good and omnipotent creator God does not exist. But such theory, whatever its logical merits, carries little moral weight in relation to those who have suffered greatly and who have found a different answer in their own experience. Still others who have suffered greatly struggle with their religious beliefs, for the kind of reasons given in this chapter. In this sense, the arguments in the first part of this chapter stand, but within a dialogue that ultimately needs to be about compassion as well as logic.

As such, in practical terms, the challenges to human life are often too great for believer and unbeliever to afford to be divided. Their dialogue about problems of evil and suffering in every sense is a rich source of understanding about how to face, and come to terms with, some of the most difficult things we face. This is where theory needs to start, from working practically with others to reduce suffering. Our thinking needs to reflect on the mutuality or dialogue of our lives as much as on the rationality of a set of related beliefs. This will take us further in our understanding and therefore in our judgment, which relies on this.

Conclusion

We have found some good philosophical reasons as to why problems of evil and suffering tell against a belief in an all-good, omnipotent God. At the same time, there is something breathtakingly superficial and ungrounded in simply drawing such a conclusion as an objective fact. Life is, thankfully, not lived on the basis of philosophical argument, though some in academe on either side of this debate appear regretful about this. In practice, individuals and communities encounter their own questions and responses in relation to problems of evil and suffering. Life experience, even very similar life experience, often takes people in very different directions. Belief in God is also, as we have seen at many points in this book, a great source of strength at times – of moral strength and sanity – while, depending on the kind of God believed in, it can also have baleful effects. The meaning, direction and support that belief in God offers to so many alongside its deleterious effects is, as such, part of the moral character of that belief. That character needs to be seen alongside the moral challenges to belief in God outlined in this chapter and those challenges on a personal level bring some people to the moral necessity of atheism. This variety of responses to problems of evil and suffering does not mean that belief in a good God is merely a subjective, personal matter. Instead, dialogue makes most moral sense when believers and non-believers join together in seeking to alleviate suffering rather than contributing to it. In our concluding chapter, I shall bring together some of the observations and arguments made throughout this book to indicate how well religion is doing morally in its dialogue of actions as well as words.

10

Beyond Conclusions

At this point I want to look to the future and raise two questions about religion mainly but not exclusively as it is found in the UK. First, what is likely to be the cultural context in which evaluations of religion will continue to be made, and what are the implications of this for such assessments and for our culture more generally? Secondly, what are the best prospects for such evaluations? Let's turn to the first of these questions.

Our Multi-cultural Prospect
We have seen that religion is not simply a growing presence on the planet but also that this presence is being increasingly felt. Encounters with different religions – either directly or as brought to our attention through all forms of media – also continue to grow. In the UK, the fastest growing ethnic group is that of 'mixed ethnicity'. This fact alone indicates that ethnic and religious interaction, diversity and awareness, are increasingly as much a mainstay of British cultural life as they are in so many places across the globe. This

remains true even as the process of secularisation holds sway across Britain and north-Western Europe more generally. We can then reasonably imagine that ethical evaluations of religion are going to be ever-more relevant to our lives, as diverse communities and perspectives (including secular ones) reflect about our ever-evolving multiculture.

What kind of a context are legislators, policy makers, local councils and schools likely to find themselves in as evaluations of religion continue to be made? Two less-than-likely prospects are as follows. First would be an assimilationist melting pot in which religious diversity will have been tamed to the point of there being similar visions of the good society and the good life. This seems unlikely to emerge any time soon, either in the UK or anywhere else that is vaguely democratic and multi-cultural. We have seen how some very conservative forces within Christianity, Judaism and Islam do everything to resist all forms of assimilation and seek through the means of religious schooling to 'protect' upcoming generations from such an outcome. Such exclusivist tendencies are not in decline, although it is often part of their psychology to often feel very much under threat.

A second less-than-likely prospect is one in which religions are confined to a series of ghettoised cultures away from more mainstream society. There are a number of reasons for regarding such a severally segregated society as unlikely. First, while a number of such isolated religious cultures do everything to segregate themselves from the wider culture, such practice is not at all the norm among those who are religiously affiliated at present. Second, as mixed ethnicity and mixed religious adherence within families and communities grow, this helps fragment and dilute particular ethnic and religious cultures. Third, work culture persistently brings together people from diverse backgrounds and, in many cases schooling, higher education and sport continue to do the same. In addition, government policy shows every sign of continuing to work against cultural ghettoisation.[373]

It is likely that there will continue to be both assimilation and persistent ghettoisation too, but much of UK culture will remain and grow as a vibrant, yet at times uncomfortable, mix of faiths and secularisms which are compelled to live together and also often feel to benefit from that fact.

The prospect for future ethical evaluation of religion is therefore likely to be one in which there will be those pushing to establish or re-establish an enclosed world in which their minority faith is as unaccountable as possible to anyone else. There will equally be many, including government organisations and inter-faith groups, working for the opposite, while at the same time the mainstream churches – not least the Church of England – will continue to decline in significance. The whole of society, ever-more multi-cultural, will be affected by and engaged in these issues at work; through education; and in policy-making and direction. Given this prospect, the whole of society is, rightly, engaged in ethically evaluating religion, because the whole of society is a stakeholder in the outcomes since these increasingly touch us all.

On this basis I want to sketch out two types of debate around the best prospects for ethical evaluation of religion that, for all the tensions between them, are both very much needed.

Best prospects for evaluation
i. Towards Better Disagreement
I take this phrase from the title of Paul Hedges's book of the same name.

At the heart of any ethical appraisal of religion is the perennial question of what is moral. As we have seen, those within and beyond the bounds of religion don't simply disagree about how to reach moral goals, they also disagree even more about what those goals should be.

The moral goals or values championed today even in Britain are diverse – and they keep changing. They include for example the will of the people, the will of God, right intent, human rights, the pursuit of truth, the pursuit of happiness, the generation of wealth and economic growth, freedom (variously defined), equality of opportunity, environmentalism… The list could be very long, and the items on the list also have many meanings. A committed, strident secularist may see 'the will of God' not at all as a type of good, but as an unhealthy projection of the human mind, a first-rate moral hazard. By the same token, those of some specific types of religious persuasion may see 'freedom' as code for narcissism, permissiveness and relativism, the loss of a moral compass.

This kind of situation appears to be a moral impasse, but I don't think it has to be. I mentioned in the Introduction the notion of the sympathetic imagination as a crucial ingredient for moral progress. The philosopher Isaiah

Berlin referred to this when he proffered his concept of the plurality of goods, meaning that there are many goods – such as the ones just mentioned – that are not always commensurable with each other. Berlin suggested that if we were to put ourselves in another's shoes, we could begin to imagine how goods that we don't ourselves regard as such could nonetheless be goods for some others. This can begin to make room for moral dialogue across strongly contested moral divides. If all can begin to imagine why some alleged goods are goods for others, people holding diametrically opposed views may be better disposed to listen and engage with people and views they have most ardently opposed.

However, why will parties, religious and non-religious who disagree about what is moral, take up the challenge of engaging with the sympathetic imagination so as to allegedly better understand those with whom they sometimes most passionately disagree? Put more strongly, there is the view that the sympathetic imagination is a deviance from both morality and truth. For ardent secularists to enter into the perspective of staunch religious believers is to enter a world of delusion and even madness. For passionate believers of some kinds, the sympathetic imagination is similarly a dangerous distraction away from the truth and the good.

Yet if the human imagination is a potential moral hazard then ghettoised cultures are surely not immune from such dangers either in how they perceive others or in how they perceive themselves. The demonising of others – as evident in derogatory language such as kafir, goyim, and heathen – is all the more difficult to check within the confines of the tribe. Self-perceptions of victimhood and self-righteousness, for their part, can also gather pace and be imagined so as to exclude other possibilities. By contrast, the sympathetic imagination can reveal how these kinds of images of the self and of the other take shape on all sides to form vicious circles that are fertile soil for violence.

Many within religion will also point out that at the heart of much religious as well as humanist ethics are sentiments such as, 'Do unto others as you would have them do unto you,' or, as the Qur'an puts it, 'Repel evil with what is better.' (Surah 41: 34). The sympathetic imagination is not a million miles away from the heart of much religious teaching about morality, in fact it is hard to see how it is not quite often commended. My point is that, as we have seen, for all that there are significant moral hazards that have often been manifest in all faiths, there are also ingredients for better understanding of others, including those of opposing religious and non-religious points of view. Such a process does not at all lead towards agreement particularly, but as Paul Hedges writes, 'better disagreement' may be made available in which goals of understanding and a mutual exploration of spiritual, theological and moral issues comes more into the foreground.

This is a key task with which we find ourselves, and it is a perennial human challenge: how to better understand and better disagree. We need to acknowledge that there are many alleged moral goods, that humanity will perennially disagree about what these are and how to implement them. In my view the longer this disagreement goes on, the better, because this is the nature of the active, critical, self-reflective mind, informed as it should be by varied experience and culture. For that reason, the only thing that would halt disagreement would be a totalitarianism, within which disagreement was forbidden. Accepting disagreement and working alongside it rather than always seeking its eradication is seen here as both a moral and a practical way forward in negotiating contrasting values between religions, between believers and non-believers and within multi-cultures. Understanding this point is important. It has a number of implications. When we move away from always seeking agreement, consensus, or resolution in some form as regards moral judgments about religion, this can open up space in which other priorities arise. For example, we may start to look more closely at how we live in multicultures with perennial and, at times, passionately opposed moral agendas that are not about to be resolved. The nature of moral dialogue in this situation since it is then seen increasingly as very much on-going comes ever more to the fore and once again the sympathetic imagination is of no small significance here. For example, it can help us to appreciate that however unsympathetic we are towards a view with which we disagree, we can all the same be sympathetic with respect to the circumstances that have led to the formation of such views. In this way, hearing more about the lives, the narratives and circumstances of people from other religions and cultures is crucial, and quite a lot of inter-faith work today in the UK has this kind of focus. An instance in point is some of the good work being done at present in what are known as 'scriptural reasoning' meetings, in which members of different faiths engage with each others' understanding of their own sacred texts, with a view to understanding each other and their approaches to their texts. The aim is not to agree, either in the short or the long term. Where non-defensive cultures of dialogue can begin to grow in this way, there is also the prospect of self-questioning and self criticism as a product of better understanding the outlooks of others.

ii. Towards rational encounter and decision-making

Nevertheless, 'living alongside each other in our disagreements' as part of an on-going process of dialogue in understanding and judgment can only ever be part of the story, it can only take us so far. Decisions, including moral ones, taken within multi-cultures, need to be made all the time. They need to be made about the inter-relationships between the constituents of the overall culture, and about the character of multi-cultures as a whole.

A few remarks about specific cases and issues might help us to think things through a little more here. Recently, a primary school in east London rescinded a ban on the hijab being worn by girls under the age of eight due to protests and a petition that called for the ban to be lifted. Government regulation leaves such matters largely down to school policy, bearing in mind the nature of the school and of local communities. Upton Park, in east London, where the school is located, is very much a Muslim area. There is every reason, time and again, to not simply give way to a specific expression of public opinion just because it is public opinion, without considering what the opinion is. Those groups demanding that girls younger than eight wear the hijab should very reasonably be asked why they seek this. The research that we saw indicating that the wearing of the hijab by young girls may well have deleterious effects on them is quite reasonably brought into the discussion. To simply say that 'my religion says that my six-year old should do this' is not actually a good enough answer in itself. In this case, it isn't a valid argument, and shouldn't hold sway for two reasons. First, there is nothing in the Qur'an or Hadith or in any of the law schools to indicate it is a requirement. Amanda Spielman, current head of the school inspectorate service OFSTED, is quite right to point out that it is a conservative cultural practice more than anything else. The second reason is, however, even more important. To say 'I must be able to do 'x' because it is my religion' isn't in itself moral justification for an action. Otherwise, anything would be morally permissible so long as it came with religious commendation. Many within religions share my view on this point all too aware that those who think otherwise – some of their co-religionists – need to explain why in principle we shouldn't allow child sacrifice, genocide or any other atrocity if all that is needed by way of a moral justification is that 'my religion commands these things.' To take the example of the official Catholic teaching that abortion is a sin, even in the case of rape, we should be clear that this is a claim to absolute truth being made not just about Catholics but about anyone who has an abortion. For this reason, among others, non-Catholics have every justification – even a moral duty – to question the claims being made about them and their behaviour or potential behaviour. They might more than reasonably question the concept of sin, alongside notions of papal infallibility as it was constructed in the nineteenth century for political reasons, before getting to grips with more generic issues about the subjugation of women in past and present Church teaching.

Let's take a rather different example, from Orthodox Judaism. Orthodox Jewish women are required to wash in a facility known as a *mikveh* after menstruation, before resuming sexual relations. I remember looking round the Jewish Museum in Camden, in north London, with a liberal Jewish friend. An example of a *mikveh* is the first exhibit you see when you enter the museum, and my friend was not impressed by the association of menstruation with impurity – an association which of course is also found in other religions, for example in Islam. Unlike Catholicism with abortion, Orthodox Judaism is not asserting that this way of life is right for all, but rather that 'this is right for our community'. Twinned with this is often the claim that, in this respect, 'our rituals are our affair', and that the secular world and those from other faiths are in no position to comment; they simply have no moral purchase on the issues. Yet such a claim carries with it the expectation that it will be listened to by the wider society. What could be the justification for such an expectation, unless reciprocally critiques of such a claim were not also listened to by the Orthodox Jewish community? One such critique runs as follows. Just as minority religious groups have moral grounds to seek protection from, for example, the state when they may be liable to persecution, by the same token individuals within such minority religious groups have equal grounds for protection from such communities when they as individuals come under threat. There is a further problem too with the kind of communal privatisation of ethics that we are considering here. On the face of it, it looks like an example of relativism when a religious group argues, 'Look, we will keep to our rituals, we are not bothering you (outsiders).' But that is not what is actually going on. It is a relativism of convenience, where to get what you want you speak the language of the outside world…but you don't believe a word of it. Instructions about *mikveh* are based on the Torah, they are part of God's law for Orthodox Judaism, and as such are absolutely true for them. So, the argument really runs: 'We have the absolute truth from God, nothing that any outsider says has any purchase on the truth by comparison, and we shall therefore ignore it.' Yet claims to absoluteness by definition concern everyone and the wider society does not particularly share this view of absolute truth, and there is every reason why they should say so where, in their eyes, moral questions are raised.

I am not suggesting that for example the UK bans *mikvehs*, but it seems not only reasonable, but morally desirable, that they be criticised by the wider society, alongside discriminatory elements within other religions such as Christianity and Islam. That said, there does come a point at which the law should, it seems to me, step in and outlaw discrimination – for example against women – in ways it fails to do at present. For example, it would do well to start with equal pay for equal work for men and women in all forms of employment in the UK and elsewhere across Western culture. Only in 2017 was it revealed that the BBC was failing to do this as regards some of its leading reporters. By the same token, closer attention should also be given to 'under the radar' marriages within Islam in the UK, where men and women are married in the eyes of the religion, but not actually so under English law, but such that rights to divorce and inheritance are unequal because they are governed by various versions of Shari'a, as we have seen. Such a parallel system of aspects of civil law is a move towards establishing elements of a state within a state, and it is reasonably outlawed on moral grounds. Crucially, Muslims needn't keep to such practices to follow their religion faithfully. In fact, we have seen how some argue that one would better keep to Islam by rejecting them and this is exactly the point at which alliances are to be made cross-culturally, and across religious divides.

But what has happened to the sympathetic imagination, and to better disagreement at this point? Perhaps I appear to be paving the way for confrontation in some of what I have just said. What I am advocating is further engagement and more diversity of engagement. In particular, liberal alliances that reach across bounds of religion and culture are important insofar as they are committed to listening, to multi-cultural exchange and to understanding. This is the kind of context in which disagreement can be most fruitful. For example, aspects of Islam have much to offer wider British society by way of moral critique. An obvious case in point would be the British love affair with alcohol, which the health service regards as excessive, causing considerable harm for individuals, families, communities and the economy. Aspects of Islam also offer very fundamental moral critiques of the generational fabric of much Western culture. For example, the twentieth century in the West would seem to have invented the teenager, a free-floating youth generation, ephemerally self-defining through music, fashion, body-image, angst and rage, but also vulnerable, adrift from the vertical moorings of parents and community, which in turn becomes vulnerable to fragmentation and disintegration. These moral critiques are important, just as are critiques of conservative forms of religion, and as a whole society we need to engage more, not less with such issues.

Disagreement about moral issues is, however, also vital even when it runs the risk of being liable to confrontation. But here it is crucial to be clear that no one begins with a monopoly on morality nor has that by default or by right. Instead, all may be equal contributors, not least because all are equal stakeholders. So I'm suggesting, coming back to the fact that people and communities have many moral goals, that open and equal debate about ethics should be key among such goals. In this respect, a democratic and egalitarian ethos, as an integral part to open, ethical debate, is what underpins my criticisms a moment ago of the unequal way in which women and others are quite often treated in religious faiths. Those within religion who would have things otherwise would need to argue why they should not be subordinated within or excluded from ethical debate if they are going to do that to others or imply as much.

I have reached a variety of conclusions about the ethical character of religion today. From what has just been said, it is essential to keep such ethical debate alive about these issues and, through our sympathetic imagination, to maintain and build upon the ethics of such debate. while also reasoning our way towards decisions that involve evaluations of religion – whether those decisions are about government policy, local schooling or simply our own commitments and attitudes. Reaching conclusions can appear far more satisfying than the graft of pursuing an understanding that will almost certainly never be complete. Yet it is precisely for this reason that we shouldn't stop the pursuit of understanding, that we must reach beyond conclusions and not make the judgment that our judgments are so secure that no further understanding is worth the effort.

Endnotes

1   Scott Atran, *Talking to the Enemy* (London: Penguin, 2011), 401.
2   Fatema, Mernissi, *Beyond the Veil: Male-Female Dynamics in Modern Muslim Society*, ebook ed., (London: Saqi, 2011), 94.
3   I refer principally to the disciplines that go to make up Religious Studies, an introduction to which is John R. Hinnells (ed.), *The Routledge Companion to The Study of Religion*, 2nd ed., (London and New York: Routledge, 2010).
4   This is even so for those who believe in reincarnation. Reincarnationists do not believe that they will have the opportunity to live this life again, and the consequence of how this life is lived can be very far-reaching.
5   Pew Research Center, *Europe's Growing Muslim Population: Muslims are projected to increase as a share of Europe's population – even with no future migration*, Nov 29, 2017, available at http://www.pewforum.org/2017/11/29/europes-growing-muslim-population/
6   Friedrich Max Müller, *Introduction to the Science of Religion* (London: Longmans, Green and Co., 1882), 13.
7   John H. Hick, *The Philosophy of Religion* (New Jersey: Prentice Hall, 1990), 2-3.
8   William T. Cavanaugh, *The Myth of Religious Violence: Secular Ideology and the Roots of Modern Conflict* (Oxford: Oxford University Press, 2009), see Chapter 1. Here we see how John Hick, Charles Kimball and Leroy Rouner are just three scholars among many others who maintain that we can meaningfully speak about religion in the abstract as something distinct from either ideology or politics. They also claim that we can meaningfully apply such distinctions to the past.
9   W. G. Aston trans., *The Nihongi: Chronicles of Japan from the Earliest Times to AD 697*, Vol. 2 (London: The Japan Society, 1896; reprint Tokyo: Tuttle, 1972), 131.
10 Paul Feyerabend, *Farewell to Reason* (London and New York: Verso, 2002), 9.
11 The Italian philosopher Giambatista Vico wrote about *fantasia*, sometimes translated as 'the sympathetic imagination', to describe the human ability to

enter, through an imaginative reconstruction, into the life of another, perhaps a historical figure. Martha Nussbaum writes in a similar way about empathy or, as she calls it, 'the participatory imagination'. She adds, however, that more is needed to realise the kind of thing I mean by the sympathetic imagination. For example, the sadist can be empathetic, that is part of their armoury against their victim. They can well imagine and exploit the impact of what they are doing. So, in addition to empathy, good intent is essential so as to seek, through the understanding of another, what is best for them, through valuing their perspective of the good. See Martha C. Nussbaum, *The New Religious Intolerance: Overcoming the Politics of Fear in an Anxious Age* (Cambridge: Harvard University Press, 2012), 144f.

12 Stewart M. Hoover, 'Why Has Religion gone public again: Towards a theory of media and religious re-publicisation' in *Religion, Media and Culture: A Reader*, Gordon Lynch and Jolyon Mitchell (eds.) with Anna Strhan (London: Routledge, 2012) 85.

13 Christopher Landau, 'What the Media Thinks about Religion: A Broadcast Perspective', in *Religion and the News*, Jolyon Mitchell and Owen Gower (eds.), (Farnham: Ashgate, 2012) 83.

14 Landau, in *Religion and the News*, Mitchell and Gower (eds.), 84.

15 Choudary was released in 2018 after serving time under the Terrorism Act 2000 for inviting support for ISIS.

16 Neil Thurman, *Does British Journalism have a diversity problem?*, online survey, May 2016 (Reuters Institute for the Study of Journalism, Oxford University), 11 available at https://drive.google.com/file/d/0B4lqRxA4qQpja kl1UEd5WEFlRGc/view?pref=2&pli=1

17 Landau 82.

18 Landau 82.

19 Owen Jones, *The Establishment: And How They Get Away with it* (London: Penguin, 2015), 122. See also J. Lewis, A. Williams, B. Franklin, J. Thomas and N. Mosdell, report entitled *The Quality and Independence of British Journalism: Tracking the Changes over 20 Years* (Cardiff University, 2008), available at https://orca.cf.ac.uk/18439/1/Quality%20%26%20Independence%20of%20 British%20Journalism.pdf

20 See Teemu Taira, Elizabeth Poole and Kim Knott, Chapter 2: 'Religion in the

British Media Today', in *Religion and the News*, Mitchell and Gower (eds.), 38.
21   Author's telephone interview with Andrew Brown at *The Guardian*, London, on 11 Apr, 2014.
22   Taira, Poole and Knott, in *Religion in the News*, Mitchell and Gower (eds.), 41.
23   Taira et al., 41.
24   Taira et al., 41.
25   Robin Gill, Chapter 3: 'Religion News and Social Context: Evidence from Newspapers', in *Religion in the News*, Mitchell and Gower (eds.), 57.
26   See Taira et al., 33.
27   Taira et al., 36.
28   Kerry Moore, Paul Mason and Justin M. W. Lewis, *Images of Islam in the UK: The Representation of British Muslims in the National Print News Media 2000-2008 [working paper]* (Cardiff University, 2008), available at http://orca.cf.ac.uk/53005/1/08channel4-dispatches.pdf
29   Chris Allen, 'A review of the evidence relating to the representation of Muslims and Islam in the British media', submitted to the All-Party Parliamentary Group on Islamophobia, October 2012 (Institute of Applied Social Studies, School of Social Policy, University of Birmingham), available at https://www.birmingham.ac.uk/Documents/college-social-sciences/social-policy/IASS/news-events/MEDIA-ChrisAllen-APPGEvidence-Oct2012.pdf.
30   Allen, report to the All-Party Parliamentary Group on Islamophobia, 9.
31   Dominic Ponsford, *Newspaper stories misrepresenting Islam would not be tolerated if they were about Judaism, regulator IPSO needs to step in*, online article from PressGazette, 27 Jan, 2017, available at https://www.pressgazette.co.uk/news paper-stories-misrepresenting-islam-would-not-be-tolerated-if-they-were-about-judaism-regulator-ipso-needs-to-step-in/.
32   See Taira et al., 38.
33   Miqdaad Versi, *The UK media too often misrepresents Muslims – with dangerous results*, *The Guardian* online, 23 Jan, 2017, available at https://www.theguardian.com/commentisfree/2017/jan/23/uk-media-misrepresents-muslims-islam-prejudice-press
34   David Chidester, *Christianity: A Global History* (London: Penguin, 2001), 534.
35   A CTVC production for Channel 4, produced by Ray Bruce, 1989.
36   Julius Streicher argued at his Nuremberg trial that if he should be standing there arraigned on such charges, so should Martin Luther, who had suggested that Jews

should be burnt in their synagogues. See also http://www.newworldencyclopedia.org/entry/Julius_Streicher. For further details about how Luther thought Jews should be dealt with, see as quoted from Luther's *The Jews and Their Lies* (1543), available at http://www.jewishvirtuallibrary.org/martin-luther-quot-the-jews-and-their-lies-quot.

37   http://www.jewishvirtuallibrary.org/martin-luther-quot-the-jews-and-their-lies-quot.
38   Chidester, Christianity, 537.
39   Diarmaid MacCulloch, *A History of Christianity: The First Three Thousand Years* (London: Penguin, 2009), 942.
40   MacCulloch, 944.
41   MacCulloch, 937-8.
42   MacCulloch, 937-8.
43   Jonathan Glover, *Humanity: A Moral History of the Twentieth Century* (London: Pimlico, 2001), 385.
44   The work of the Council of Christians and Jews as well as broader interfaith work are cases in point.
45   See Yuri Tabak's article 'Relations between the Russian Orthodox Church and Judaism: Past and Present' (undated, copyrighted 2000), explaining some of the problems in the Russian Orthodox Church in recent times. Available at Jewish-Christain Relations, online inter-faith site, owned and operated by the International Council of Christians and Jews, http://www.jcrelations.net/Relations+between+the+Russian+Orthodox+Church+and+Judaism%3A+Past+and+Present.2227.0.hyml?L=3.
46   Brian E. Close, *Judaism (Student's Approach to World Religions)* (London: Hodder Arnold H&S, 1991), 113.
47   Christopher Hitchens, *God Is Not Great: How Religion Poisons Everything* (London: Atlantic Books, 2007), 176. There is good reason to regard Hitchens's characterisation of both Judaism and Jesus as mistaken here.
48   Hitchens 175f.
49   John Hick's theology is just one example of this kind of approach. See his *Evil and the God of Love* (Collins, 1979).
50   Martin Luther King, Jr., *Stride Toward Freedom: The Montgomery Story* (New York: Harper Row, 1958), 137-8.

51 King, 137-8.
52 According to the Encyclopaedia Britannica, satyagraha '(Sanskrit and Hindi: "holding onto truth")' is a 'concept introduced in the early 20th century by Mahatma Gandhi to designate a determined but nonviolent resistance to evil. Gandhi's satyagraha became a major tool in the Indian struggle against British imperialism and has since been adopted by protest groups in other countries', available at https://www.britannica.com/topic/satyagraha-philosophy
53 Richard Deats, *Martin Luther King, Jr.: Spirit-Led Prophet – A Biography* (London: New City Press, 1999), 67.
54 *The Words of Martin Luther King, Jr.*, selected by Coretta Scott King; Clayborne Carson and Peter Holloran (ed.), (New York: Newmarket Press, 1983), 74.
55 Martin Luther King, Jr., *Strength to Love* (Minneapolis: Fortress Press, 2010), 99-108.
56 King, *Strength to Love*, 105.
57 Chidester, *Christianity*, 564-7.
58 Andrew Bradstock, *Saints and Sandanistas: The Catholic Church in Nicaragua and Its Response to the Revolution* (London: Epworth Press, 1987), 2.
59 See Steve Bruce, *Politics and Religion* (Cambridge: Polity, 2003), 98, for further details. For a defence of Catholicism see Edward Bell, 'Catholicism and Democracy: A Reconsideration', *Journal of Religion & Society*, vol. 10, 2008, 1–22; available at http://www.luc.edu/media/lucedu/dccirp/pdfs/articlesforresourc/Article_-_Bell,_Edward.pdf
60 Bruce Politics and Religion 136.
61 Bruce Politics and Religion 136.
62 See Deane William Ferm's précis in 'Third-World Liberation Theology: Challenge to World Religions', in *World Religions and Human Liberation*, Dan Cohn-Sherbok (ed.), (Maryknoll: Orbis Books, 1992).
63 *Religion and Politics in Comparative Perspective: The One, the Few and the Many*, Ted Gerard Jelen and Clyde Wilcox (eds.), (New York: Cambridge University Press, 2002), 228.
64 Penny Lernoux, 'The Fundamentalist Surge in Latin America', first published in *Christian Century*, January 20, 1988, 51, republished by permission by Religion Online and available at https://www.religion-online.org/article/the-fundamentalist-surge-in-latin-america/

65 Lernoux, 'The Fundamentalist Surge in Latin America.' 2.
66 *The Bible*, New Revised Standard Version, Romans 13:1. https://www.biblestudytools.com/nrs/
67 Paul Freston, remarks made at a conference entitled 'Christianity and Conflict in Latin America', held at the National Defense University Washington, D.C., Apr 6, 2006. 'The discussion was part of a joint project on religion and security undertaken by the Pew Forum and National Defense University's School for National Security Executive Education,' writes the Pew Research Center. See http://www.pewforum.org/2006/04/06/christianity-and-conflict-in-latin-america.
68 Freston, conference remarks.
69 Freston, conference remarks.
70 The UCKG describes itself on its website as formed in 1977 in Brazil. For a non-partisan account of what it is and its work, contact INFORM at King's College London; it is a research centre studying new religious movements.
71 There is of course the ethical question of the elimination of indigenous religion due to religious importation. The parties involved are best placed to begin this conversation.
72 Jelen and Wilcox (eds.), *Religion and Politics in Comparative Perspective*, 229.
73 Jelen and Wilcox, *Religion and Politics*, 230. This is very much in line with the arguments of Max Weber in *The Protestant Ethic and the Spirit of Capitalism* (first published 1904-5).
74 Mark Johnston, *Saving God: Religion After Idolatry* (Princeton, New Jersey: Princeton University Press, 2009), 51.
75 UCKG are an example of this including in their UK operation where they appear to target the poor and needy in their advertising and publicity while also making financial demands on such people too.
76 Stephanie Kirchgaessner in Rome and Jonathan Watts in Rio de Janeiro, 'Catholic Church warms to liberation theology as founder heads to Vatican', *The Guardian*, Monday 11 May, 2015; available at https://www.theguardian.com/world/2015/may/11/vatican-new-chapter-liberation-theology-founder-gustavo-gutierrez
77 This is my paraphrase of Gary Potter. See the link below for the full text. https://bit.ly/2Uly3Id

78 Hitchens, *God Is Not Great*, 24-5. (Italics original to the text)
79 Robert D. Lee, *Religion and Politics in the Middle East: Identity, Ideology, Institutions, and Attitudes* (Boulder: Westview Press, 2014), 79.
80 Lee, *Middle East*, 80.
81 Declaration of the Establishment of the State of Israel, 14 May, 1948; available at http://www.mfa.gov.il/mfa/foreignpolicy/peace/guide/pages/declaration%20of%20establishment%20of%20state%20of%20israel.aspx
82 Lee, Middle East, 83.
83 Charles S. Liebman and Eliezer Don-Yehiya, Religion and Politics in Israel (Bloomington: Indiana University Press, 1984), 50.
84 Liebman and Don-Yehiya, Religion and Politics in Israel, 97.
85 Ilan Pappé, *A History of Modern Palestine: One Land, Two Peoples* (Cambridge: Cambridge University Press, 2006), 200.
86 Lee, *Middle East*, 98.
87 Lee, *Middle East*, 98.
88 Lee, *Middle East*, 100.
89 According to the Pew Research Center, 62% of Haredi Jews in Israel think that the word Zionist is either 'not too' accurate a description of them or 'not at all' an accurate description of them. From a Pew study entitled *Israel's Religiously Divided Society*, 8 Mar, 2016; available at http://assets.pewresearch.org/wp-content/uploads/sites/11/2016/03/Israel-Survey-Full-Report.pdf. 23.
90 Jewish religious law both written and oral beginning with the 613 *mitzvot* or commandments in the Torah but including the Talmud as well.
91 Bennett Zimmerman, Roberta Seid and Michael Wise of the American Research Initiative presented their demographic findings on January 23, 2005. A critique by leading Hebrew University demographer, Professor Sergio DellaPergola, followed. Published as 'What is the True Demographic Picture in the West Bank and Gaza? – A Presentation and a Critique', in *Jerusalem Issue Brief*, Vol. 4, No. 19, 10 Mar, 2005; available at the Jerusalem Center for Public Affairs, http://www.jcpa.org/brief/brief004-19.htm.
92 Pappé, *Modern Palestine*, 155.
93 See the Palestine National Charter of 1964, the PLO's founding declaration, listing its objectives in a series of articles; available at http://www.palwatch.org/main.aspx?fi=640&doc_id=8210 https://web.archive.org/web/20101130144018/

http://www.un.int/wcm/content/site/palestine/pid/12363
94 Pappé, *Modern Palestine*, 247.
95 Pappé, *Modern Palestine*, 246.
96 Laleh Khalili, *Heroes and Martyrs of Palestine: The Politics of National Commemoration* (Cambridge: Cambridge University Press, 2007), 147.
97 Hamid Dabashi gives us a glimpse of the Shi'a mind-set as regards the meaning of martyrdom. See Hamid Dabashi, *Shi'ism: A Religion of Protest* (Cambridge, Massachusetts: Belknap Press of Harvard University Press, 2011), 84.
98 Seen very much as a terrorist organisation in the West, Palestinian Islamic Jihad was formed in 1981 with the objective of the destruction of the state of Israel and the founding of a Palestinian state.
99 A Palestinian Islamist movement.
100 Pappé, *Modern Palestine*, 284.
101 Pappé, *Modern Palestine*, 284.
102 Pappé, *Modern Palestine*, 284.
103 Scott Atran, *Talking to the Enemy* (London: Penguin, 2011), 384. More will be said about interpretations of the Qur'an in Chapter 6 . I will also have more to say about concepts of jihad in Chapter 8.
104 Pappé, *Modern Palestine*, 283.
105 Atran, *Talking to the Enemy*, 363.
106 Forms of Sufism for example often eschew the exoteric suggesting that believers can become too attached to the externals of religion, such as ritual, place, dress and outward appearance. For these kinds of believer the true pilgrimage is really a journey within not to a sacred site such as the Ka'ba in Mecca or and the Dome of the Rock on the Temple Mount. A good example of a British based Jewish organisation that opposes confrontation over sacred space is Jews for Justice for Palestinians http://jfjfp.com
107 Harold G. Koenig, Summary and Conclusions, in Harold G. Koenig (ed.), *Handbook of Religion and Mental Health*, (San Diego, CA: Academic Press, 1998), 392.
108 Simon Dein, 'Religion and Mental Health: Current Findings', Royal College of Psychiatrists, 2013, 1; available at https://www.rcpsych.ac.uk/pdf/Simon%20Dein%20Religion%20and%20Mental%20Health.%20Current%20Findings.pdf.

109 Dein, 'Religion and Mental Health', 1.
110 Simon Dein, 'Religion, spirituality and mental health', in *The Psychiatric Times*, 10 Jan, 2010; available at http://www.psychiatrictimes.com/schizophrenia/religion-spirituality-and-mental-health.
111 Jeff Levin, 'Religion and mental health: Theory and research', in *International Journal of Applied Psychoanalytic Studies*, Vol. 7, Issue 2, Jan 2010; available online at Wiley InterScience https://onlinelibrary.wiley.com/doi/pdf/10.1002/aps.240, 7.
112 This was certainly the view of Dr. Grace M. Jantzen (from King's College London) who speacialised in the study of religious experience.
113 William James, *The Varieties of Religious Experience: A Study in Human Nature* (London: Penguin, 1982), 444.
114 Richard Dawkins, *The God Delusion* (London: Bantam Press 2006), 61-4.
115 I am thinking here in particular of the via negativa or apophatic tradition of for example Pseudo-Dionysius, Moses Mendelssohn and Meister Eckhart. Roughly speaking their theologies maintain that if God can be conceptualised and understood through language then this is not God. If God can be imagined, be made an object of desire and hope then this is not God. The stage by stage emancipation of the mind and heart from such constraints is the true spiritual path.
116 John Maltby, C.A. Lewis, and Liza Day, 'Prayer and subjective well-being: the application of a cognitive-behavioural framework', in *Mental Health Religion and Culture*, Vol. 11, Issue 1, 2008, 119-129; online version used, Sheffield Hallam University Research Archive at http://shura.shu.ac.uk/6056/1/Day_Prayer_and.pdf, 5.
117 Maltby *et al.*, 'Prayer and subjective well-being', 5.
118 Maltby *et al.*, 5.
119 Leslie J. Francis and Thomas E. Evans, 'The Psychology of Christian Prayer: A Review of Empirical Research', in *Religion*, Vol. 25, Issue 4, Oct 1995, 371-88; available at https://www.tandfonline.com/doi/abs/10.1016/S0048-721X(05)80021-1.
120 Markus H. Schafer, 'Close Ties, Intercessory Prayer, and Optimism Among American Adults: Locating God in the Social Support Network', *Journal for the Scientific Study of Religion*, Vol. 52, Issue 1, Mar 2013, 35–56; available online at https://onlinelibrary.wiley.com/doi/abs/10.1111/jssr.12010.

121 Christopher G. Ellison, Matt Bradshaw, Kevin J. Flannelly, Kathleen C. Galek, 'Prayer, Attachment to God, and Symptoms of Anxiety-Related Disorders among US Adults', in *Sociology of Religion*, Vol. 75, Issue 2, 2014, 208-33; available at http://www.baylorisr.org/wp-content/uploads/Sociology-of-Religion-2014-Ellison-208-33.pdf.

122 Dein, 'Religion and Mental Health', 2.

123 Voltaire actually said 'If there were no God it would be necessary to invent him'.

124 Had Hitchens been able to read Stephen Batchelor's *Confessions of a Buddhist Atheist* before he wrote *God Is Not Great*, he might have had the odd positive word to add about Buddhist meditation. See the following link: https://www.theguardian.com/commentisfree/belief/2010/mar/10/buddhism-atheism-hitchens

125 Walpola Rahula, *What the Buddha Taught* (New York: Grove Press, 1974), 48.

126 J. Kabat-Zinn, A. L. Massion, J. Kristeller, L. G. Peterson, K. E. Fletcher, L. Pbert, W. R. Lenderking, S. F. Santorelli, 'Effectiveness of a Meditation-Based Stress Reduction Program in the Treatment of Anxiety Disorders', in *American Journal of Psychology*, Vol. 149, Issue 7, Jul 1992, 936-43; available at http://citeseerx.ist.psu.edu/viewdoc/download?doi=10.1.1.474.4968&rep=rep1&type=pdf.

127 J. D. Teasdale, Z.V. Segal, J. M. Williams, V. A. Ridgeway, J. M. Soulsby, M. A. Lau, 'Prevention of Relapse/Recurrence in Major Depression by Mindfulness-Based Cognitive Therapy', in *Journal of Consulting and Clinical Psychology*, Vol. 68, Issue 4, Aug 2000, 615-23; available at http://psycnet.apa.org/record/2000-05084-010.

128 J. D. Teasdale, Z. Segal, M. G. Williams, 'How Does Cognitive Therapy Prevent Depressive Relapse and Why Should Attentional Control (Mindfulness) Training Help?', in *Behaviour Research and Therapy Journal*, Vol. 33, Issue 1, Jan 1995, 25-39; available at https://www.sciencedirect.com/science/article/pii/0005796794E00117?via%3Dihub.

129 D. L. Beauchamp-Turner, D. M. Levinson, 'Effects of Meditation on Stress, Health and Affect', in *Medical-Psychotherapy: An International Journal*, Vol. 5, 1992, 123-31; abstract available at http://psycnet.apa.org/record/1994-18824-001.

130 Robert Booth, 'Mindfulness therapy comes at a high price for some say experts', *The Guardian*, 25 Aug 2014; available at https://www.theguardian.com/society/2014/aug/25/mental-health-meditation.

131 Michal Baime, 'This is Your Brain On Mindfulness: Meditators Say Their Practice

Fundamentally Changes the Way They Experience Life – Michael Baime reports on how modern neuroscience is explaining this in biological terms', *Shambhala Sun*, July 2011, 47; available at http://www.uphs.upenn.edu/pastoral/events/Baime_SHAMBHALA_2011.pdf.

132 J. J. Miller, K. Fletcher, J. Kabat-Zinn, 'Three-Year Follow-up and Clinical Implications of Mindfulness Meditation-Based Stress Reduction Intervention in the Treatment of Anxiety Disorders', *General Hospital Psychiatry*, Vol. 17, Issue 3, May 1995, 192-200, 192; available at https://pdfs.semanticscholar.org/dda0/0bafa0dbeb4bc6ac12c9b5d63d9315230191.pdf.

133 P. Grossman, L. Niemann, S. Schmidt, H. Walach, 'Mindfulness-Based Stress Reduction and Health Benefits: A Meta-Analysis', in *Journal of Psychosomatic Research*, Vol. 57, Issue 1, Jul 2004, 35-43, 35; available at https://www.cancerwa.asn.au/resources/2015-07-07-Grossman-2004MBSR-and-health-benefits-meta-analysis.pdf.

134 What arguably has least credit is the commercialisation of mindfulness as basic courses in this proliferate. Dubbed McMindfulness there appear to be serious concerns about the qualifications of some teachers on basic mindfulness courses as business appears keen to cash in on the growing mental health needs of the population.

135 Heidi A. Wayment, Bill Wiist, Bruce M. Sullivan, Meghan A. Warren, in the *Journal of Happiness Studies*, Vol. 12, Issue 4, Aug 2011, 575-89; abstract available at https://www.researchgate.net/publication/225470995_Doing_and_Being_Mindfulness_Health_and_Quiet_Ego_Characteristics_Among_Buddhist_Practitioners.

136 Gauri Verma and Ricardo Araya, 'The Effect of Meditation on Psychological Distress Among Buddhist Monks and Nuns', in the *International Journal of Psychiatry in Medicine*, Vol. 40, Issue 4, Dec 2010, 461-8; available at http://journals.sagepub.com/doi/abs/10.2190/PM.40.4.h.

137 See Daisetz T. Suzuki *Zen Doctrine of No-Mind* for a more detailed account of *mushin*.

138 As defined by the Encyclopedia Britannica Civil religion is 'a public profession of faith that aims to inculcate political values and that prescribes dogma, rites, and rituals for citizens of a particular country.' https://www.britannica.com/topic/civil-religion

139 We are looking here specifically at Christian mission, defined according to the Encyclopedia Britannica – 'as an organised effort for the propagation of the Christian faith'

140 World Council of Churches, Pontifical Council for Interreligious Dialogue, World Evangelical Alliance, 'Christian Witness in a Multi-Religious World: Recommendations for Conduct', jointly issued in June 2011 by the three bodies, 'the document represents a broad consensus on appropriate missionary conduct "according to gospel principles" when sharing the Christian faith', 4; available at https://bit.ly/2Uj2nOw; abstract quoted here available at http://journals.sagepub.com/doi/abs/10.1177/239693931103500403.

141 The Parliament of World Religions, the Interfaith Encounter Association, the Interfaith Network for the UK.

142 See www.interfaith.org.uk for their statement of mission, vision and values.

143 See the section about religious harmony spoken by the Dalai Lama athttps://www.dalailama.com/messages/religious-harmony-1.

144 Anonymous, 'Pope Francis says atheists can do good and go to heaven too!', Catholic Online, 30 May 2013; available at www.catholic.org/news/hf/faith/story.php?id=51077

145 http://www.vatican.va/roman_curia/congregations/cfaith/documents/rc_con_cfaith_doc_20000806_dominus-iesus_en.html

146 Pope John Paul II, *Crossing the Threshold of Hope*, (New York: Knopf, 2013), 48-49.

147 Pew Research Center, *Tolerance and Tension: Islam and Christianity in Sub-Saharan Africa*, 13 Apr 2010, 15. The report indicates this to be the case across Africa as regards the two dominant religions of Islam and Christianity. Available at http://www.pewforum.org/2010/04/15/executive-summary-islam-and-christianity-in-sub-saharan-africa/.

148 Andrew Wingate, 'Inter-religious conversion', in *Understanding Inter-religious Relations*, David Cheetham, Douglas Pratt and David Thomas (eds), (Oxford: Oxford University Press, 2014), 190.

149 Stanley Hauerwas, *The Hauerwas Reader*, John Berkman and Michael Cartwright (eds.), (Durham: Duke University, 2001), 619.

150 Nicky Gumbel *Searching Issues: What About Other Religions?* (London: Alpha International, 2009) 7 - 11.

151 For example, *The Concise Oxford Dictionary of the Christian Church* gives the

following definition of redaction criticism: 'the investigation of the editorial work done by Biblical writers on earlier material, e.g. of the use made of the Marcan material by Matthew and Luke.' *The Concise Oxford Dictionary of the Christian Church* ed. E. A. Livingstone (Oxford: Oxford University Press, 1987)

152 Evangelical Christian missionary activity in India today is very easily seen and portrayed as neo-colonialism readily giving rise to the kind of hostile response we see in the incumbent BJP government's strictures.

153 I referred in the last chapter to Reagan cults, US-inspired evangelical Christianity that was part of a political campaign to counter communist and left-wing influence in Latin America.

154 Terry Sanderson, president of the National Secular Society, posted a blog on 8 June, 2014, entitled 'BBC poll shows that religious people give more to charity than non-religious. Maybe…'; available at https://www.secularism.org.uk/opinion/2014/06/bbc-poll-shows-that-religious-people-give-more-to-charity-than-non-religious-maybe.

155 Ingrid Storm, 'Civic Engagement in Britain: The Role of Religion and Inclusive Values', Oxford University Press, open-access article, 28 Oct 2014, 1; also published in *European Sociological Review*, Vol. 31, Issue 1, 1 February 2015, 14–29; available at https://academic.oup.com/esr/article/31/1/14/458836.

156 Storm, 'Civic Engagement', 2.

157 Storm, 'Civic Engagement', 15.

158 Greg Smith, 'Faith and Volunteering in the UK: Towards a Virtuous Cycle for the Accumulation of Social, Religious and Spiritual Capital?', in *Diaconia*, Vol. 2, Issue 2, Nov 2011, 175-209, 183; available at http://gregsmith.synthasite.com/resources/Diaconia_02_2011_Smith.pdf.

159 Charities Aid Foundation, 'One Pound in Six Given to Charity Goes to Religious Charities – Research', 29 Mar, 2013; available at https://www.cafonline.org/about-us/media-office/2903-religious-charities.

160 Tom McKenzie is now Assistant Professor of Economics, College of Business, at the Antalya Bilim University in Turkey.

161 Tom McKenzie and Cathy Pharoah, 'UK Household Giving: New Results on Regional Trends 2001-08', CGAP Briefing Note 6, July 2010. Available at http://www.cgap.org.uk/uploads/reports/CGAP_Briefing_Note_6%20(Regional%20Giving).pdf. As quoted in Steve Lodge, 'Giving to charity: who digs the deepest?',

Cass Knowledge, 1 Jul 2011, available at https://www.cass.city.ac.uk/faculties-and-research/research/cass-knowledge/inbusiness/2011/giving-to-charity-who-digs-the-deepest.

162 McKenzie and Pharoah in Lodge,
163 McKenzie and Pharoah in Lodge,
164 *The Huffington Post UK*, 'Muslims "give most to charity", ahead of Christians, Jews and Atheists, poll finds', 21 Jul, 2013; available at https://www.huffingtonpost.co.uk/2013/07/21/muslims-give-most_n_3630830.html.
165 As quoted in 'Would aid flourish without religion?', anonymous, *The Guardian* online, 20 Sep, 2010; available at https://www.theguardian.com/commentisfree/belief/2010/sep/20/religion-generosity-humanitarian-aid.
166 Chloe Stothart, 'The religious give more to charity, according to CAF report', *Third Sector* online news site for the not-for-profit sector, 23 Feb, 2012; available at https://www.thirdsector.co.uk/religious-give-charity-according-caf-report/fundraising/article/1118732.
167 Stothart, 'The religious give more'.
168 Simon Rogers, 'Britain's Top 1,000 Charities Ranked by Donations. Who raises the most money?', *The Guardian*, 24 Apr, 2012
169 Author's interview with David Ainsworth, 29 May, 2015.
170 See also B. Schmid, E. Thomas, J. Olivier and J. R. Cochrane, *The contribution of religious entities to health in sub-Saharan Africa*, on behalf of ARHAP, the African Religious Health Assets Programme; unpublished report, May 2008, of study commissioned by the B. & M. Gates Foundation. Available at https://s3.amazonaws.com/berkley-center/08ARHAPGatesContributionReligiousSubsaharanAfrica.pdf.
171 'Caspar Melville, 'Ditching the baggage of scripture', *The Guardian* online, 13 Mar, 2009; available at https://www.theguardian.com/commentisfree/belief/2009/mar/13/religion-charitable-giving.
172 Melville, 'Ditching the baggage',
173 Melville, 'Ditching the baggage',
174 Melville, 'Ditching the baggage',
175 Storm, 'Civic Engagement',
176 Ian Linden 'The Debate Is Lacking Facts: Finding accurate statistics to make the case for the religious contribution to international development is a problem', *The*

Guardian online, 22 September 2010; available at https://www.theguardian.com/commentisfree/belief/2010/sep/22/debate-lacking-facts-religion-international-development

177 "The World's Billionaires: 2015 Ranking - #1638 Edir Macedo & family".*Forbes*. 2015. The bulk of Macedo's fortune stems from his ownership of Rede Record, Brazil's second-largest broadcaster, which he acquired in 1990 from entertainer Silvio Santos.

178 David V. Barrett, *The New Believers: Sects, 'Cults', and Alternative Religions* (London: Cassell & Co., 2001), 229-30. For in-depth research about new religious movements, INFORM at King's College, London is a valuable source of information.

179 https://www.secularism.org.uk/news/2014/01/suspect-fundraising-methods-of-evangelical-church-under-spotlight-again

180 Frank Cranmer, 'The Charity Commission and information on religious charities', at online forum *Law and Religion UK*, 7 Mar, 2015; available at http://www.lawandreligionuk.com/2015/03/07/the-charity-commission-and-information-on-religious-charities/

181 See *Faith Schools in England*, 1998-2015, a report by British Religion in Numbers, an Academy Research Project hosted at the University of Manchester. Available at http://www.brin.ac.uk/figures/faith-schools-in-england-1998-2015 for statistics about the percentage of primary and secondary school pupils in religious schools between 1998 and 2015.

182 The Bible, King James Version, Matthew 7:20 (NB v. 16 reads "Ye shall know them by their fruits. Do men gather grapes of thorns, or figs of thistles?" v. 20 is the one Grayling is quoting: "Wherefore by their fruits ye shall know them."

183 'Parenting and the Different Ways It Can Affect Children's Lives: Research Evidence', paper edited by David Utting, commissioned by the Joseph Rowntree Foundation, 2007; 9 available at https://www.jrf.org.uk/sites/default/files/jrf/migrated/files/2132-parenting-literature-reviews.pdf See the following link for the full report: https://www.jrf.org.uk/report/parenting-and-different-ways-it-can-affect-childrens-lives-research-evidence.

184 Jean Decety, Jason M. Cowell, Kang Lee, Randa Mahasneh, Susan Malcolm-Smith, Bilge Selcuk and Xinyue Zhou, in *Current Biology*, Vol. 25, Issue 22, 2951-55, Nov 16, 2015; available at http://www.cell.com/current-biology/abstract/S0960-9822(15)01167-7.

185 Harriet Sherwood, 'Religious children are meaner than their secular counterparts, study finds', *The Guardian*, 6 Nov, 2015; available at https://www.theguardian.com/world/2015/nov/06/religious-children-less-altruistic-secular-kids-study

186 Michael Ungar, 'Does Religion Make Children Resilient? – It can, but it depends on the experience', *Psychology Today* online, posted Jun 26, 2014; available at www.psychologytoday.com/blog/nurturing-resilience/201406/does-religion-make-children-resilient.

187 In the social sciences there are often clearly both experimental and ethical constraints. For example, one cannot change a variable (the independent variable) such as the religious schooling of a child and then wait to see what are the behavioural consequences (the dependent variable).

188 Those demographic trends about the decline of religious adherence in the UK are well set out in a recent article in *The Economist* entitled 'Backwards, Christian Soldiers' (print edition) and 'A majority of Britons now follow no religion' (online edition), 9 Sep, 2017; available at https://www.economist.com/britain/2017/09/09/a-majority-of-britons-now-follow-no-religion.

189 Stanley Milgram's famous experiment can be found described at www.simplepsychology.org. It makes clear some very alarming consequences that follow from being too willing to obey authority figures regardless of the consequences.

190 This is a key conclusion of his short book Stephen Law, *The War for Children's Minds: Liberal Values and Why We Should Defend Them* (London: Routledge, 2006)

191 S. P. Oliner and P. M. Oliner, *The Altruistic Personality – Rescuers of Jews in Nazi Europe* (New York: The Free Press, 1992), 156.

192 Naomi Ackerman, '"Teach philosophy in primary schools," says academic', *The Daily Telegraph*, 12 Mar, 2015; available at http://www.telegraph.co.uk/education/primaryeducation/11466547/Teach-philosophy-in-primary-schools-says-academic.html

193 For example, as an R.E. teacher for over 25 years, idly scouring the pages of the Times Educational Educational Supplement on Fridays, I never once came across an advert for an R.E. teacher in a Catholic School that did not state that a practising Catholic was required to fill the post. The adoption of 'religious character status' by, for example, the vast majority of Catholic and Church of England primary and junior schools also means that such schools are able

and willing to discriminate in the appointment of teaching staff on grounds of religious/non-religious affiliation and commitment. These facts indicate more of an authoritarian than a liberal set of intentions.

194 I am in absolute sympathy with Richard Dawkins in this respect when he points out that creationists such as Michael Behe have had their notions of 'intelligent design' critiqued in 57 peer reviews. Even in the US with its many millions of Christian fundamentalists, creationism doesn't really figure at all in serious scientific circles.

195 John Teehan, *In the Name of God: The Evolutionary Origins of Religious Ethics and Violence* (Chichester: Wiley-Blackwell, 2010), 206.

196 Mark Juergensmeyer, *Terror in the Mind of God: The Global Rise of Religious Violence* (Berkeley and Los Angeles: University of California Press, 2001) 149.

197 Juergensmeyer, *Terror in the Mind of God* 163.

198 Edna Fernandes, 'Inside the Muslim Eton – Special Report', *The Mail on Sunday*, 20 Jun, 2010; available at http://www.dailymail.co.uk/news/article-1288053/Inside-Muslim-Eton-Their-day-starts-3-45am-goes-disciplined-20-hours-Their-aim-produce-Muslim-elite-leaders-.html.

199 Innes Bowen, *Medina in Birmingham, Najaf in Brent: Inside British Islam* (London: Hurst & Co., 2014), 16-7.

200 https://www.bbc.co.uk/news/10407559

201 https://www.bbc.co.uk/news/world-44209971

202 See summary of the Supreme Court's decision in Wisconsin V. Yoder *et al.*, 406 US 205, May 15, 1972, Decided, available at http://law2.umkc.edu/faculty/projects/ftrials/conlaw/yoder.html.

203 This it strikes me is a dubious argument since whether or not this is a bad thing comes down to the content of the schooling and upbringing. We rightly don't allow fascist schools in the UK for very good reason. There are strong arguments too as we have seen for ensuring that religious communities are not beyond wider ethical critique. Some traditions should perhaps be encouraged and others not. This as well, in a democracy, cannot be simply imposed, but needs to be the consequence of on-going dialogue as this book implies.

204 https://bit.ly/2Uly3Id

205 This is questionable not least because such exclusivist interpretations of, for example, the Bible in Christianity are, as we have seen, not at all universal. Inclusivist and pluralist forms of Christianity are not difficult to find. For

example, the majority of Quakers who also consider themselves to be Christian – because not all Quakers identify with Christianity – are very rarely exclusivist.

206 Anthony Grayling, *What is Good? The Search for the Best Way to Live* (London: Phoenix, 2007), 236.

207 See Jonathan Glover, *Humanity: A Moral History of the Twentieth Century* (London: Pimlico, 2001),

208 I attended the National Secular Society Conference in September 2016 and was impressed to hear a lecture that made clear how secularism has been, and still is, variously defined. This – as was pointed out – was great ammunition to its detractors, but it is important to be clear about this. Some secularists try to make out that secularism is a simple, clear concept. This is false.

209 There is a very small group of Muslims known as Qur'anists, who seek guidance from the Qur'an alone and regard the Hadith to be apocryphal. The vast majority of Muslims, however, are very much guided by Hadith. For example, the Hadith are important as part of teaching within madrasahs. Alongside the Qur'an they also form the basis for the Friday midday sermons (khutbah).

210 Sam Harris, *The End of Faith: Religion, Terror, and the Future of Reason* (London: The Free Press, 2004), 110.

211 Harris, *End of Faith*, 123.

212 See Patricia Crone, *Roman, Provincial and Islamic Law, The Origins of the Islamic Patronate*, (Cambridge: Cambridge University Press, 2010)

213 Wilfred Cantwell Smith, 'The Concept of Shari'a among Some Mutakallimun', in *Arabic and Islamic Studies in Honour of Hamilton A. R. Gibb*, George Makdisi (ed.), (Cambridge: Department of Near Eastern Languages and Literatures of Harvard University, 1965), 581-602, 585 and 588-9.

214 Shahab Ahmed, *What Is Islam? The Importance of Being Islamic* (Princeton: Princeton University Press, 2016), 125.

215 Ahmed *What Is Islam?* 129.

216 Ahmed *What Is Islam?* 72 gives a fuller account of the coin.

217 Ahmed, *What is Islam?* 57.

218 Qur'an 5: 92 Dawood, N. J., translator, *The Qur'an* (Harmondsworth and New York: Penguin, 1990).

219 Ahmed 62.

220 Ahmed 62.

221 John L. Esposito *The Future of Islam* (Oxford: Oxford University Press, 2010) 123-124. Here Esposito explains how traditionalist scholarship can eclipse the Qur'an by putting an overriding emphasis on the consensus of scholars (ijma). This explains how the hijab came to be regarded as compulsory when there is no mention of it in the Qur'an.
222 Author's interview with Shabbir Akhtar July 28 2016.
223 Author's interview with Shuruq Naguib May 17 2016.
224 The following link explains the Ismaili version of this view. https://iis.ac.uk/approaches-qur#anchor6
225 Reza Aslan, *No God But God: The Origins, Evolution, and Future of Islam* (London: Heinemann, 2005), 201.
226 Tariq Ramadan, *Western Muslims and the Future of Islam* (Oxford: Oxford University Press, 2004), 27.
227 Esposito, *Future of Islam*, 123-4.
228 Khaled M. Abou El Fadl, *The Great Theft: Wrestling Islam from the Extremists* (New York: Harper Collins, 1st ed., 2005), 45.
229 Abou El Fadl, *Great Theft*, 55.
230 Abou El Fadl, *Great Theft*, 55.
231 Sam Harris *The End of Faith* 117-123. Here Harris describes a litany of militant Qur'anic exhortations but nearly every one he cites is about how God will punish unbelievers on Judgment Day. He offers nothing that I haven't included above about how Muslims should fight unbelievers in this world. Many commentators view the Qur'anic emphasis on God's judgment against unbelievers in an afterlife as emphasising that humans, unlike God, are in no position now, to make such judgments. As such there is no reason to be aggressive towards unbelievers unless one is first attacked.
232 See Asma Afsaruddin, *Contemporary Issues in Islam* (Edinburgh: Edinburgh University Press, 2015), 45.
233 Jamal al-Banna provides a good example of such an argument against Harris. See Afsaruddin, *Contemporary Issues*, 45.
234 See Afsaruddin, *Contemporary Issues*, 45.
235 Laleh Bakhtiar, translator and author, *The Sublime Qur'an*, (Chicago: Kazi Publications, 2006), Surah *xliii*.
236 Marshall G. S. Hodgson, *The Venture of Islam: Conscience and History in a World*

Civilization, Volume 1: The Classical Age of Islam (Chicago: University of Chicago Press, 1974), 327.

237 Muhammad Khalid Masud, *Ikhtilaf al-Fuqaha: Diversity in Fiqh as a Social Construction*, published online at Musawah, 76; available at http://www.musawah.org/sites/default/files/Wanted-MKM-EN.pdf.
238 Afsaruddin *Contemporary Issues*, 123.
239 Neal Robinson, *Discovering the Qur'an: A Contemporary Approach to a Veiled Text* (London: SCM, 1996), 66.
240 Robinson, *Discovering the Qur'an*, 67.
241 Hodgson, *Venture of Islam*, 328.
242 Abou El Fadl *Great Theft* 153.
243 Afsaruddin, *Contemporary Issues*, 41.
244 Cyril Glasse (ed.) *The Concise Encyclopedia of Islam* (London: Stacey International, 1989) – see the entry under Hadith, 141.
245 Shi'a Muslims constitute between 10 and 15 percent of Muslims world-wide. They differ in their beliefs from Sunnis because they believe that the initial leadership of the Islamic community (ummah) after the death of Muhammad should have followed in the family line and been given to Ali - Muhammad's son-in-law. Shi'as believe that this family line of leaders, following on from Ali, is also a spiritual succession of figures known as Imams. By contrast Sunnis believed the succession was to take place as it did, by the elders (or ulama) of the community appointing the person best-placed to know the sunnah of the Prophet. So, the first leaders were known as Rightly Guided Caliphs.
246 Andrew Rippin, *Muslims: Their Religious Beliefs and Practices*, (London: Routledge, 2005), 53-54. See also the entry for 'hadith', in Cyril Glasse, *The Concise Encyclopedia of Islam* (London: Stacey International, 1989), 141.
247 Mansud, *Ikhtilaf al-Fuqaha: Diversity in Fiqh as a Social Construction*, 75. http://www.musawah.org/sites/default/files/Wanted-MKM-EN.pdf
248 G. H. A. Juynboll, *Studies on the Origins and Uses of Islamic Hadith, (1st edition)* (Abingdon: Routledge, 1996), Section VI, 381.
249 Al-Bukhari's Sahih: *The Correct Traditions of Al-Bukhari*, Vol. 1, Bk 6 (Beirut: Dar Al-Kotob Al-ilmiyah, 2003), no. 304.
250 Afsaruddin, *Contemporary Issues*, 96.
251 Afsaruddin, *Contemporary Issues*, 96.

252 M. Steven Fish, *Are Muslims Distinctive? – A Look at the Evidence* (Oxford: Oxford University Press, 2011), 208.
253 Amina Wadud, *Inside the Gender Jihad: Women's Reform in Islam* (Oxford: Oneworld, 2006), 7.
254 Afsaruddin, *Contemporary Issues*, 38.
255 M. Steven Fish, *Are Muslims Distinctive? – A Look at the Evidence* (Oxford: Oxford University Press, 2011), 182.
256 Fish, *Are Muslims Distinctive?*, 186-9.
257 Fish, *Muslims*, 189-93.
258 Fish, *Muslims*, 192.
259 Fish, *Muslims*, 194.
260 Fish, *Muslims*, 201.
261 *OECD Social Institutions and Gender Index, 2014 Synthesis Report*, prepared by the OECD Development Centre's Social Cohesion Unit, 10; available at https://www.oecd.org/dev/development-gender/BrochureSIGI2015-web.pdf.
262 Ida Lichter, *Muslim Women Reformers: Inspiring Voices Against Oppression* (New York: Prometheus Books, 2009), 125.
263 Lichter, *Muslim Women Reformers*, 240.
264 Lichter, *Muslim Women*, 278.
265 Lichter, *Muslim Women*, 280.
266 Abdal Hakim Murad (a.k.a. Timothy Winter), 'Boys Will Be Boys', undated essay, posted on massud.co.uk, 10; available at http://masud.co.uk/ISLAM/ahm/boys.htm. Some of Murad's similar views are also found quoted by John L. Esposito, *The Future of Islam* (Oxford: Oxford University Press, 2010), 125.
267 Seyyed Hossein Nasr, *Islam in the Modern World: Challenged by the West, Threatened by Fundamentalism, Keeping Faith with Tradition* (New York: Harper Collins, 2010), 70.
268 Khaled M. Abou El Fadl, *The Great Theft: Wrestling Islam from the Extremists* (New York: Harper Collins, 1st ed., 2005), 131.
269 Abou El Fadl, *The Great Theft*, 150.
270 Lichter, in *Muslim Women* p. 98. recounts that in March 2007, thirty women took the oath before the Supreme Judicial Council thereby became judges.
271 Abou El Fadl, *The Great Theft*, 273.
272 As quoted by Lichter, in *Muslim Women*, p. 407.

273 Amina Wadud, *Inside the Gender Jihad: Women's Reform in Islam* (Oxford: Oneworld, 2006), 200.
274 Wadud, *Gender Jihad*, 200.
275 I mentioned in Chapter 5 how the conservative London based scholar Haitham Hadad has levelled this accusation of 'innovator' against Wadud.
276 Asma Afsaruddin, *Contemporary Issues in Islam* (Edinburgh: Edinburgh University Press, 2015), 108. She also argues that a more equitable understanding of Surah 2: 282 is more consistent with Q 33: 35 and 9: 71
277 See Michael Crawford, *Ibn 'Al Wahhab (Makers of the Muslim World)* (London: One World, 2014), 77.
278 Owen Bennett Jones 'The Overlooked: Owen Bennett Jones on the Deobandhis' in *The London Review of Books*, Vol. 38. No. 17. 8th September 2016, 22
279 John L. Esposito and Natana J. Delong-Bas *Shariah: What Everyone Needs to Know* (New York: Oxford University Press, 2018) 213-15.
280 Esposito and Delong-Bas *Shariah* 214.
281 https://www.theguardian.com/world/2015/feb/06/female-genital-mutilation-egypt
282 Lichter, *Muslim Women*, 98.
283 John L. Esposito *What Everyone Needs to Know About Islam* (Oxford: Oxford University Press, 2002), 95-96.
284 See *The Independent*, The faces behind the veil: Muslim women speak out against ban *12 September 2013*, article about the veil. https://www.independent.co.uk/incoming/the-faces-behind-the-veil-muslim-women-speak-out-against-ban-8812767.html
285 See Anabel Inge's lecture at the British Islam Conference 2018 https://www.youtube.com/watch?v=g4EVFtlUTUw
286 The two Qur'anic passages about which there is contestation here are Surah 33: 59-60 and 24: 30-31. The view that no head or face covering is mandated is taken by Muhammad Asad, a key twentieth-century Islamic scholar in his *The Message of the Qur'an* (Dar al Andalus Limited, 1980), 734-35, and is in agreement with Zaki Badawi and John Esposito. See the Asad text at: http://www.muhammad-asad.com/Message-of-Quran.pdf See Omar Hussein Ibrahim, *The Myth of the 'Islamic' Headscarf* (London: Omar Hussein Ibrahim and FELD Productions, 2008 and 2010), 1; and John L. Esposito, *What*

Everyone Needs to Know about Islam (Oxford: Oxford University Press, 2002), 95. These views are also shared by Leila Ahmed and the Shi'a scholar Reza Aslan. See Aslan, *No God But God: The Origins, Evolution, and Future of Islam* (London: Heinemann, 2005), 66.
287 John L. Esposito, *What Everyone Needs to Know about Islam* (Oxford: Oxford University Press, 2010), 95.
288 Lichter, *Muslim Women*, 133.
289 Lichter, *Muslim Women*, 278.
290 Yasmin Alibhai-Brown, 'Revealed: The Brutal Truth that hides inside the burka', London's *Evening Standard* newspaper, 30 Nov, 2005; an extract of which is available at https://www.questia.com/newspaper/1G1-139274654/revealed-the-brutal-truth-that-hides-inside-the-burqa.
291 Lichter, *Muslim Women*, 127, 133, 257.
292 See http://www.arabnews.com/node/1053516/saudi-arabia
293 Jack O'Sullivan 'Defender of his faith', *The Guardian* 15 January 2003. https://www.theguardian.com/world/2003/jan/15/terrorism.religion
294 https://www.revolvy.com/page/International-propagation-of-Salafism-and-Wahhabism-by-region
295 John L. Esposito, *The Future Of Islam*, (Oxford: Oxford University Press, 2010), 129.
296 William Dalrymple *The Return of A King: The Battle For Afghanistan*, (London: Bloomsbury, 2014)
297 James Mill, *The History of British India in 6 Volumes*, (London: Baldwin, Cradock, and Joy, 1826), Vol. 1, 225-6.
298 Reza Aslan, *No God But God: The Origins, Evolution, and Future of Islam* (New York: Heinemann, 2005), 225.
299 Atran *Talking to the Enemy*, 87.
300 Abdel Bari Atwan *Islamic State: The Digital Caliphate*, (London: Saqi, 2015), 176.
301 Aslan, *No God But God*, 259.
302 United Nations Conciliation Commission for Palestine, *General Progress Report and Supplementary Report of the United Nations Conciliation Commission for Palestine, Covering the Period from 11 December 1949 to 23 October 1950*, in the General Assembly's Official Records: Fifth Session, Supplement No.18 (A/1367/Rev.1), New York, 1951. Available at https://bit.ly/2KMTtto
303 https://www.hrw.org/reports/2007/lebanon0907/3.htm#_Toc175028478

Notes

304 Avi Shlaim *The Iron Wall: Israel and the Arab World* (London: Penguin, 2014), 802 - 803.
305 https://www.theguardian.com/world/2009/jan/07/gaza-israel-palestine
306 David Cook *Understanding Jihad* (Berkeley: University of California Press, 2005),114.
307 M. Steven Fish, *Are Muslims Distinctive? – A Look at the Evidence* (Oxford: Oxford University Press, 2011), 151.
308 Shiraz Maher, *Salafi Jihadism: The History of an Idea* (London: Hurst & Co., 2016), 111-2.
309 Scott Atran, *Talking to the Enemy*, 101.
310 Maher, *Salafi Jihadism* 67.
311 Maher, *Salafi Jihadism* 68.
312 Khaled M. Abou El Fadl, *The Great Theft: Wrestling Islam from the Extremists* (New York: Harper Collins, 1st ed., 2005), 166.
313 Abou El Fadl, *The Great Theft*, 166.
314 It was the philosopher David Hume who made clear that you can't get an 'ought' from an 'is'. To explain is to describe whereas to justify is to speak about what ought to be. Nothing at all follows about how people ought to behave from how they *actually* behave.
315 https://www.theguardian.com/world/2014/oct/15/female-british-muslims-vulnerable-radicalisation-men
316 Marc Sageman *Leaderless Jihad: Terror Networks in the Twenty-First Century* (University of Pennsylvania Press: Philadelphia, 2008), 11.
317 William James's *The Varieties of Religious Experience* and Edwin Starbuck's *The Psychology of Religion* are the classic texts on religious conversion.
318 Abou El Fadl, *The Great Theft*, 36.
319 Atwan, *Islamic State*, 2.
320 Atwan, *Islamic State*, 2.
321 Atran, *Talking to the Enemy*, 273.
322 Scott Atran (*Talking to the Enemy*, p. 35) takes this view regarding this kind of greater jihad to be the focus of the vast majority of Muslims worldwide. See also Bruce B. Lawrence, *Shattering the Myth: Islam Beyond Violence* (Princeton: Princeton University Press, 1998), 157-85.
323 Lindsey Jones ed., *The Encyclopedia of Religion*, 2nd ed., Vol. 7 (Detroit: Thomson Gale, 2005). See entry on 'jihad' by Rudolf Peters 4917.

324 Cyril Glasse ed., *The Concise Encyclopedia of Islam* (London: Stacey International, 1989), article on 'jihad', 209.

325 Asma Afsaruddin contests this view in her *Contemporary Issues in Islam* (Edinburgh: Edinburgh University Press, 2015), p.115-21. In support of the view that the Qur'an mandates an offensive jihad, see David Cook's *Understanding Jihad* (Berkeley: University of California Press, 2005).

326 Hamilton A. R. Gibb *Whither Islam* (London: Victor Gollancz, 1932), 379.

327 Bernard Lewis The Multiple Identities of the Middle East (London: Weidenfeld and Nicholson, 1998), 129.

328 Marshall G. S. Hodgson, *The Venture of Islam: Conscience and History in a World Civilization, Volume 2: The Expansion of Islam in the Middle Periods* (Chicago: University of Chicago Press, 1974), 538.

329 Maher, *Salafi Jihadism*, 87.

330 Cook, *Understanding Jihad*, 129.

331 Cook *Understanding Jihad*, 123-124.

332 Wahbah Al-Zuhaylī, *Al-Muʿāmalāt al-Māliyyah al-Islāmiyyah: Buʿūth wa Fatāwā wa Hulūl* (Beirut: Dar al-Fikr al-Muʾasir, 2002), 255.

333 Tariq Ramadan, *Western Muslims and the Future of Islam* (Oxford: Oxford University Press, 2004), 65.

334 Doris Lessing's novel *The Good Terrorist* (New York: Alfred A. Knopf, 1985), explores these questions.

335 Ted Honderich's *Humanity, Terrorism, Terrorist War: Palestine, 9-11, Iraq, 7-7…* also makes for interesting reading about the justification of terrorism.

336 Sam Harris, *The End of Faith: Religion, Terror, and the Future of Reason* (London: The Free Press, 2004) 127.

337 Scott D. Sagan and Benjamin A. Valentino, 'Would the US Drop the Bomb Again?', *Wall Street Journal* online, 19 May, 2016; available at https://www.wsj.com/articles/would-the-u-s-drop-the-bomb-again-1463682867.

338 'US Remembers 9/11 But Not 1.3 Million Dead from "War on Terror"', teleSUR website, 11 Sep, 2014; available at http://www.telesurtv.net/english/news/US-Remembers-911-But-Not-1.3-Million-Dead-from-War-on-Terror-20150911-0011.html.

339 James Paul and Céline Nahory (principal authors), *War and Occupation in Iraq, in Chapter 7: Killing Civilians, Murder and Atrocities*, report prepared by Global

Policy Forum, June 2007, available at https://www.globalpolicy.org/component/content/article/168/37151.html.

340 Spencer Ackerman 'Obama claims US drones strikes have killed up to 116 civilians' 1 July 2016 The Guardian https://www.theguardian.com/us-news/2016/jul/01/obama-drones-strikes-civilian-deaths

341 A clear shortcoming of this is that a great many terrorist fatalities go unnoticed since so many attacks kill fewer than 15 people. According to Dr. Monty G. Marshall's survey, he understands a terrorist attack to be one meted out against a) civilians, b) public officials/politicians/demonstrators c) armed soldiers/the police/barracks but it excludes occupying soldiers. In this report the identification of those responsible depends both upon self-ascription and admission of responsibility, plus at least two independent sources of evidence to support those who claim responsibility. See Steven Fish's Are Muslims Distinctive p. 151

342 Fraser Egerton, *Jihad in the West* (Cambridge: Cambridge University Press, 2011), 97.

343 Terry McDermott, *Perfect Soldiers: The 9/11 Hijackers: Who They Were, Why They Did It* (New York: Harper Collins, 2006), 87.

344 Atran, *Talking to the Enemy*, 418.

345 Omar Hussein Ibrahim, *The Myth of the 'Islamic' Headscarf* (London: Omar Hussein Ibrahim and FELD Productions, 2008 and 2010), 53.

346 Atran, *Talking to the Enemy*, 418.

347 Richard Wike, Pew Global Attitudes Project and Nilanthi Samaranayake, Pew Research Center for the People & the Press, *Where Terrorism Finds Support in the Muslim World: That May Depend on How You Define It – and Who Are the Targets*, the Pew Research Center, May 2006; available at: www.pewglobal.org/2006/05/23/where-terrorism-finds-support-in-the-Muslim-world/

348 Both Steven Pinker's *The Better Angels of Our Nature* and, more specifically, Scott Atran's *Talking to the Enemy*, point distinctively in this direction.

349 We noted in the last chapter Abou El Fadl's view that every form of belligerent Islamist group that has become internationally known has been significantly influenced by Wahhabism. Abou El Fadl, *The Great Theft*, 45.

350 Atwan, *Islamic State*, 185.

351 Atwan, *Islamic State*, 195.

352 See http://www.globalsecurity.org/military/world/para/isil-2.htm
353 Atwan, *Islamic State*, 194.
354 Atwan, *Islamic State*, 191.
355 Atwan, *Islamic State*, 196.
356 Robert Fisk, 'For the first time, Saudi Arabia is being attacked by both Sunni and Shia leaders', *The Independent* online, 22 Sep, 2016; available at http://www.independent.co.uk/voices/saudi-arabia-attacked-sunni-shia-leaders-wahhabism-chechenya-robert-fisk-a7322716.html.
357 Atran, *Talking to the Enemy*, 412.
358 Atran, *Talking to the Enemy*, 412.
359 Atran, *Talking to the Enemy*, 415.
360 Richard Dawkins, *The God Delusion* (London: Bantam Press, 2006), 64.
361 We get this idea from Genesis 1, where all created things come about as a result of God's will.
362 C. Stephen Evans, *Philosophy of Religion: Thinking About Faith* (Leceister: InterVarsity Press, 1985), 138.
363 St. Augustine *The Enchiridion on Faith, Hope, and Love*, Albert C. Outler (ed.), (Dallas: 1955) iii, 11 Online edition accessed http://www.tertullian.org/fathers/augustine_enchiridion_02_trans.htm
364 See Terry Eagleton's use of Augustine on pages 125-7 in *On Evil* (New Haven: Yale University Press, 2010).
365 John Mackie, 'Evil and Omnipotence', in *The Philosophy of Religion*, edited by Basil Mitchell, (Oxford: Oxford University Press, 1982), 100.
366 Peter Vardy, *The Puzzle of Evil* (London: Fount, 1992), 142.
367 Mackie, 'Evil and Omnipotence', in Mitchell (ed.), 97.
368 John Stuart Mill in *Nature; The Utility of Religion; and Theism* in *The Existence of God*, ed. John Hick (New York: MacMillan 1964), 118.
369 For a full account of Hick's theodicy, see *Evil and the God of Love* (Glasgow: Collins, 1979), 279-400.
370 The idea that any form of resolution to problems of evil and suffering is too high a price to pay, and not within anyone's gift, is expressed in an excerpt taken from Fyodor Dostoevsky's *The Brothers Karamazov*, in *The Problem of Evil: Selected Readings*, edited by Michael L. Peterson (Indiana: University of Notre Dame Press, 1992), 57-66.

371 See also my article 'Between Dawkins and God', *Philosophy Now Magazine*, Issue 86, Sep/Oct 2011, for an appraisal of different concepts of religious faith. Available at https://philosophynow.org/issues/86/Between_Dawkins_and_God.
372 Beverley Clack and Brian R. Clack, *The Philosophy of Religion: A Critical Introduction* (Cambridge: Polity, 2008), 81-6. The sub-section here entitled 'Critiquing Theodicy' gives us a range of views like the ones I have just enumerated.
373 As has been mentioned, the persistence of some religious schools of a very conservative nature is reason to question how far our culture will avoid a tendency towards ghettoisation in some respects, but I am suggesting that ghettoisation which amounts toa quite rigid isolation from the wider society will be marginal among those who are religiously affiliated in the UK.

Bibliography

Primary

Al'Bukhari's Sahih: The Correct Traditions of Al'Bukhari (Beirut: Dar Al-Kotob Al-ilmiyah, 2003)

The Bible, New Revised Standard Version https://www.biblestudytools.com/nrs/

Dawood, N. J., translator, *The Qur'an* (Harmondsworth: Penguin, 1990)

Arberry Arthur J. *The Koran Interpreted* (London: George Allen and Unwin, 1955)

The Words of Martin Luther King, Jr., selected by Coretta Scott King; Clayborne Carson and Peter Holloran (eds.) (New York: Newmarket Press, 1983)

Secondary

Abou El Fadl, Khaled M., *The Great Theft: Wrestling Islam from the Extremists* (New York: Harper Collins, 1st Ed., 2005)

Afsaruddin, Asma, *Contemporary Issues in Islam* (Edinburgh: Edinburgh University Press, 2015)

Ahmed, Leila, *A Quiet Revolution: The Veil's Resurgence from the Middle East to America* (New Haven: Yale University Press, 2011)

Ahmed, Shahab, *What Is Islam? The Importance of Being Islamic* (Princeton: Princeton University Press, 2016)

Aldridge, Alan, *Religion in the Contemporary World* (Cambridge: Polity, 2013)

Armstrong, Karen, *Fields of Blood: Religion and the History of Violence* (New York: Penguin, 2015)

Armstrong, Karen, *Islam: A Short History* (New York: Random House, 2002)

Aston, W. G., translator, *The Nihongi: Chronicles of Japan from the Earliest*

Times to AD 697, Vol. 2 (London: The Japan Society, 1896; reprint Tokyo: Tuttle, 1972)

Aslan, Reza, *No God But God: The Origins, Evolution, and Future of Islam* (London: Heinemann, 2005)

Asad, Muhammad, *The Message of the Qur'an* (Bristol: The Book Foundation, 2003)

Atran, Scott, *Talking to the Enemy* (London: Penguin, 2011)

Atwan, Abdel Bari, *Islamic State: The Digital Caliphate* (London: Saqi, 2015)

St. Augustine *The Enchiridion on Faith, Hope, and Love*, Albert C. Outler (Ed.), (Dallas: 1955)

Bakhtiar, Laleh, translator, The *Sublime Qur'an*, English translation of the Qur'an (Chicago: Kazi Publications, 2006)

Barrett, David V., *The New Believers: Sects, 'Cults', and Alternative Religions* (London: Cassell & Co., 2001)

Berlin, Isaiah *The Crooked Timber of Humanity* (London: Pimlico, 2003)

Berlin, Isaiah *The Power of Ideas* (London: Pimlico, 2000)

Berlin, Isaiah *Vico and Herder* (London: Chatto and Windus, 1976)

Birnbaum, Philip, ed. *Encyclopedia of Jewish Concepts* (New York: Hebrew Publishing Co., 1979)

Bonhoeffer, Dietrich, *Letters and Papers from Prison* (London: SCM, 1971)

Bonhoeffer Dietrich *The Cost of Discipleship* (London: SCM, 1964)

Bowen, Innes, *Medina in Birmingham, Najaf in Brent: Inside British Islam* (London: Hurst & Co., 2014)

Bradstock, Andrew, *Saints and Sandanistas: The Catholic Church in Nicaragua and Its Response to the Revolution* (London: Epworth Press, 1987)

Brown, Raymond, Joseph Fitzmyer and Roland Murphy ed. *The New Jerome Biblical Commentary* (London: Geoffrey Chapman, 1997)

Bruce, Steve, *Politics and Religion* (Cambridge: Polity, 2003)

Bullivant, Stephen and Michael Ruse *The Oxford Handbook of Atheism* ed. (Oxford: Oxford University Press, 2013)

Camus, Albert, *The Plague* (Harmondsworth: Penguin, 1982)

Cavanagh, William, T., *The Myth of Religious Violence: Secular Ideology and the Roots of Modern Conflict* (Oxford: Oxford University Press, 2009)

Cheetham, David, Douglas Pratt and David Thomas, *Understanding Interreligious Relations* (Oxford: Oxford University Press, 2014)

Chidester, David, *Christianity: A Global History* (London: Penguin, 2001)

Clack, Beverley and Brian R. Clack, *The Philosophy of Religion: A Critical Introduction* (Cambridge: Polity, 2008)

Clarke, Peter B. and Peter Byrne, *Religion Defined and Explained* (New York: St. Martin's Press, 1993)

Close, Brian E., *Judaism (Student's Approach to World Religions)* (London: Hodder Arnold H&S, 1991)

Cohn-Sherbok, Dan, *World Religions and Human Liberation* (Maryknoll: Orbis Books, 1992)

Commins, David, *Islam in Saudi Arabia* (London and New York: I. B. Tauris, 2015)

Cook, David, *Understanding Jihad* (Berkeley, Los Angeles, London: University of California, 2005)

Cook, Michael, *The Kor'an: A Very Short Introduction* (Oxford: Oxford University Press, 2000)

Cornwell, John, *Darwin's Angel* (London: Profile Books, 2007)

Crossman, Richard, ed. *The God That Failed* (Chicago: Regnery Gateway, 1983)

Critchley, Simon, *The Faith of the Faithless* (London and New York: Verso, 2014)

Cupitt, Don, *Taking Leave of God* (London: SCM, 1980)

Dabashi, Hamid, *Shi'ism: A Religion of Protest* (Cambridge Massachusetts and London: Belknap Press of Harvard University Press, 2011)

Dalrymple, William, *From the Holy Mountain: A Journey in the Shadow of Byzantium* (London: Harper Collins, 1997)

Dalrymple, William, *The Last Mughal: The Fall of a Dynasty, Delhi 1857* (London: Bloomsbury, 2007)

Dalrymple, William, *The White Mughals: Love and Betrayal in Eighteenth Century India* (London: Harper Collins, 2002)

Davies, Brian, ed., *Philosophy of Religion: A Guide and Anthology* (Oxford: Oxford University Press, 2000)

Dawkins, Richard, *The God Delusion* (London: Bantam Press, 2006)

Deats, Richard, *Martin Luther King Jr.: Spirit Led Prophet - A Biography* (London: New City, 1999)

Dennett, Daniel, *Breaking the Spell* (London: Penguin, 2007)

Eagleton, Terry, *Culture and the Death of God* (New Haven and London: Yale, 2014)

Eagleton, Terry, *On Evil* (New Haven and London: Yale, 2010)

Eagleton, Terry, *The Idea of Culture* (Oxford: Blackwell, 2000)

Eagleton, Terry, *Reason Faith and Revolution: Reflections on the God Debate* (New Haven and London: Yale, 2009)

Egerton, Fraser, *Jihad in the West: The Rise of Militant Salafism* (Cambridge: Cambridge University Press, 2011)

Esposito, John, and Ibrahim Kalin, ed., *Islamophobia: The Challenge of Pluralism in the 21st Century* (Oxford: Oxford University Press, 2011)

Esposito, John, *The Future of Islam* (Oxford: Oxford University Press, 2010)

Evans, C. Stephen, Philosophy of Religion: Thinking About Faith (Leceister: InterVarsity Press, 1985)

Feuerbach, Ludwig, translated by George Eliot, *The Essence of Christianity* (New York: Harper Row, 1957)

Feyerabend, Paul, *Farewell To Reason* (London and New York: Verso, 2002)

Fish, Steven M., *Are Muslims Distinctive? – A Look At the Evidence* (Oxford: Oxford University Press, 2011)

Flew, Anthony, ed., *A Dictionary of Philosophy* (London: Pan, 1979)

Ford, David F., *The Modern Theologians Vol. 1 and 2* (Oxford: Blackwell, 1994)

Frances, Bryan, *Gratuitous Suffering and the Problem of Evil* (New York: Routledge, 2013)

Gellner, Ernest, *Nationalism* (London: Phoenix, 1997)

Gellner, Ernest, *Nations and Nationalism* (Oxford: Blackwell, 2006)

Gethin, Rupert, *The Foundations of Buddhism* (Oxford and New York: Oxford University Press, 1998)

Gill, Robin, ed., *A Textbook of Christian Ethics 4th Edition* (London: Bloomsbury 2014)

Girard, Rene, translated by Patrick Gregory, *Violence and the Sacred* (Baltimore: John Hopkins University Press, 1977)

Goodin, Robert and Philip Petit, ed., *Contemporary Political Philosophy: An Anthology* (Oxford: Blackwell, 2001)

Glasse, Cyril, ed., *The Concise Encyclopedia of Islam* (London: Stacey International, 1989)

Glover, Jonathan, *A Moral History of the Twentieth Century* (London: Pimlico, 2001)

Gray, John, *Black Mass: Apolcalyptic Religion and the Death of Utopia* (London: Penguin, 2007)

Grayling, Anthony, *What Is Good? The Search for the Best Way to Live* (London: Phoenix, 2007)

Gutierrez, Gustavo, *A Theology of Liberation: History Politics and Salvation* (London: SCM, 1988)

Haidt, Jonathan, *The Happiness Hypothesis: Putting Ancient Wisdom and Philosophy to the Test of Modern Science* (London: Arrow Books, 2006)

Haidt, Jonathan, *The Righteous Mind: Why Good People are Divided by Politics and Religion* (New York: Vintage, 2012)

Harris, Sam, *Letter to a Christian Nation* (New York: Vintage, 2008)

Harris, Sam, *The End of Faith: Religion Terror and the Future of Reason* (London: The Free Press 2006)

Hart, David Bentley, *Atheist Delusions: The Christian Revolution and Its Fashionable Enemies* (New Haven and London: Yale University Press, 2009)

Hartung, Jan-Peter, *A System of Life: Maududi and the Ideologisation of Islam* (London: Hurst and Co. 2013)

Bibliography 289

Harvey, Peter, *An Introduction to Buddhism: Teachings History and Practices* (Cambridge: Cambridge University Press, 1995)

Harvey, Peter, *An Introduction to Buddhist Ethics: Foundations Values and Issues* (Cambridge: Cambridge University Press, 2009)

Hauerwas, Stanley, *The Hauerwas Reader*, John Berkman and Michael Cartwright eds. (Durham: Duke University, 2001)

Hick, John, *An Interpretation of Religion* (London: MacMillan, 1991)

Hick, John, *Evil and the God of Love* (Glasgow: Collins, 1979)

Hick, John, *The Myth of God Incarnate* (London: SCM Press, 1985)

Hinnells, John R., ed.,*The Routledge Companion to the Study of Religion 2nd* edition (London and New York: Routledge, 2010)

Hitchens, Christopher, *God Is Not Great: The Case Against Religion* (London: Atlantic Books, 2007)

Hodgson, Marshall G. S., *The Venture of Islam: Conscience and History in a World Civilization Vols. 1 – 3* (Chicago and London: University of Chicago, 1974)

Holloway, Richard, *Godless Morality* (Edinburgh: Canongate 2000)

Honderich, Ted, *Humanity Terrorism and Terrorist War: Palestine,9/11, Iraq, 7/7...*(London and New York: Continuum, 2006)

Hume, David, *Dialogues Concerning Natural Religion* (Indianapolis: The Library of Liberal Arts 1979)

Ibrahim, Omar Hussein, *The Myth of the Islamic Headscarf* (London: Omar Hussein Ibrahim and FELD Productions, 2008 and 2010)

James, William, *The Varieties of Religious Experience* (New York and London, Penguin 1985)

Jelen, Ted Gerard, and Wilcox, Clyde (eds.), *Religion and Politics in Comparative Perspective: The One, the Few and the Many* (New York: Cambridge University Press, 2002)

Johnston, Mark, *Saving God: Religion After Idolatry* (Princeton: Princeton University Press, 2009)

Jones, Lyndsey, ed., *Encyclopedia of Religion 2nd ed.* (Detroit: Thomson Gale 2005)

Jones, Owen, *The Establishment: And How They Get Away With It* (London: Penguin, 2015)

Jurgensmeyer, Mark, *Terror in the Mind of God: The Global Rise of Religious Violence* 4th edition (Berkeley: University of California Press, 2017)

Juynboll G. H. A. *Studies on the Origins and Uses of Islamic Hadith* (Abingdon: Routledge, 1996)

Kant, Immanuel, translated by Lewis White Beck, *Critique of Practical Reason* (New York: The Library of Liberal Arts, 1956)

Kant, Immanuel, translated by Lewis White Beck, *Foundations of the Metaphysics of Morals* (New York: The Library of the Liberal Arts, 1980)

Keown, Damien, ed. *A Dictionary of Buddhism* (Oxford: Oxford University Press, 2003)

Khalili, Laleh, *Heroes and Martyrs of Palestine: The Politics of National Commemoration* (Cambridge: Cambridge Middle Eastern Studies, Cambridge University Press, 2009)

King, Jr., Martin Luther, *Strength to Love* (Minneapolis: Fortress Press, 2010)

King, Jr., Martin Luther, *Stride Toward Freedom: The Montgomery Story* (New York: Harper, 1958)

Koenig, H. G., ed., *Handbook of Religion and Mental Health* (San Diego CA: Academic Press, 1998)

Kung, Hans, translated by Edward Quinn, *Does God Exist?* (London: Collins, 1980)

Kunin, Seth D., *Religion: The Modern Theories* (Edinburgh: Edinburgh University Press, 2005)

Kymlicka, Will, *Contemporary Political Philosophy: An Introduction 2nd Edition* (Oxford: Oxford University Press, 2002)

Lakoff, George, and Mark Johnson, *Philosophy In the Flesh* (New York: Basic books, 1999)

Law, Stephen, ed., *Israel, Palestine and Terror* (London and New York: Continuum, 2008)

Law, Stephen, *The War for Children's Minds* (London and New York: Routledge, 2006)

Lawrence, Bruce B., *Shattering the Myth: Islam Beyond Violence* (Princeton: Princeton University Press, 1998)

Lee, Robert D., *Religion and Politics in the Middle East: Identity, Ideology, Institutions and Attitudes* (Boulder CO: Westview Press, 2013)

Lichter, Ida, *Muslim Women Reformers: Inspiring Voices Against Oppression* (New York: Prometheus Books, 2009)

Livingstone, E. A., ed., *The Concise Oxford Dictionary of the Christian Church* (Oxford: Oxford University Press, 1987)

Lynch, Gordon and Jolyon Mitchell, ed. with Anna Strhan, *Religion Media and Culture: A Reader* (Abingdon: Routledge, 2012)

MacCulloch, Diarmaid, *A History of Christianity: The First Three Thousand Years* (London: Penguin, 2009)

Makdisi, George ed., *Arabic and Islamic Studies in Honour of Hamilton A. R. Gibb*, (Cambridge: Department of Near Eastern Languages and Literatures of Harvard University, 1965)

Maher, Shiraz, *Salafi Jihadism: The History of an Idea* (London: Hurst & Co., 2016)

Martin, David, *Does Christianity Cause War?* (Vancouver: Regent College, 2006)

McDermott, Terry, *Perfect Soldiers: The 9/11 Hijackers: Who They Were, Why They Did It* (New York: Harper Collins, 2006)

McGrath, Alister E., *Dawkins' God: Genes Memes and the Meaning of Life* (Oxford: Blackwell, 2005)

McGrath, Alister E. ed., *The Christian Theology Reader* (Oxford: Blackwell, 2000)

Meister, Chad and Paul Copan Ed., *The Routledge Companion to the Philosophy of Religion* (Abingdon and New York: Routledge, 2007)

Mernissi, Fatema, *Beyond the Veil* ebook edition, (London: Saqi, 2011)

Midgley, David ed., *The Essential Mary Midgley* (Abingdon and New York: Routlege, 2006)

Midgley, Mary, *The Myths We Live* (Abingdon and New York: Routledge 2004)

Mill, James, *The History of British India in 6 Volumes*, (London: Baldwin, Cradock, and Joy, 1826)

Mitchell, Basil ed., *The Philosophy of Religion* (Oxford: Oxford University Press, 1982)

Mitchell, Basil, *The Justification of Religious Belief* (Oxford: Oxford University Press, 1981)

Mitchell, Jolyon and Owen Gower ed., *Religion and the News* (Farnham: Ashgate, 2012)

Muller, Friedrich Max, *Introduction to the Science of Religion* (London: Longmans, Green and Co., 1882)

Nasr, Seyyed Hossein, *Islam in the Modern World: Challenged by the West, Threatened by Fundamentalism, Keeping Faith with Tradition* (New York: Harper Collins, 2010)

Nietzsche, Friedrich, translated by Francis Golffing, *The Birth of Tragedy and the Genealogy of Morals* (New York: Doubleday, 1956)

Nussbaum, Martha C., *The New Religious Intolerance: Overcoming the Politics of Fear in an Anxious Age* (Cambridge: Harvard University Press, 2012)

Oliner, S. P. and P. M. Oliner, *The Altruistic Personality – Rescuers of Jews in Nazi Europe* (New York: The Free Press, 1992)

Otto, Rudolf, translated by John W. Harvey, *The Idea of the Holy* (Oxford: Oxford University Press, 1980)

Pappé, Ilan, *A History of Modern Palestine: One Land, Two Peoples* (Cambridge: Cambridge University Press, 2006)

Palmer, Michael, *Freud and Jung on Religion* (London: Routledge, 1997)

Palmer, Michael, *The Question of God* (London and New York: Routledge 2001)

Pals, Daniel L., *Seven Theories of Religion* (Oxford and New York: Oxford University Press, 1996)

Peterson, Michael L, ed.,*The Problem of Evil: Selected Readings* (Notre Dame: University of Notre Dame Press, 1992)

Phillips, Dewi Z., *The Concept of Prayer* (Oxford: Blackwell, 1981)

Pinker, Steven, *The Better Angels of Our Nature* (London and New York: Penguin, 2011)

Rahula, Walpola, *What the Buddha Taught* (New York: Grove Press, 1974)

Ramadan, Tariq, *The Arab Awakening: Islam and the new Middle East* (London: Penguin, 2012)

Ramadan, Tariq, *Western Muslims and the Future of Islam* (Oxford: Oxford University Press, 2004)

Rawls, John, *A Theory of Justice* (Oxford: Oxford University Press, 1980)

Rhees, Martin, *Our Final Century: Will the Human Race Survive the 21st Century?* (London: Heinemann, 2003)

Rippin, Andrew, *Muslims: Their Religious Beliefs and Practices* (Abingdon and New York: Routledge, 2005)

Robinson, Neal, *Discovering the Qur'an: A Contemporary Approach to a Veiled Text* (London: SCM, 1996)

Robinson, Neal, *Islam: A Concise Introduction* (Richmond: Curzon, 1999)

Ruether, Rosemary Radford, *Faith and Fratricide: The Theological Roots of Anti-Semitism* (New York: The Seabury Press, 1979)

Ruthven, Malise, *Encounters with Islam: On Religion, Politics and Modernity* (London and New York: I.B. Tauris, 2012)

Ryan, Phil, *After the New Atheist Debate* (Toronto, Buffalo, London: University of Toronto, 2014)

Sardar, Ziauddin, *Reading the Qur'an: The Contemporary Relevance of the Sacred Text of Islam* (Oxford: Oxford University Press, 2011)

Said, Edward, *Orientalism* (London: Penguin, 2003)

Sandel, Michael J., *Justice: What's The Right Thing To Do?* (London: Penguin, 2009)

Scruton, Roger, *Modern Culture* (London and New York: Continuum, 2000)

Sen, Amartya, *Identity and Violence: The Illusion of Destiny* (London and New York: Penguin, 2007)

Silverstone, Roger, *Media and Morality: On the Rise of the Mediapolis* (Cambridge: Polity, 2013)

Singer, Peter, ed., *A Companion to Ethics* (Oxford: Blackwell, 2008)

Singer, Peter, *One World: The Ethics of Globalization* (New Haven and London: Yale University Press, 2002)

Singer, Peter and Renata Singer ed., *The Moral of the Story: An Anthology of Ethics through Literature* (Oxford: Blackwell, 2005)

Smart, Ninian, *The Religious Experience of Mankind* (New York: Fount, 1980)

Smith, Greg, *Faith and Volunteering in the UK: Towards a Virtuous Cycle for the Accumulation of Social, Religious and Spiritual Capital?* (V&R eLibrary, 2011)

Stevenson, J. ed., *A New Eusebius: Documents Illustrative of the History of the Church to A.D. 337* (London: SPCK, 1980)

Stiver, Dan, *The Philosophy of Religious Language: Sign, Symbol and Story* (Oxford: Blackwell, 1997)

Storm, Ingrid, *Civic Engagement in Britain: The Role of Religion and Inclusive Values* (Oxford: Oxford University Press, 2014)

Surber, Jere Paul, *Culture and Critique: An Introduction to the Critical Discourses of Cultural Studies* (Oxford: Westview Press, 1998)

Suzuki, Daisetz T., *The Zen Doctrine of No-Mind* (York Beach, Maine: Weiser Books, 1972)

Swinburne, Richard, *The Existence of God* (Oxford: Oxford University Press, 1991)

Taji-Farouki, Suha, and Basheer M. Nafi ed., *Islamic Thought in the Twentieth Century* (London: I. B. Tauris, 2004)

Taylor, Charles, *A Secular Age* (Cambridge, Massachusetts and London, Harvard University Press, 2007)

Taylor, Charles, *Modern Social Imaginaries* (Durham and London: Duke University Press, 2007)

Teehan, John, *In the Name of God: The Evoutionary Origins of Religious Ethics and Violence* (Oxford: Wiley-Blackwell, 2010)

Unterman, Alan, *Jews: Their Religious Beliefs and Practices* (London and New York: Routledge, 1990)

Vardy, Peter, *Good and Bad Religion* (London: SCM Press, 2010)

Victoria, Brian Daizen, *Zen at War* 2nd ed., (Lanham, Md, Oxford: Rowman and Littlefield, 2008)

Wadud, Amina, *Inside the Gender Jihad: Women's Reform in Islam* (Oxford: Oneworld, 2008)

Wadud, Amina, *Qur'an and Women: Rereading the Sacred Text from a Woman's Perspective* (Oxford: Oxford University Press, 1999)

Ward, Keith, *Is Religion Dangerous?* (Oxford: Lion Hudson, 2011)

Ward, Keith, *Is Religion Irrational?* (Oxford: Lion Hudson, 2011)

Ward, Keith, *Why There Almost Certainly Is A God: Doubting Dawkins* (Lion Hudson, 2008)

Watts, Alan, *The Way of Zen* (New York: Vintage Books, 1985)

Weil, Simone, *Waiting on God* (Abingdon and New York: Routledge, 2010)

Wiesel, Elie, *Night* translated by Stella Rodway, (New York: Bantam, 1982)

Wilson, Bryan R. ed., *Rationality* (Oxford: Basil Blackwell, 1981)

Woodhead, Linda ed., *Religions in the Modern World* (London and New York: Routledge, 2002)

Websites

www.adherents.com

The Internet Encyclopedia of Philosophy www.iep.utm.edu/

Stanford Encyclopedia of Philosophy https://plato.stanford.edu/

http://www.theosthinktank.co.uk/

www.worldvaluessurvey.org/

Index

Page numbers with n refer to endnotes. For example, 268n152 means note 152 on page 268. Names beginning with 'Al-' are filed under the second element. For example, 'Al-Qaeda' will be found under Q.

9/11 terrorist attacks, 37, 192, 217–18, 221

Abbas, Tahir, 212
Abduh, Muhammad, 154–55, 172
abortion, 109–10, 252
Abou El Fadl, Khaled
    on Hadith, 154, 157
    on militancy, 197, 204, 205
    on misogyny, 157, 175
    on the Qur'an, 141, 150
    on Wahhabism, 142, 150, 172, 177, 222
absolutism, 24, 26–29, 252, 253
abuse
    child abuse, 43, 89, 120–21, 233–34
    indoctrination as, 118
    see also domestic violence
Al Afghani, Jamal ad Din, 190
Afghanistan, 190, 191–92, 198, 208
Africa, 109–11, 168
Afsaruddin, Asma, 141, 150, 158, 160, 176, 203–4, 209, 210
afterlife, 146, 241–42

Ahmed, Shahab, 135–36
AIDS/HIV, 110
Ainsworth, David, 108, 111–12
Akhtar, Shabbir, 137, 146
al-wala'wa-l-bara (loyalty and disavowal), 195–96
Algeria, 191, 196
Alibhai-Brown, Yasmin, 185
Allen, Chris, 45–46
Alpha course, 101–3
altruism, 116, 238
American civil rights movement, 57–63
Amish community, 122–23
animal suffering, 240–41
Annis, Sheldon, 70
anti-Semitism, 50–57, 258–59n36
Anwar, Zainab, 173
Arafat, Yasser, 76, 77, 82, 83
Asim, Qari, 153, 174, 211
Aslan, Reza, 191–92
atheists, 227–28 *see also* Dawkins, Richard; Harris, Sam; Hitchens, Christopher
Atkins, Peter, 227

Index

Atran, Scott, 81, 191, 200, 202, 206–7, 209, 217, 224, 225
Atwan, Abdel Bari, 191, 220–21
Augustine of Hippo, St., 231–32, 237
Auschwitz, 56
authoritarianism, 117–18, 121–22, 125, 271–72n193
al-Awlaki, Anwar, 202
Azzam, Abdallah, 208

Badawi, Zaki, 182, 185–86, 217–18
Al Baghdadi, Abu Bakr, 193, 198
al Banna, Hasan, 191
al Banna, Jamal, 146
Barlas, Asma, 157
Barth, Karl, 54
Benedict XVI, Pope (Joseph Ratzinger), 100
Bentham, Jeremy, 28
Berlin, Isaiah, 248–49
al-Betawi, Hamed, 81
Bible, 58, 80, 102, 118
bin Laden, Osama, 142, 221
Bonhoeffer, Dietrich, 54
Brazil, 67, 68–69
British imperialism, 190–91
Brown, Andrew, 39, 43–44
Bruce, Steve, 63–64
Buddhism, 93–98, 100, 107
burkas *see* veiling of women
Butler, Tom, 38

Catholic Church
    child abuse within, 89, 120–21
    and inter-faith relations, 99, 100
    in Latin America, 63–67, 71, 72–73
    media coverage of, 41
    moral absolutism of, 110, 252
    in Nazi Germany, 50, 52–53, 55
    school R.E. teachers, 271–72n193
Cavanaugh, William, 19
CEDAW (Convention on the Elimination of all forms of Discrimination against Women), 174
chadors *see* veiling of women
charity, 104–12
    contribution of religious charities, 108
    giving, 106–8
    outcomes, 109–12
    volunteering, 105–6
children
    abuse of, 43, 89, 120–21, 233–34
    altruism in, 116
    school fire in Saudi Arabia, 183
    see also religious upbringing
Chile, 67
Choudary, Anjem, 40
Christian Science, 230–31
Christianity
    and American civil rights movement, 57–63
    decline in UK mainstream denominations, 36, 116–17
    and Israeli–Palestinian conflict, 77, 81
    in Latin America, 63–73

media representation, 41–45
mission and evangelising,
    66–73, 98–104, 109–11,
    268n152
    and Nazi Germany, 50–57
    rivalry between churches, 72–73
    see also Catholic Church;
    Christian Science
civil rights movement, American,
    57–63
Clark, Lynn Schofield, 40–41
Close, Brian, 56
Cohn-Sherbok, Dan, 71
colonialism and neo-colonialism,
    190–93
community rights, 122–23, 124–25,
    170, 185, 252–53
Convention on the Elimination of
    all forms of Discrimination
    against Women (CEDAW), 174
conversion, religious, 200 see also
    mission and evangelising
Cook, David, 205, 208
corruption, 111–12
Cranmer, Frank, 112
cultural relativism, 24–26
culture, 163–64, 176–80, 210–11,
    246–55 see also community rights

Dalai Lama, 100
Dar al Islam and Dar al Harb,
    210–13
Dar al Salam, 210
Dawkins, Richard, 90, 91, 92, 93,
    118, 227
Day, Liza, 91–92
Deats, Richard, 59

Dein, Simon, 87–88
Delong-Bas, Natana J., 179
Deobandhi Islam, 139, 178
dialogue, 30–32
digital media, 40–41, 201–3,
    223–24
divorce, 147–48, 169, 174, 253
domestic violence, 148, 168, 169,
    171, 174, 175–76, 185

Eagleton, Terry, 231
Eddy, Mary Baker, 230–31
Edison-Dew, Mark, 101–2
education, 166–67, 220–21 see also
    religious upbringing
Egerton, Fraser, 201, 216–17,
    223–24
Egypt, 179, 187, 197, 200–201,
    207–8
empathy, 30, 128, 238, 257n11
Esposito, John L., 179, 183
ethical judgments, 23–29, 246–55
    cultural context for, 246–48
    decision-making in multi-
        cultural context, 251–55
    disagreement over moral
        values, 128, 133–34, 193,
        248–51
    nature and purpose of, 23
    status of, 24–29
evangelical Christianity, 66–70, 71,
    72–73
evangelising, 66–73, 98–104,
    109–11, 146, 268n152 see also
    religious conversion
Evans, Stephen, 229
Evans, Thomas, 92

INDEX 299

evil and suffering, problem of, 226–45
   introduction, 226–28
   evil as illusion or non-existent, 230–32
   free-will defence, 232–37, 239–40, 241
   natural evil and the 'for a greater good' defence, 237–43
   philosophical theory, 228–30
   sufferers' perspective, 242, 243–45
evolution
   human freedom and, 235–36, 241
   teaching against, 118
exclusivism
   Christian, 72–73, 100, 101–4, 272–73n205
   in education, 125, 247
   in Israeli–Palestinian conflict, 76, 80–81
   tribalism (in-group/out-group mentality), 118–20, 23–24, 127, 128, 249
Ezzat, Heba Raouf, 187

Faraj, Muhammad abd-al-Salam, 207, 222
Female Genital Mutilation (FGM), 178–79
Feyerabend, Paul, 28–29
FGM (Female Genital Mutilation), 178–79
Fish, M. Steven, 158–59, 165–67, 215–16, 224
Fisk, Robert, 222

forgiveness, 58–59
Francis, Leslie, 92
Francis, Pope, 100
free-will, 232–37, 239–40, 241
Freston, Paul, 68–69
Freud, Sigmund, 31, 123

Galton, Sir Francis, 89
Gibb, Hamilton, 205
Gibbs, Gary, 99
Gill, Robin, 44
Gledhill, Ruth, 43
Glover, Jonathan, 53
God, 90–91, 92, 264n115 *see also* evil and suffering, problem of
Graham, Billy, 62
Grayling, Anthony, 126, 127
Green, Linda, 70
Guatemala, 67–68, 70
Gumbel, Nicky, 101, 102
Gutierrez, Gustavo, 64–65

al-Haddad, Haitham, 119, 170, 180
Hadith, 80, 132–33, 153–60, 176, 182, 203, 216, 273n209
Haidt, Jonathan, 107
Hallum, Anne, 69
Hamas, 79, 80, 81, 83, 194, 218
Hare, Richard, 28
Haredi Jews, 76–77, 262n89
Harnack, Adolf von, 52
Harries, Richard, 100
Harris, Sam, 96–97, 132–33, 146, 188, 212, 214, 274n231
Harrison, Richard, 107
Hauerwas, Stanley, 101
headscarves *see* veiling of women

Hezbollah, 79, 80, 83, 194
Hick, John, 20–21, 239–42
hijab *see* veiling of women
Hinduism, 101, 103–4, 107
Hitchens, Christopher, 57–63, 73, 91, 93
Hitler, Adolf, 28, 50, 51, 52–53, 54, 213
HIV/AIDS, 110
Hodgson, Marshall, 206
Holocaust, 50–57, 117, 227–28
Holy Land *see* Israeli–Palestinian conflict
Hoodbhoy, Pervez, 192
Hoover, Stewart, 37
hospitals, 109–10
Howard, Michael, 194–95
hypermedia, 201–3, 223–24

Ibn Kathir, Ismail, 158
Igwe, Leo, 109–10
impartiality, 26–29
India, 190–91, 268n152
individual experience, 30–32, 36–37, 39
individual rights, 124, 170, 185, 252–53
indoctrination of children, 118
Indonesia, 168, 179, 185, 187–88, 219
Inge, Anabel, 182
institutions, inclination to defend, 121
inter-faith relations, 99–104, 146, 250–51
intercessionary prayer, 90–91
internet, 40–41, 201–3, 223–24

intolerance *see* exclusivism
Iran, 79, 83, 169, 183, 185, 221
Iraq, 192–93, 214
IS (ISIS, ISIL) (Islamic State (of Iraq and Syria/the Levant)), 193, 198, 200, 202, 223–24
Islam
    al-wala'wa-l-bara (loyalty and disavowal), 195–96
    alcohol, attitude to, 135–36, 254
    charitable giving, 107
    Deobandhi, 139, 178
    education, attitude to, 120, 165–67
    inter-faith relations, 146
    and Israeli–Palestinian conflict, 77–81, 206–7, 218
    jihad, 80, 196, 203–10, 217, 224
    media representation, 40, 43, 45–48
    Mutazilites, 172
    post-colonial reformation, 200–201
    religion, culture and politics, 163–64, 176–80, 210–11
    Shari'a law, 134–35, 171, 217–18, 253
    Shi'a, 79, 138, 155, 221, 275n245
    Sufism, 134, 135, 138, 140, 155, 197, 263n106
    Sunni, 136–38, 155, 160, 275n245 (*see also* Wahhabism)
    takfir (excommunicate), 196, 208, 220
    tatarrus (human shields), 196

see also Hadith; militancy in
    Islam; misogyny in Islam;
    Qur'an; Salafism;
    Wahhabism
Islamic State *see* IS (ISIS, ISIL)
Islamophobia, 45–46
Israeli–Palestinian conflict, 73–83
    chronology of events, 82–83
    as factor in Islamic militancy,
        193–94
    Israel, Jews and Zionism,
        73–77, 80–81, 119
    Palestinians and Islam,
        77–81, 206–7, 218

James, William, 89
Jews and Judaism, 73–77, 80–81,
    105, 106–7, 119, 252–53, 262n89
    see also anti-Semitism
jihad, 80, 196, 203–10, 217, 224
John Paul II, Pope, 100
Joseph Rowntree Foundation, 116
journalism, 36–37, 38–41
Judaism *see* Jews and Judaism
judging religion, 17–34
    introduction, 17–18
    defining religion, 19–23
    dialogue, role of, 30–32
    ethical judgments, 23–29
Juergensmeyer, Mark, 119
Juynboll, G. H. A., 157

Kahane, Meir, 76
Kant, Immanuel, 28
Kazi, Temina, 180
Khalili, Laleh, 78–79
King, Martin Luther, 57, 58–63

Kittel, Gerhard, 52
Knott, Kim, 44, 45, 46
Koenig, H. G., 87, 88
Kook, Abraham Isaac, 75
Kook, Zvi Yehuda, 75
Kymlicka, Will, 123, 185

Landau, Christopher, 39–40, 41
Latin America, 63–73
Law, Stephen, 117, 118, 122,
    125–26, 128
Lazar, Sara, 95
Lebanon, 79, 82, 83, 194, 219, 224
Lee, Robert, 73–74, 75
Levin, Jeffrey, 88
Lewis, Bernard, 205–6
Lewis, Christopher, 91–92
liberation theology, 63–73, 70–71, 72
Lichter, Ida, 185
life after death, 146, 241–42
Linden, Ian, 111
Luther, Martin, 51, 258–59n36
Lynch, Gordon, 202

MacCulloch, Diarmaid, 52–53
Macedo, Edir, 111
MacIntyre, Alasdair, 121–22
Mackie, John, 232–33, 238
Madrid bombers, 201–2, 217
al-Magdisi, Abu Muhammad,
    195–96
Maher, Shiraz, 195–96
Malaysia, 173, 179
Maltby, John, 91–92
Maqsood, Raqiyyah Waris, 170
marriage, 146–48, 158, 168, 169,
    174–76, 186–87, 253

see also domestic violence
Marshall, Monty, 216
martyrdom, 61, 79, 204
Marx, Karl, 31
Masud, Muhammad Khalid, 149, 156
Maududi, Syed Abu A'la, 178, 191
McDermott, Terry, 217
McKenzie, Tom, 106
media, 35–48
    introduction, 35–38
    hypermedia, 201–3, 223–24
    journalists and their credentials, 38–41
    reporting on Christianity, 41–45
    reporting on Islam, 40, 43, 45–48
    role in radicalisation, 201–3
    Western colonisation of, 193
meditation, 91–92, 93–98
Melville, Caspar, 109–10
mental health, 87–89, 91–93, 94–96
Mernissi, Fatema, 174, 175, 183
Middle East, 190–94, 197–98, 213–15, 219, 224 *see also* Israeli–Palestinian conflict; *and individual countries*
militancy in Islam, 189–225
    contributory factors, 190–203
    colonialisms and neo-colonialisms, 190–93
    internet and social media, 201–3, 223–24
    Islamic reformations, 200–201
    Israel, 193–94
    war as catalyst, 194–98, 208–9
    youth psychology, 198–200
    Dar al Islam and Dar al Harb, 210–13
    Hadith and, 159–60
    jihad, 80, 196, 203–10, 217, 224
    Qur'an and, 80, 139, 140, 141–46, 148–49, 151, 152–53, 209, 216, 217, 274n231
    terrorism, 213–25, 281n341
    Islamic condemnation of, 139, 141, 217–19
    Islamic condoning of, 140, 141
    and justification, 213–15
    media linking with Islam, 45–46
    suicide bombing, 79, 80, 81, 139, 144, 213–25
    tatarrus (human shields) in, 196
    Wahhabism and, 142, 212, 220–22, 223
Mill, James, 190
Mill, John Stuart, 28, 238
Miller, John J., 95
mindfulness, 93–98, 266n134
misogyny in Islam, 163–88
    introduction, 163–64
    evidence of, 165–69
    Hadith and, 157–59
    Muslim views on, 170–76
    on-going struggle and dialogue, 186–88, 253

origins of, 176–80
Qur'an and, 139–41, 143–44, 146–48, 149, 175–76, 182, 277n286
the veil, 169, 180–86, 251, 274n221, 277n286
mission and evangelising, 66–73, 98–104, 109–11, 146, 268n152
see also religious conversion
moral absolutism, 24, 26–29, 252, 253
moral agendas, imposition of, 109–10
moral judgments *see* ethical judgments
moral relativism, 24–26, 133, 253
moral values, differing, 128, 133–34, 193, 248–51
MPV (Muslims For Progressive Values), 174
Muhammad, Prophet, 154, 155, 158–59, 171, 173, 174, 182–83, 203, 204
Müller, Max, 20
multi-cultures, 246–55
Murad, Abdal Hakim, 133, 170, 171, 217
murder, 28, 146 *see also* terrorism
Muslim Brotherhood, 191, 197, 207
Muslims *see* Islam
Muslims For Progressive Values (MPV), 174
Mutanen, Annikka, 44
Mutazilites, 172

Naguib, Shuruq, 137–38, 174, 175
Nasr, Seyyed Hossein, 170
Nasser, Gamal Abdel, 197, 207–8
Nazi Germany, 50–57

Neo-Pentecostalism, 69–70
new atheists, 227–28 *see also* Dawkins, Richard; Harris, Sam; Hitchens, Christopher
Nicaragua, 64
Nietzsche, Frederick, 199
Nigeria, 109–11
niqabs *see* veiling of women
non-violence, 59–61
Northern Ireland, 106, 119
Nussbaum, Martha C., 257n11

objectivity, 26–29
Oliner, Pearl, 117
Oliner, Samuel, 117

pacifism, 59–61
Paisley, Ian, 103
Pakistan, 185
Palau, Luis, 66
Palestinians *see* Israeli–Palestinian conflict
Pappé, Ilan, 77, 78, 79–80
Pentecostalism, 66–67, 69, 70, 72, 99
personal experience of religion, 30–32, 36–37, 39
Peters, Rudolf, 204
Peters, Ruud, 217
Pharoah, Cathy, 106–7, 108
PLO (Palestine Liberation Organization), 77–78, 82
pluralism, 100, 125
polygamy, 146, 169, 175
Poole, Elizabeth, 45
Potter, Gary, 73, 125
poverty, 64–65, 69–70
prayer, 89–93

prison populations, 116–17
proselytising *see* mission and
   evangelising
prosperity theology, 69–70
Protestant churches
   and American civil rights
      movement, 62, 63
   in Latin America, 66–70, 71,
      72–73
   and Nazi Germany, 51–52,
      54, 55

Al-Qaeda, 196, 198, 202, 217
al-Qaradawi, Yusuf, 182, 187, 218
Qur'an, 131–53
   introduction, 131–32, 133–34
   abrogation, 149–53
   as ally of women's rights, 171
   interpretation of, 134–43,
      149–53, 171–72
   jihad in, 203–4, 209
   and militancy, 80, 139, 140,
      141–46, 148–49, 151, 152–53,
      209, 216, 217, 274n231
   and misogyny, 139–41,
      143–44, 146–48, 149,
      175–76, 182, 277n286
   terrorists' ignorance of, 217
   see also Hadith
Qutb, Sayyid, 197, 207–8, 222

Rabin, Yitzak, 76
racism, 57–63
radicalisation, 197, 198–200,
   216–17, 220–25
Rahman, Fazlur, 155
Ramadan, Tariq, 139–40, 211–12

Raouf, Heba, 171
Ratzinger, Joseph (later Pope Benedict
   XVI), 100
Rawls, John, 26–28, 29
reason, 27–29, 30, 121–22
relativism, 24–26, 126, 133, 253
religion
   and charity, 104–12
   defining, 19–23
   and mental health, 55–56,
      87–89, 91–93, 94–96
   personal experience (or lack)
      of, 30–32, 36–37, 39
   victims of, 88–89, 120–21
religious conversion, 55, 146, 200,
   206 *see also* mission and evangelising
religious faith, as psychological and
   spiritual resource, 55–56, 87–89,
   91–93
religious rivalry, 72–73
religious upbringing, 115–30
   introduction, 115–17
   moral critiques of, 111, 117–21,
      251
   response to critiques, 111,
      121–28
   in Saudi Arabia, 220–21
   see also children
Rigby, Lee, 40
Robinson, Neal, 151
Romero, Oscar, 65–66
Ronson, Jon, 102
Rosensaft, Yossel, 56

Sacks, Jonathan, 121–22
sacred texts *see* Bible; Hadith; Qur'an
sacred values, rivalry over, 80–81

Sageman, Marc, 200
Salafism
    and Hadith, 154–55
    and militancy, 190, 196, 205, 209, 212
    and Qur'anic interpretation, 136–37, 139–42, 172, 209
Sanderson, Terry, 104
satyagraha, 59–60
Saudi Arabia, 169, 183–84, 185, 186–87, 218, 220–22
Schindler, Oscar, 54
Schleiermacher, Friedrich, 52
Schlink, Bernhard, 33
schools, 111, 117–21, 122–23, 124, 125–28, 183, 251, 271–72n193
scripture *see* Bible; Hadith; Qur'an
Sen, Amartya, 119–20
sexual abuse, 43, 89, 120–21
sexual morality, 110
al-Shafi'i, 136, 156, 210–11
Shaikh, Sa'diyya, 160
Shari'a law, 134–35, 171, 217–18, 253
Shi'a Islam, 79, 138, 155, 221, 275n245
Shlaim, Avi, 194
Sisters in Islam, 173, 179
slavery, 233
Smith, Greg, 105, 106
Smith, Wilfred Cantwell, 135
social media, 40, 201–3, 223–24
Soviet Union, 192
Spanish Inquisition, 55
Sri Lanka, 224
Stein, Edith, 55
stereotyping, 41, 43, 44, 45–47, 188
Storm, Ingrid, 105
subjective perspectives, 30–32, 36–37, 39
suffering *see* evil and suffering, problem of
Sufism, 134, 135, 138, 140, 155, 197, 263n106
suicide bombing, 79, 80, 81, 139, 144, 213–25
Sunni Islam, 136–38, 155, 160, 275n245 *see also* Wahhabism
Swaggart, Jimmy, 66, 67, 71
Swinburne, Richard, 227
sympathetic imagination, 30, 248–51, 256–57n11

Taha, Mahmud Muhammad, 152
Taira, Teemu, 45
takfir (excommunicate), 196, 208, 220
Taliban, 202
Tamil Tigers, 224
tatarrus (human shields), 196
Teehan, John, 119, 127
television, 40, 45
terrorism, 213–25, 281n341
    Islamic condemnation of, 139, 141, 217–19
    Islamic condoning of, 140, 141
    and justification, 213–15
    media linking with Islam, 45–46
    suicide bombing, 79, 80, 81, 139, 144, 213–25
    tatarrus (human shields) in, 196
    Wahhabism and, 142, 212, 220–22, 223
theodicy *see* evil and suffering, problem of

torture, as factor in radicalisation, 196–97, 201–2
tribalism (in-group/out-group mentality), 118–20, 123–24, 127, 128, 249
Tzortsis, Hamza, 180

UCKG (United Church of the Kingdom of God), 111, 261n75
United States
    Amish community, 122–23
    charitable giving, 107
    evangelical missions, 66–70, 71, 72
    Middle Eastern intervention, 191–93, 198, 214–15

Vardy, Peter, 235
veiling of women, 169, 180–86, 251, 274n221, 277n286
victims of religion, 88–89, 120–21
Victoria, Brian, 97
violence, 103, 119, 127, 201–2
    see also domestic violence; Israeli–Palestinian conflict; war and war crimes
volunteering, 105–6

Wadud, Amina, 119, 159, 171, 175–76
Wahhabism
    and abrogation of the Qur'an, 150–51
    extreme puritanism of, 142, 143, 171, 172
    militancy of, 142, 195, 212, 220–22, 223
    misogyny of, 143, 177–78, 186–87
war and war crimes, 50–57, 97–98, 190–93, 194–98, 214–15 *see also* Dar al Islam and Dar al Harb; Israeli–Palestinian conflict
Wayment, Heidi, 96
Western imperialism, 190–93
Wiles, Maurice, 90
Winter, Timothy *see* Murad, Abdal Hakim
women's rights
    abortion and reproductive health, 109–10, 252
    inheritance, 138, 148, 175, 183, 253
    literacy, 166–67
    marriage and divorce, 146–48, 157–59, 168, 169, 174–76, 186–87, 253
    witness testimony, 148, 157, 169, 176
    see also domestic violence; misogyny in Islam

young people, radicalisation of, 198–200

Zionism, 74–77, 81, 119
al Zuhayli, Wahbah, 211

www.ingramcontent.com/pod-product-compliance
Ingram Content Group UK Ltd.
Pitfield, Milton Keynes, MK11 3LW, UK
UKHW031020181224
452569UK00004B/401